MATH

WEEKLY

PRACTICE

Grade 4

Credits
Author: Christy M. Flora
Copy Editor: Christine Schwab

Visit *carsondellosa.com* for correlations to Common Core, state, national, and Canadian provincial standards.

Carson-Dellosa Publishing, LLC
PO Box 35665
Greensboro, NC 27425 USA
carsondellosa.com

978-1-4838-2797-1
01-053167784

Table of Contents

Introduction

The Weekly Practice series provides 40 weeks of essential daily practice in either math or language arts. It is the perfect supplement to any classroom curriculum and provides standards-based activities for every day of the week but Friday.

The activities are intended as homework assignments for Monday through Thursday and cover a wide spectrum of standards-based skills. The skills are presented at random to provide comprehensive learning but are repeated systematically throughout the book. The intention is to offer regular, focused practice to ensure mastery and retention.

Each 192-page book provides 40 weeks of reproducible pages, a standards alignment matrix, flash cards, and an answer key. The reproducible pages are perfect for homework but also work well for morning work, early finishers, and warm-up activities.

About This Book

Each page contains a variety of short, fun exercises that build in difficulty across the span of the book. The activities are divided into two sections:

- The Daily Extension Activities at the front of the book are intended to engage both student and family. These off-the-page activities are simple and fun so that students will look forward to this practice time at home. The activities span one week at a time. The instructions are clear and simple so that students can follow them with or without assistance in their homes. None need be returned to school.

- The daily practice section involves more comprehensive learning. Because of the simplicity of directions and straightforward tasks, students will be able to complete most tasks independently in a short period of time. There are four pages of activities per week, allowing for testing or a student break on Friday if desired. These pages are intended to be brought back to school.

Pages can be offered in any order, making it possible to reinforce specific skills when needed. However, skills are repeated regularly throughout the book to ensure retention over time, making a strong case for using pages sequentially.

An answer key is included for the daily practice section. You can check answers as a group for a quick follow-up lesson or monitor students' progress individually. Follow the basic page layout provided at the beginning of the answer key to match answers to page placement. Also included in the book is a set of flash cards. Reproduce them to give to students for at-home practice, or place them in classroom centers.

Common Core State Standards
Alignment Matrix

Standard	W1	W2	W3	W4	W5	W6	W7	W8	W9	W10	W11	W12	W13	W14	W15	W16	W17	W18	W19	W20
4.OA.A.1	•	•		•	•		•	•	•	•		•	•		•	•	•		•	
4.OA.A.2	•	•			•	•			•			•			•		•	•		
4.OA.A.3		•			•	•	•	•	•			•		•	•	•	•			
4.OA.B.4	•	•	•		•	•	•	•	•	•	•		•	•	•	•	•	•	•	•
4.OA.C.5	•	•	•	•	•	•		•	•			•	•		•	•	•		•	•
4.NBT.A.1	•	•	•		•	•		•	•	•	•		•	•	•	•	•	•	•	•
4.NBT.A.2	•	•		•		•	•		•	•		•	•	•		•	•	•	•	•
4.NBT.A.3	•	•	•	•	•	•	•	•	•	•	•	•	•	•		•	•	•	•	•
4.NBT.B.4	•	•	•		•	•		•	•	•	•		•	•	•	•	•	•	•	•
4.NBT.B.5	•	•	•	•	•	•	•	•	•	•	•	•	•	•	•	•	•	•	•	•
4.NBT.B.6		•	•	•	•	•	•	•	•	•	•	•	•	•		•	•	•	•	•
4.NF.A.1	•	•	•		•	•	•	•	•	•		•	•	•	•	•	•		•	•
4.NF.A.2	•	•	•	•	•	•	•	•	•			•	•	•	•	•		•	•	•
4.NF.B.3	•	•	•	•	•	•	•	•	•			•	•	•	•	•	•		•	•
4.NF.B.4		•				•		•			•		•	•	•		•			•
4.NF.C.5		•		•		•		•		•	•		•	•	•	•			•	•
4.NF.C.6	•	•	•	•	•	•	•	•	•	•		•	•	•	•	•	•	•	•	•
4.NF.C.7		•		•		•		•	•	•		•	•		•	•	•			•
4.MD.A.1	•	•		•	•	•	•	•	•	•		•	•	•	•			•	•	
4.MD.A.2	•	•	•	•	•	•	•	•	•	•		•	•	•	•	•	•	•	•	•
4.MD.A.3	•	•				•	•	•	•	•			•		•	•	•	•	•	
4.MD.B.4				•			•			•						•				
4.MD.C.5								•	•		•	•			•					
4.MD.C.6										•		•	•	•		•		•		
4.MD.C.7												•				•				
4.G.A.1	•	•	•	•	•	•	•	•	•	•	•	•	•	•	•	•			•	•
4.G.A.2	•				•			•	•		•		•	•		•	•	•	•	
4.G.A.3	•			•	•		•	•	•	•	•	•			•		•	•	•	•

W = Week

Common Core State Standards
Alignment Matrix

Standard	W21	W22	W23	W24	W25	W26	W27	W28	W29	W30	W31	W32	W33	W34	W35	W36	W37	W38	W39	W40
4.OA.A.1	•	•		•		•	•		•			•		•	•	•		•	•	
4.OA.A.2	•				•				•					•			•			
4.OA.A.3	•		•	•	•	•		•		•	•		•	•		•			•	
4.OA.B.4		•	•	•	•	•	•	•	•	•	•	•	•	•	•					
4.OA.C.5	•	•	•	•	•	•	•	•	•	•	•	•	•	•	•	•	•	•	•	•
4.NBT.A.1	•	•	•	•	•	•	•	•	•	•	•		•	•		•	•	•	•	•
4.NBT.A.2	•		•	•	•	•	•		•	•			•	•				•	•	•
4.NBT.A.3	•	•	•	•	•	•	•	•	•		•	•	•			•	•	•	•	•
4.NBT.B.4	•	•	•		•	•	•	•		•	•	•	•	•	•	•		•		•
4.NBT.B.5	•	•	•	•		•	•	•	•	•	•	•		•	•	•	•	•	•	•
4.NBT.B.6	•	•	•	•	•		•	•		•				•	•	•	•	•	•	•
4.NF.A.1	•	•	•	•	•	•	•	•	•	•	•	•	•	•	•	•		•	•	
4.NF.A.2		•	•	•	•	•		•	•		•		•	•	•	•	•		•	•
4.NF.B.3	•	•	•	•	•	•		•		•			•		•	•	•	•	•	•
4.NF.B.4	•	•	•	•	•	•	•	•	•	•	•	•	•	•	•	•	•	•	•	•
4.NF.C.5	•	•	•			•	•		•			•			•			•	•	•
4.NF.C.6	•	•	•	•	•	•	•	•	•	•	•	•	•	•	•	•	•	•	•	•
4.NF.C.7	•	•					•	•										•		
4.MD.A.1		•	•	•	•	•				•	•	•	•	•	•	•	•	•	•	•
4.MD.A.2	•	•	•	•		•	•	•	•	•	•	•	•	•	•	•	•	•	•	•
4.MD.A.3	•				•			•			•		•		•		•		•	
4.MD.B.4		•	•			•	•		•			•		•		•		•		•
4.MD.C.5		•				•	•			•				•		•		•	•	•
4.MD.C.6	•	•	•	•	•	•	•	•	•	•	•	•	•	•	•	•	•	•	•	•
4.MD.C.7	•							•	•		•	•	•	•	•	•	•	•	•	
4.G.A.1	•	•		•	•	•	•	•	•	•	•	•	•	•	•	•	•	•	•	•
4.G.A.2		•	•	•		•	•			•	•	•		•		•	•	•	•	
4.G.A.3	•	•	•	•	•			•		•			•			•	•		•	

W = Week

School to Home Communication

The research is clear that family involvement is strongly linked to student success. Support for student learning at home improves student achievement in school. Educators should not underestimate the significance of this connection.

The activities in this book create an opportunity to create or improve this school-to-home link. The activities span a week at a time and can be sent home as a weeklong homework packet each Monday. Simply clip together the strip of fun activities from the front of the book with the pages for Days 1 to 4 for the correct week.

Most of the activities can be completed independently, but many encourage feedback or interaction with a family member. The activities are simple and fun, aiming to create a brief pocket of learning that is enjoyable to all.

In order to make the school-to-home program work for students and their families, we encourage you to reach out to them with an introductory letter. Explain the program and its intent and ask them to partner with you in their children's educational process. Describe the role you expect them to play. Encourage them to offer suggestions or feedback along the way.

A sample letter is included below. Use it as is or create your own letter to introduce this project and elicit their collaboration.

Dear Families,

I anticipate a productive and exciting year of learning and look forward to working with you and your child. We have a lot of work to do! I hope we—teacher, student, and family—can work together as a team to achieve the goal of academic progress we all hope for this year.

I will send home a packet of homework each week on _____. There will be two items to complete each day: a single task on a strip plus a full page of focused practice. Each page or strip is labeled Day 1 (for Monday), Day 2, Day 3, or Day 4. There is no homework on Friday.

Please make sure that your student brings back the completed work _____. It is important that these are brought in on time as we may work on some of the lessons as a class.

If you have any questions about this program or would like to talk to me about it, please feel free to call or email me. Thank you for joining me in making this the best year ever for your student!

Sincerely,

_____
Name

_____
Phone

_____
Email

	Day 1	Day 2	Day 3	
Week 1	Find five sets of parallel lines. Explain what makes the lines parallel.	Locate a store receipt. Round the prices and the total to the nearest whole dollar amounts.	Roll two dice. Use the numbers rolled to create a two-digit number. Round this number to the nearest ten.	Fin mu in ar p expand

$115.77 ↗ $116.00

	Day 1	Day 2	Day 3	Day 4
Week 2	Roll three dice. Add the first two numbers together. Multiply by the number on the third die.	Find three right triangles. Explain what makes the triangles right triangles.	Is your house or apartment number a multiple of the number 2? How do you know?	Write down your phone number. Multiply the first set of three digits by your age. Then, multiply the second set of four digits by your age.
Week 3	Find two multi-digit numbers in a magazine or a newspaper. Determine which number is larger.	Collect 24 pennies. Organize them to show different factor pairs for the number 24. For instance, organize them in a 2-by-12 array. Record the factors. What other factor pairs are there?	A prime number has only two factors—itself and 1. Find three prime numbers in print around your house.	Cut out pictures of objects in a book, magazine, or newspaper. Would you weigh the objects in—kilograms or grams? Glue the pictures on a T-chart to show the correct unit for each.
Week 4	Look at a clock. Round the time to the nearest half hour.	Make up fractions stories in the kitchen. For example, if you ate 1 banana from a bunch with 6 bananas, you ate of $\frac{1}{6}$ the bunch.	Find four triangles. Is each one acute, right, or obtuse? Explain.	Is your age a multiple of the number 3? Why or why not?

	Day 1	Day 2	Day 3	Day 4
Week 5	Organize small objects in a pattern. Describe the pattern.	Roll three dice. Use the numbers rolled to make three different three-digit numbers. Subtract the smallest number from the greatest. Multiply by the remaining number.	Practice math at the store. For example, how many crackers does your family need so that everyone can have a full serving?	Find a multi-digit number in a newspaper, in an address, or on a package. Write it in word form.
Week 6	Find two composite numbers in a newspaper, in an address, or on a package. List all of the factor pairs of each number.	Make a list of 10 different items in your room or home. Decide if you would measure each one in inches or feet.	Use blocks or other small objects to build an array. Write the multiplication sentence related to the array.	Find two receipts. Compare the total prices. Which is greater?
Week 7	Roll three dice. Use the numbers rolled to create three different three-digit numbers. Round each number to the nearest ten.	Practice family fractions. What fraction of your family are you? What fraction of your family is younger than five? Older than 18?	Find two multi-digit numbers in a newspaper, in an address, or on a package. Determine which number is smaller.	Compare prices of similar items in two different sales flyers. Which item costs less?
Week 8	Think of two places that you go to every week. Would you measure how long it takes to get there in minutes or hours?	Count the steps it takes to cross two rooms in your home. Write a subtraction sentence to show how much bigger one room is than the other.	Choose two items from a sales flyer. Add the prices. How much money would you need to buy both items?	Identify two figures, or shapes, in your home. Can you find a line of symmetry for each figure? Why or why not?

	Day 1	Day 2	Day 3	Day 4
Week 9	Find two receipts. Compare the total prices. Which is smaller?	Use a deck of playing cards. Face cards equal 10. Flip two cards over and multiply. How quickly can you go through the entire deck?	Roll three dice. Use the numbers rolled to create three different three-digit numbers. Round each number to the nearest hundred.	Look at a clock. Round the time to the nearest quarter hour.
Week 10	Roll a single die. Write a number pattern by adding, subtracting, or multiplying that number by a number of your choice. Continue until you have 10 terms in your pattern.	Compare prices of similar items in two different sales flyers. Which store charges more? How much more?	What time is it now? How long ago did you get home from school?	Practice math at the dinner table. Divide the items on the table into equal parts for each person.
Week 11	Write down two phone numbers as seven-digit numbers (555-4567 would be 5,554,567). Which number is greater?	Count the number of chairs in your home. Multiply to find the total number of chair legs.	Measure the height of each family member in feet. Convert each measurement to inches.	Roll two dice to make a two-digit number. Write all of the factor pairs of the number.
Week 12	What time is it? How many minutes is it to the nearest half hour? How many seconds?	Find fractions related to your family. For example, find the number of adults out of the total number of people or the number of females out of the total number of people.	Write your house or apartment number in expanded form.	Open a deck of cards. Remove the face cards. Flip over two cards and use them to make a two-digit number. Identify all of the number's factor pairs.

	Day 1	Day 2	Day 3	Day 4
Week 13	Choose two items from a sales flyer. Add their prices. What is the smallest whole-dollar amount you would need to purchase the items?	What time is it now? How many minutes are there until it is time for you to go to bed?	With a partner, open a deck of cards. Face cards equal 10. Each partner flips over two cards at the same time and multiplies. The player with the highest product wins and keeps all cards for the round.	Measure the height of each family member in feet. Find the total height of your family.

	Day 1	Day 2	Day 3	Day 4
Week 14	Round the ages of each of your family members to the nearest ten.	Open a deck of cards. Face cards equal 0. Flip over four cards. Arrange three of them to create a three-digit number. Multiply it by the value of the remaining card.	Draw a number line. Plot the age of each family member on it.	Write all of your family members' ages in word form.

	Day 1	Day 2	Day 3	Day 4
Week 15	With a partner, open a deck of cards. Face cards equal 0. Each partner flips over three cards and makes a three-digit number. The greater number wins.	Measure the height of each family member in meters. Convert the number to centimeters.	What time is it? How many hours are there until school starts? How many minutes?	Do you spend more time at school or at home every day? How much more?

	Day 1	Day 2	Day 3	Day 4
Week 16	Write your house or apartment number in base ten numerals. Then, write it in word form.	Roll two dice to make a fraction. Be sure to use the greater number as the denominator. Write the fraction. Repeat the steps to create a second fraction. Which fraction is greater?	Choose three items from a sales flyer. Add the prices. If you were going to pay with quarters, how many quarters would you need?	What time do you go to bed? What time do you get up? How much time do you sleep each night?

	Day 1	Day 2	Day 3	Day 4
Week 17	How does your family measure up? Measure the height of each family member in feet and inches. Who is tallest? Who is shortest?	Roll two dice to make a fraction. Be sure to use the larger number as the denominator. Is it greater than, less than, or equal to $\frac{1}{2}$?	Draw a number line. Plot the shoe size of each family member on it.	Measure 10 of the shoes in your house to the nearest centimeter.

	Day 1	Day 2	Day 3	Day 4
Week 18	Write fractions to show parts of groups of like items in your home. For example, write a fraction showing the number of red books out of total books.	Find an address in a phone book. Write the street address number in expanded form.	Roll two dice to make a fraction. Be sure to use the greater number as the denominator. List at least five equivalent fractions.	Open a deck of cards. Face cards equal 10. Flip over a card. Multiply the card by 100.

	Day 1	Day 2	Day 3	Day 4
Week 19	Choose four rooms in your house. Measure each room's width in feet. Which room is the widest?	Write an equation to show a way to quickly total how many shoes are in your house altogether.	Roll two dice to make a fraction. Be sure to use the greater number as the denominator. Repeat the steps to create a second fraction. Rewrite the fractions to contain a common denominator.	Open a deck of cards. Remove the face cards. Flip three cards over to make a mixed number. Change it to an improper fraction.

	Day 1	Day 2	Day 3	Day 4
Week 20	Roll two dice to make a fraction. Be sure to use the greater number as the denominator Decompose the fraction into an addition sentence. For example, $\frac{2}{4}$ would decompose to $\frac{1}{4} + \frac{1}{4}$.	If each person in your family ate half of an orange, how many oranges would your family need to buy? Explain.	Measure the height of each family member in feet and inches. Add the heights of the adults together. Then, add the heights of the children. How much taller are the adults?	Find an image in a magazine or newspaper. Place a straw or toothpick on the image as a line of symmetry. If you cannot, why not?

	Day 1	Day 2	Day 3	Day 4
Week 21	Use a bathroom scale to find the weight of a bag of groceries in pounds. How many ounces is it?	Find four images of quadrilaterals in magazines or a newspaper. Which type of quadrilateral is in each shape?	Roll one die. Write a fraction using that number as the numerator and 10 as the denominator. Write an equivalent fraction with a denominator of 100.	Roll two dice to make a fraction. Be sure to use the greater number as the denominator. Is it greater than, less than, or equal to $\frac{1}{4}$?

	Day 1	Day 2	Day 3	Day 4
Week 22	Open a deck of cards. Remove the face cards. Flip six cards over to make two mixed numbers. Add them.	Roll two dice to make a fraction. Be sure to use the greater number as the denominator. Repeat the steps to create a second fraction. Compare the fractions.	Find the prices of two food items. Write each price as a mixed number. Use a number line to compare the prices.	If each person in your family walked $2\frac{1}{4}$ kilometers a day, how far would your family have walked in all?

	Day 1	Day 2	Day 3	Day 4
Week 23	Glue straws or toothpicks onto a sheet of paper to model an acute angle.	Use a ruler to measure three items in your home in feet. Express each length in inches.	Roll two dice to make a fraction. Be sure to use the greater number as the denominator. Repeat the steps to create a second fraction. Add the fractions.	If each family member drinks 1 pint of milk at breakfast, how many gallons of milk are needed each week?

	Day 1	Day 2	Day 3	Day 4
Week 24	Roll two dice to make a fraction. Be sure to use the greater number as the denominator. Repeat the steps to create a second fraction. Find the difference.	Find the prices of two toys. Change the cents to fractions. Which fraction is greater?	Use a ruler to measure three items in your home in centimeters. If a meter is 100 cm, what fraction of a meter does each item measure?	Open a deck of cards. Remove the face cards. Flip over three cards to make a mixed number. Repeat the steps to create a second fraction. Add the mixed numbers.

	Day 1	Day 2	Day 3	Day 4
Week 25	Use play money to show $24,000. Then, imagine you must divide it between 24 people. How much money will each person get?	Roll two dice to make a fraction. Be sure to use the greater number as the denominator. Multiply it by your age.	Write the age of an adult family member or friend. List all of the factors of his age.	Identify three examples of right angles in a newspaper or magazine.
Week 26	Find four items in the kitchen that show their weight in grams, such as a bag of flour or a jar of salsa. Which weighs less? How much less?	Find your house or apartment number. Is it a prime number? Why or why not?	Ask a family member to choose a number from 1 to 179. Use a protractor to draw an angle with that measure.	Use four sets of cards numbered from 0 to 9. Shuffle them. Have two or three people draw three cards each. Arrange the cards into three-digit numbers. Compare the numbers.
Week 27	Measure the length and width of one room of your home in feet. Then, calculate the area.	Choose a number from 1 to 100. Ask a friend or family member to guess the number. Give her three hints about the number.	Use play money to show $10,000. Then, imagine you must divide it between 10 people. How much money will each person get?	Choose some toys. Divide them into groups of five. Is there a remainder?
Week 28	Measure the distance around two rooms in your home in meters to find the perimeter of each room.	Use four sets of cards numbered from 0 to 9. Shuffle them. Have two or three people draw four cards each. Arrange the cards into four-digit numbers. Compare the numbers.	Roll four dice. Use the numbers rolled to make a four-digit number. Then, roll a single die. Multiply the four-digit number by the single number.	Glue straws or toothpicks onto a sheet of paper to model a ray. Use a marker to draw the end point and arrow.

	Day 1	Day 2	Day 3	Day 4
Week 29	Roll two dice. Write an improper fraction using the numbers rolled. Use play dough to model the fraction.	Use play money to show $8,000. Then, imagine you must divide it between 100 people. How much money will each person get?	Glue straws or toothpicks onto a sheet of paper to model an obtuse angle.	Roll four dice. Use the numbers rolled to make a four-digit number. Then, roll a single die. Multiply the four-digit number by the single number.

	Day 1	Day 2	Day 3	Day 4
Week 30	Write your age. Is it a prime number? Why or why not?	Write a two-digit by two-digit multiplication problem. Solve it. Erase three digits. ask a friend or family member to solve for the missing digits.	Gather some books together. Divide them into groups of four. Is there a remainder?	Measure the length and width of a rectangular table in your home in feet. How many square feet would a tablecloth need to be to cover the table?

	Day 1	Day 2	Day 3	Day 4
Week 31	Use play money to show $500. Then, imagine you must divide it between 10 people. How much money will each person get?	Make a set of hundredths cards from 0.10 to 0.20—one card for each hundredth (0.10, 0.11, 0.12, etc.). Draw two cards. Which is greater? By how much?	Find your zip code. Use a calculator to figure out if it is a prime number. Why or why not?	Roll two dice. Use the numbers rolled to make an improper fraction. Rename it as a mixed number.

	Day 1	Day 2	Day 3	Day 4
Week 32	Using a number chart from 1 to 50, cross out all of the numbers divisible by 2. Then, cross out all of the numbers divisible by 3. Continue in this manner to reveal the prime numbers.	Roll three dice. Use the numbers rolled to make a mixed number. Be sure to use the greater number as the denominator. Multiply the mixed number by your age.	Roll two dice. Use the numbers rolled to make a two-digit number. Roll two dice to make another two-digit number. Multiply them.	Ask a partner to draw an angle. Use a protractor to measure the angle.

	Day 1	Day 2	Day 3	Day 4
Week 33	Draw two cards. Face cards are worth 10. Use the numbers drawn to make an improper fraction. Rename it as a mixed number.	Use four sets of cards numbered from 0 to 9. Shuffle them. Have two or three people draw five cards each. Arrange the cards into five-digit numbers. Compare the values.	Create a line plot showing the ages of your family and five friends.	Roll two dice. Write a decimal, to the hundredths, with the numbers rolled. Rewrite it as a fraction. Is the fraction greater or less than 0.5?

	Day 1	Day 2	Day 3	Day 4
Week 34	Use play money to show $1,890. How much more do you need to reach $2,000?	Draw a random amount of play dollar bills. Express the value in amounts of quarters, dimes, and nickels.	Identify three examples of parallel lines in a magazine or newspaper.	Make a set of tenths decimal cards from 0.1 to 1.0. Draw three cards. Order them from least to greatest.

	Day 1	Day 2	Day 3	Day 4
Week 35	Write a division problem where a three-digit number is divided by a one-digit number. Solve it. Erase three digits. Ask a friend or family member to solve for the missing digits.	Measure 10 kitchen utensils such as forks, spatulas, and tongs to the nearest $\frac{1}{8}$ inch. Make a line plot to display the data.	Measure the length, in meters, of the total distance it takes you to walk 10 steps. Convert the number to centimeters. About how many centimeters do you travel with each step?	Gather some shoes together. Divide them into groups of three. Is there a remainder?

	Day 1	Day 2	Day 3	Day 4
Week 36	Roll three dice. Use the numbers rolled to make a mixed number. Use several sheets of paper to model the mixed number. Cut the paper as needed to show the correct fraction.	Draw three cards. Face cards are worth 0. Use the numbers drawn to make a three-digit number. Draw one card to make a one-digit number. Divide the greater number by the smaller number.	Roll two dice to create a decimal to the hundredths place. Repeat three times. Order the decimals from least to greatest. What is the difference between the greatest and smallest decimals?	Measure the length and width of a square or rectangular table in inches. If a tablecloth is to hang over by 4 inches all around, how large of a tablecloth do you need?

	Day 1	Day 2	Day 3	Day 4
Week 37	Use straws or toothpicks to model an angle less than 90°. What type of angle did you model?	Write a three-digit by one-digit multiplication problem. Solve it. Erase three digits. Ask a friend or family member to solve for the missing digits.	Measure the length and width of a room in yards. Find the perimeter.	Divide a deck of 52 cards into 13 equal piles. How many cards are in each pile?

	Day 1	Day 2	Day 3	Day 4
Week 38	Ask an adult to help you measure the height of a ceiling in feet. What is the height in inches?	What time is it? Draw a clock face and use a ruler to show the time. Then, use a protractor to measure the angle formed by the hands of the clock.	Count human, pet, table, and chair legs in your home. Write a number sentence to find the total number of legs in your home.	Gather some kitchen utensils together. Divide them into groups of six. Is there a remainder?

	Day 1	Day 2	Day 3	Day 4
Week 39	Gather 24 of one type of cracker and 16 of another. Divide them into the largest number of groups possible so that each group has the same number of each item. How many items are in each group?	Find the weights of four items from the kitchen. What is the total weight? Convert that weight to a smaller unit.	Find a recipe that uses fractions. How much of each ingredient would you need if you doubled the recipe?	Measure the length and width of two rooms in the unit of your choice. Find the area of each. How much larger is the bigger room?

	Day 1	Day 2	Day 3	Day 4
Week 40	Select a number from 0 to 90. Use a protractor to see the measure of the angle. Model the angle using a door and an adjacent wall.	Measure the length and width of two different book covers in centimeters. What is the difference in their perimeters?	Measure three steps of a family member in feet. How many inches is each of your family member's steps?	Write a four-digit by one-digit multiplication problem. Solve it. Erase three digits. Ask a friend or family member to solve for the missing digits.

Divide the rectangle to show an equal fraction.

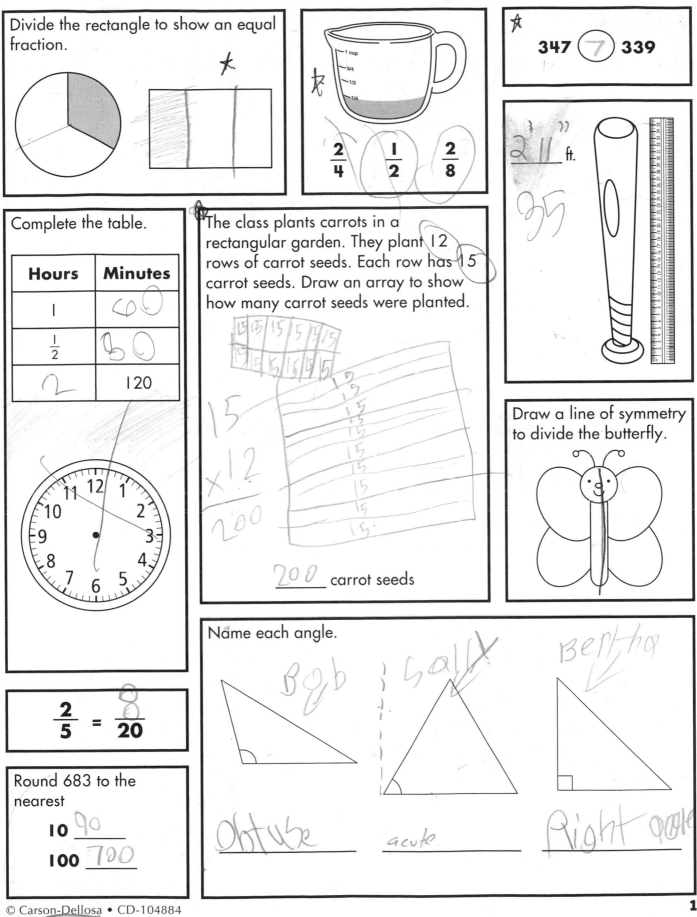

$\frac{2}{4}$ $\frac{1}{2}$ $\frac{2}{8}$

347 ⑦ 339

2 11 ft.

35

Complete the table.

Hours	Minutes
1	60
$\frac{1}{2}$	30
2	120

The class plants carrots in a rectangular garden. They plant 12 rows of carrot seeds. Each row has 15 carrot seeds. Draw an array to show how many carrot seeds were planted.

15
×12
200

_200_ carrot seeds

Draw a line of symmetry to divide the butterfly.

$\frac{2}{5} = \frac{8}{20}$

Round 683 to the nearest

10 _90_

100 _700_

Name each angle.

Bob   Sally   Bertha

Obtuse   acute   Right angle

Write 1,438 in expanded form.

Find all of the factor pairs.

20

What is the place value of the **7**?

732

_____

937

_____

879

_____

10 toy cars fit in each box.

This box is (less than, equal to, more than) $\frac{1}{2}$ full.

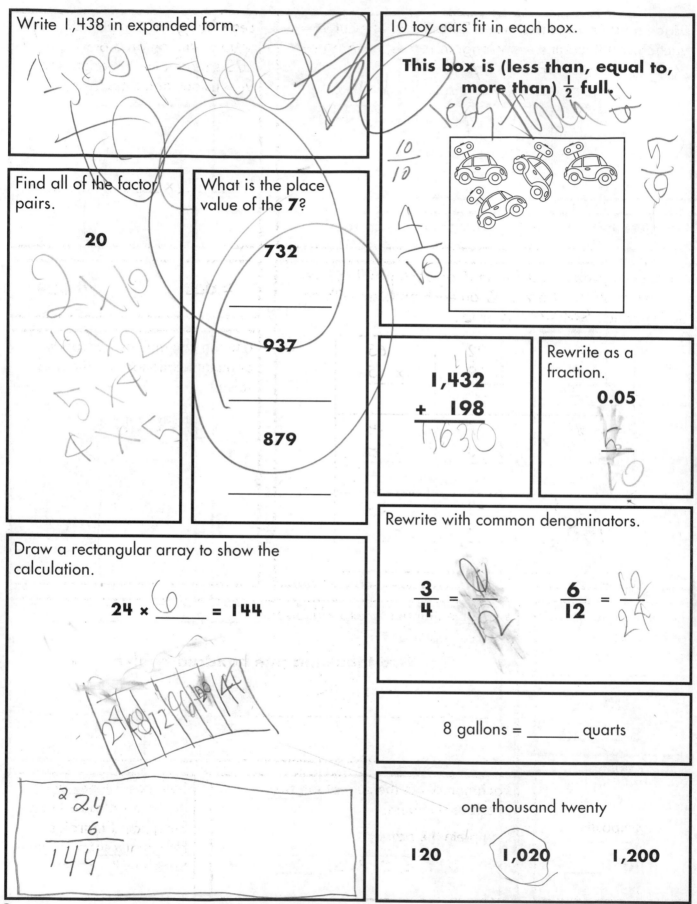

$\begin{array}{r} 1{,}432 \\ +\ \ 198 \\ \hline \end{array}$

Rewrite as a fraction.

0.05

Rewrite with common denominators.

$$\frac{3}{4} = \frac{}{} \qquad \frac{6}{12} = \frac{}{}$$

Draw a rectangular array to show the calculation.

24 × _____ = 144

8 gallons = _____ quarts

one thousand twenty

120　　　**1,020**　　　**1,200**

Claudia had a rope that was 12 feet long. She cut it into 24 equal lengths. How long, in inches, is each new rope? Show your work.

Lee's backyard is a perfect square with an area of 225 square feet. What are the dimensions of his backyard?

_____ × _____ = _____

Solve each problem. Draw an **X** on each problem with an even product. Draw an **O** on each problem with an odd product. Who won, **X** or **O**?

32 × 4	22 × 9	65 × 5
51 × 3	17 × 3	14 × 8
14 × 8	83 × 3	34 × 3

4,009 + _____ = 4,309

Use the commutative property of multiplication to rewrite and solve.

4 × 137 =

Is this number prime or composite?

23

prime

composite

Write the number in expanded form.

two thousand one hundred twelve

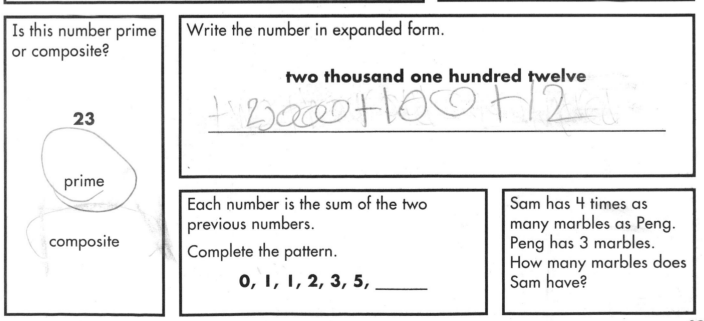

Each number is the sum of the two previous numbers.

Complete the pattern.

0, 1, 1, 2, 3, 5, _____

Sam has 4 times as many marbles as Peng. Peng has 3 marbles. How many marbles does Sam have?

Rewrite the weights in grams.

20.5 kg _____

35 kg _____

Morgan picked three times the strawberries that Tyrell picked. They picked 45 strawberries altogether. How many strawberries did Tyrell pick?

Underline the words that tell you which operation to use.

$\frac{3}{6}$ ◯ $\frac{1}{3}$

There were $3\frac{1}{4}$ pizzas. Five students ate lunch. Each of them ate $\frac{1}{4}$ of a pizza. How much pizza is left?

There are 38 students. If there are 6 seats at each table, how many tables would be needed for all of the students to be able to sit at a table? Show your work.

ten 80s = _____

Add **276** and **39**.

Circle the right triangle.

Round to the nearest thousand.

9,499

Circle the figures that have perpendicular lines.

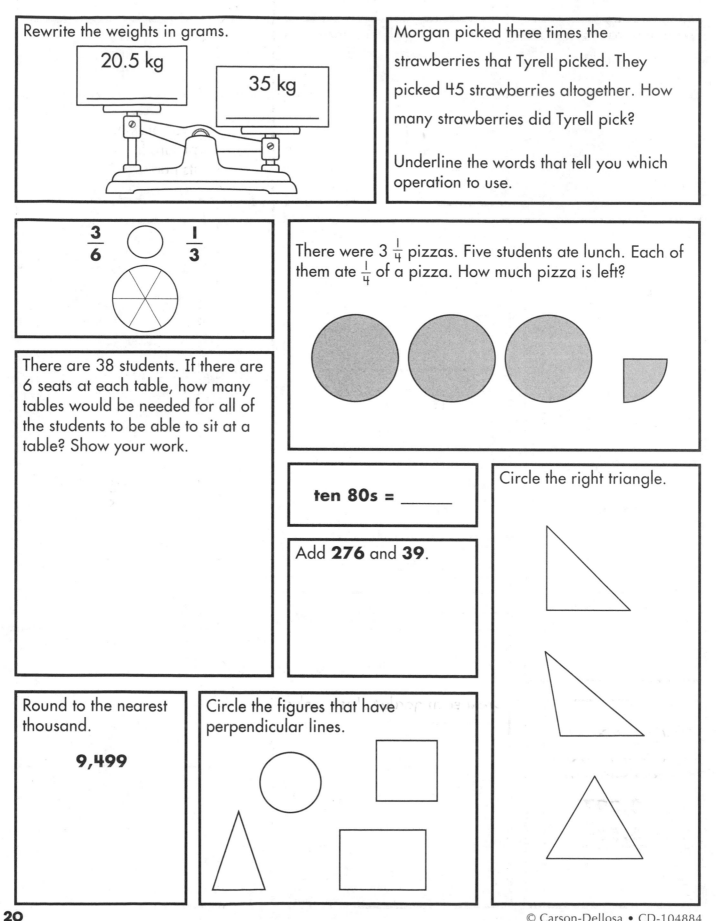

Write the fraction as a sum of other fractions.

$$\frac{3}{4} = \underline{} + \underline{} + \underline{}$$

List the factor pairs of 10.

$\boxed{||\blacksquare} = \dfrac{}{6}$

Look at Jasmine's picture frame. What is its perimeter?

7 in.

5 in.

1,584
×   2

2,326
×   5

Draw a line segment AB that is perpendicular to CD.

C ●————————————● D

How was this equivalent fraction made?

$$\frac{3}{5} = \frac{n \times 3}{n \times 5} = \frac{9}{15}$$

$n = \underline{}$

250 ÷ 5 =

3,397
+ 3,584

Darren's garden is 10 feet by 35 feet, and Trista's garden is 9 feet by 40 feet. How much larger is Trista's garden?

Draw each garden. Then, solve.

What number is 5 times as many as 2? Write an equation to show your answer.

Is **14** composite or prime?

_____

Prove your answer.

It takes 2 oranges to make a glass of orange juice. How many oranges are needed to make 13 glasses of juice?

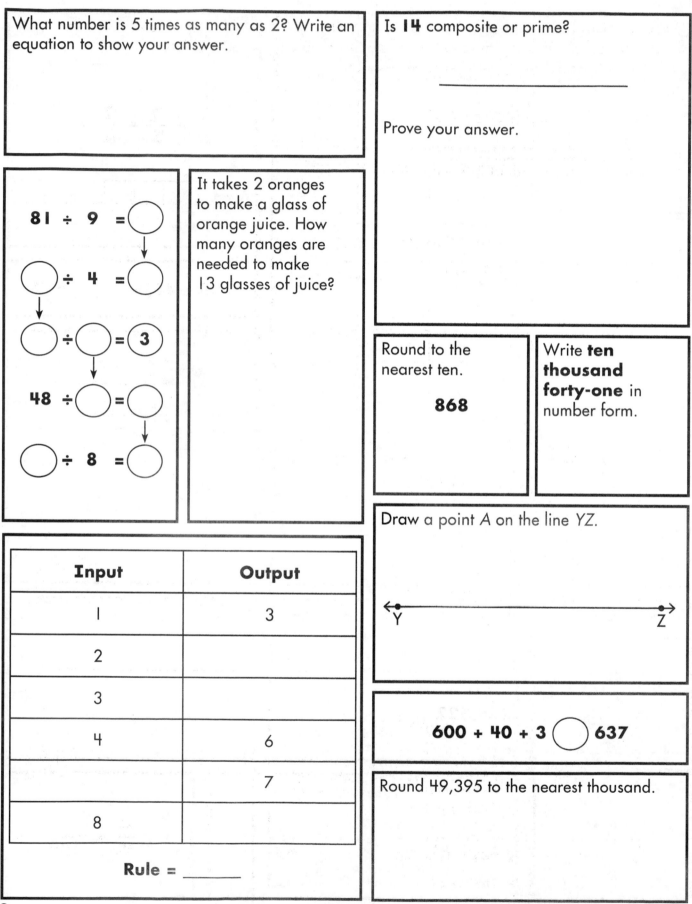

$81 \div 9 = \bigcirc$

$\bigcirc \div 4 = \bigcirc$

$\bigcirc \div \bigcirc = 3$

$48 \div \bigcirc = \bigcirc$

$\bigcirc \div 8 = \bigcirc$

Round to the nearest ten.

868

Write **ten thousand forty-one** in number form.

Draw a point A on the line YZ.

←•————————————————•→
 Y   Z

Input	Output
1	3
2	
3	
4	6
	7
8	

Rule = _____

$600 + 40 + 3 \bigcirc 637$

Round 49,395 to the nearest thousand.

Trudy practices basketball for 1 hour every day. She shoots 90 baskets. If she practiced half of that time, how many baskets would she shoot? Show your work.

Add the fractions. Color the model to match.

$$\frac{1}{8} + \frac{2}{8} + \frac{3}{8} = \underline{}$$

The pattern rule is increase by two. Draw the next term of the pattern.

$$(700 + 80) \div \underline{} = 78$$

$$\frac{7}{9} \bigcirc \frac{7}{12}$$

Draw a model to prove your answer.

Draw a model. Then, solve.

$$4 \times \frac{1}{3} = \underline{}$$

Write each number in expanded form.

6,788 _____

124,422 _____

Rewrite each improper fraction as a mixed number

$$\frac{5}{3} = \qquad \frac{11}{4} =$$

$$\frac{4}{10} = \frac{}{100}$$

The basketball backboard is 72 inches wide. The basketball is 1 foot wide. How many times wider is the basketball backboard than the basketball? Show your work.

Write **5,080** in word form.

_____

_____

Rewrite as a decimal.

$$\frac{32}{100} =$$

Locate 0.45 on the number line.

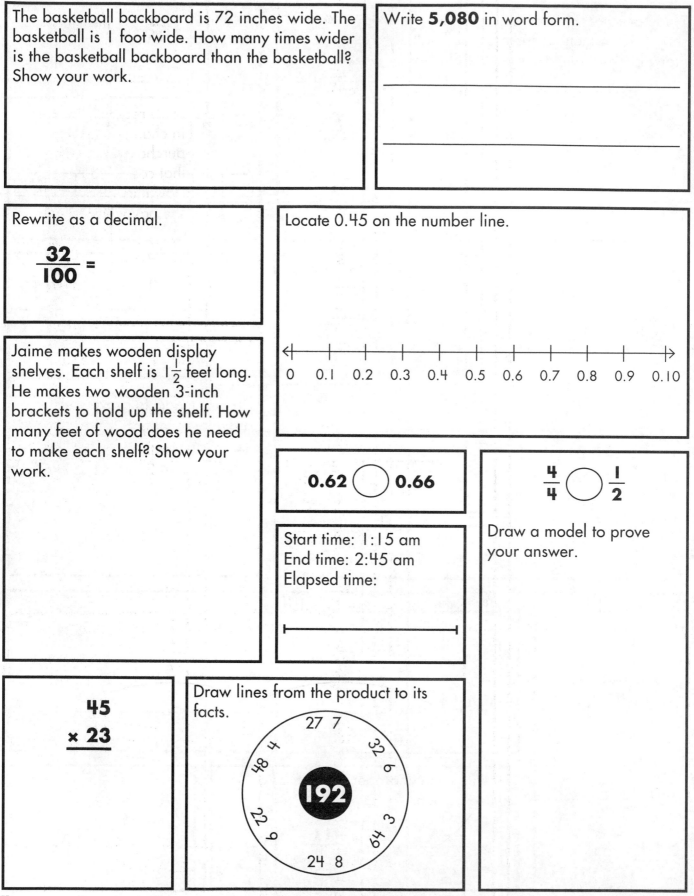

0   0.1   0.2   0.3   0.4   0.5   0.6   0.7   0.8   0.9   0.10

Jaime makes wooden display shelves. Each shelf is $1\frac{1}{2}$ feet long. He makes two wooden 3-inch brackets to hold up the shelf. How many feet of wood does he need to make each shelf? Show your work.

0.62 ◯ 0.66

$\frac{4}{4}$ ◯ $\frac{1}{2}$

Draw a model to prove your answer.

Start time: 1:15 am
End time: 2:45 am
Elapsed time:

45
× 23

Draw lines from the product to its facts.

27   7
4
48   32
6
192
22
9   3
49
24   8

Express as a decimal.

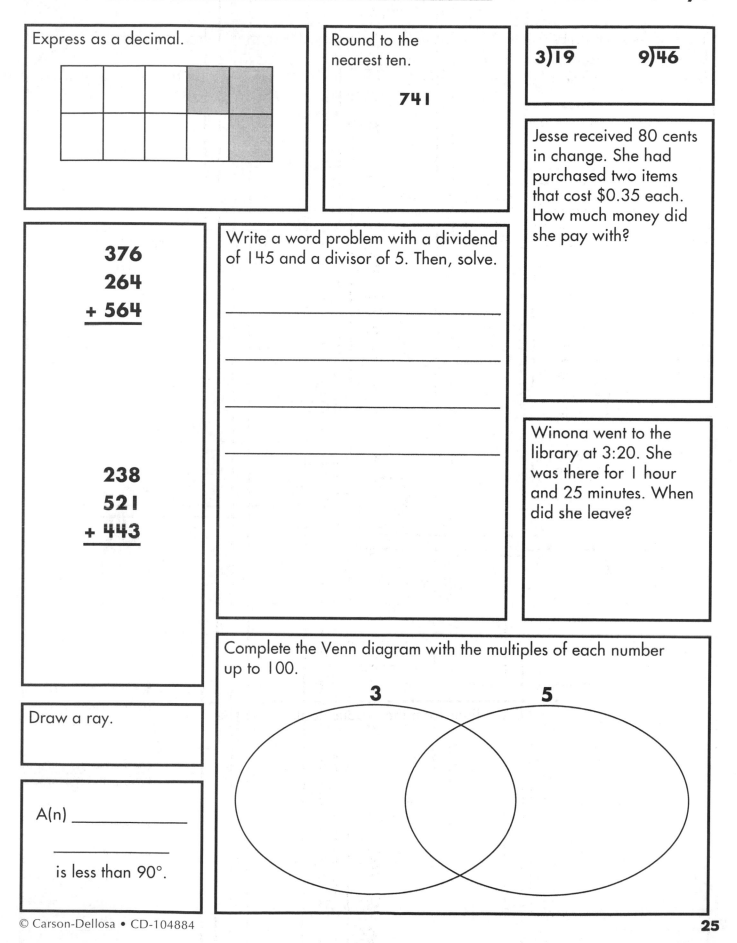

Round to the nearest ten.

741

$3\overline{)19}$ $9\overline{)46}$

Jesse received 80 cents in change. She had purchased two items that cost $0.35 each. How much money did she pay with?

376
264
+ 564

238
521
+ 443

Write a word problem with a dividend of 145 and a divisor of 5. Then, solve.

_____

_____

_____

_____

Winona went to the library at 3:20. She was there for 1 hour and 25 minutes. When did she leave?

Draw a ray.

A(n) _____

_____

is less than 90°.

Complete the Venn diagram with the multiples of each number up to 100.

3   **5**

In 3,609, what is the value of the **3**? _____
How do you know?

_____

_____

Twelve apples fit into the basket.

This basket is (less than, equal to, more than) $\frac{1}{2}$ full?

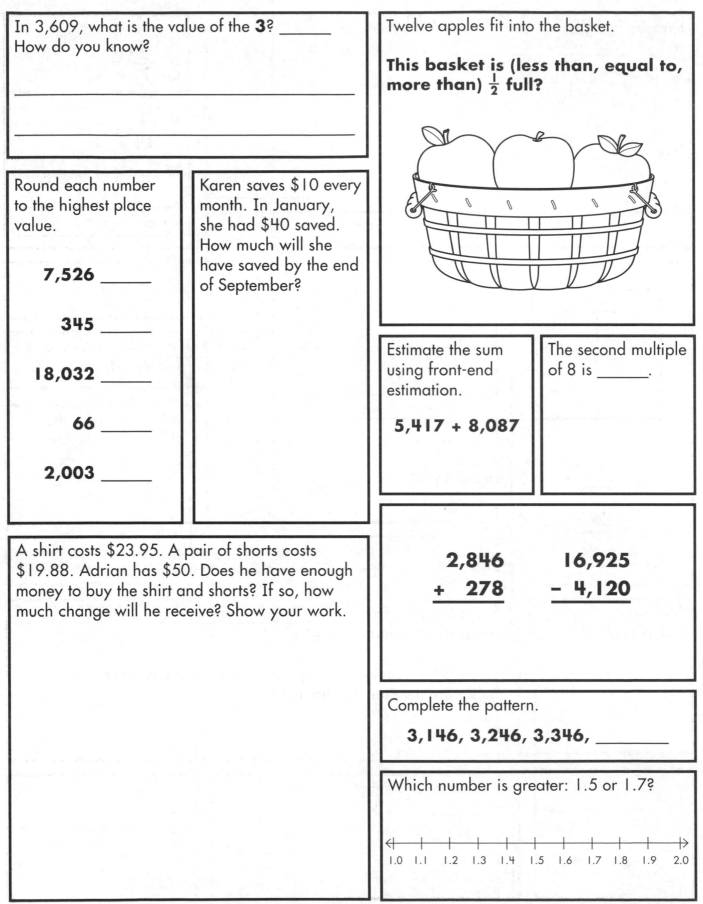

Round each number to the highest place value.

7,526 _____

345 _____

18,032 _____

66 _____

2,003 _____

Karen saves $10 every month. In January, she had $40 saved. How much will she have saved by the end of September?

Estimate the sum using front-end estimation.

5,417 + 8,087

The second multiple of 8 is _____.

A shirt costs $23.95. A pair of shorts costs $19.88. Adrian has $50. Does he have enough money to buy the shirt and shorts? If so, how much change will he receive? Show your work.

$$\begin{array}{r} 2,846 \\ +\ \ 278 \\ \hline \end{array} \qquad \begin{array}{r} 16,925 \\ -\ 4,120 \\ \hline \end{array}$$

Complete the pattern.

3,146, 3,246, 3,346, _____

Which number is greater: 1.5 or 1.7?

1.0 1.1 1.2 1.3 1.4 1.5 1.6 1.7 1.8 1.9 2.0

Find the multiples of each number through 50.

3 _____

4 _____

8 _____

Subtract the fractions.

$$\frac{6}{7} - \frac{2}{7} = \text{—}$$

$$\frac{12}{14} - \frac{4}{14} = \text{—}$$

How are the problems related?

_____

_____

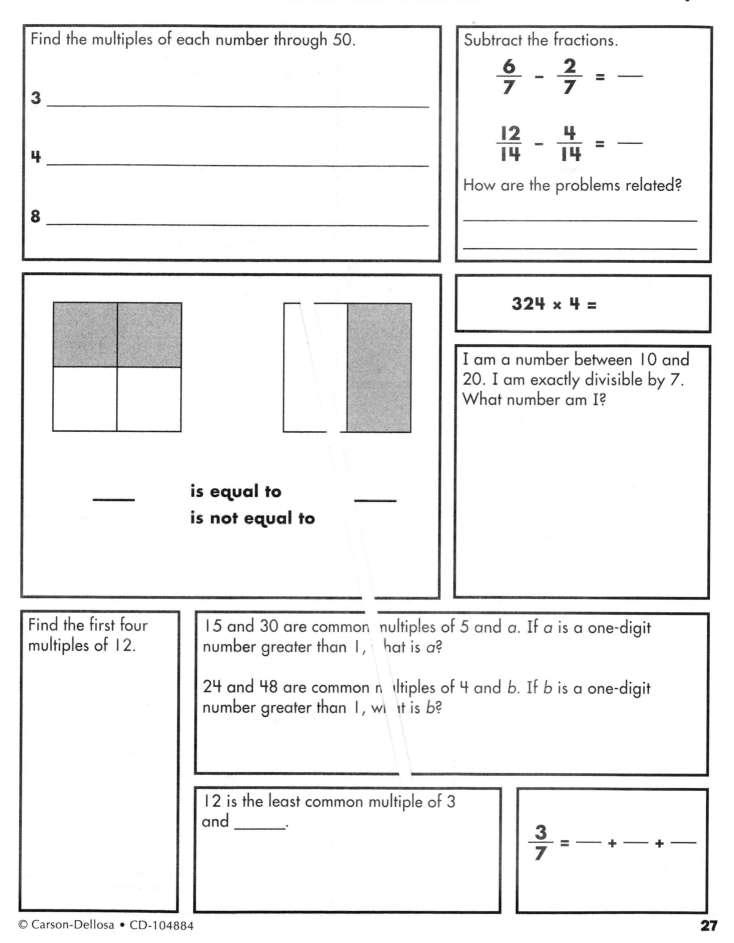

____   **is equal to**   ____
      is not equal to

$$324 \times 4 =$$

I am a number between 10 and 20. I am exactly divisible by 7. What number am I?

Find the first four multiples of 12.

15 and 30 are common multiples of 5 and a. If a is a one-digit number greater than 1, what is a?

24 and 48 are common multiples of 4 and b. If b is a one-digit number greater than 1, what is b?

12 is the least common multiple of 3 and _____.

$$\frac{3}{7} = \text{—} + \text{—} + \text{—}$$

Find the least common multiple of 30 and 48.

$$3,578$$
$$+ 826$$ ⟋ ☐ $$+ 1,936$$ ⟋ ☐ $$+ 6,532$$

2 hundreds = _____ **tens**

20 hundreds = _____ **tens**

Complete the Venn diagram with the factors of each number.

10   **25**

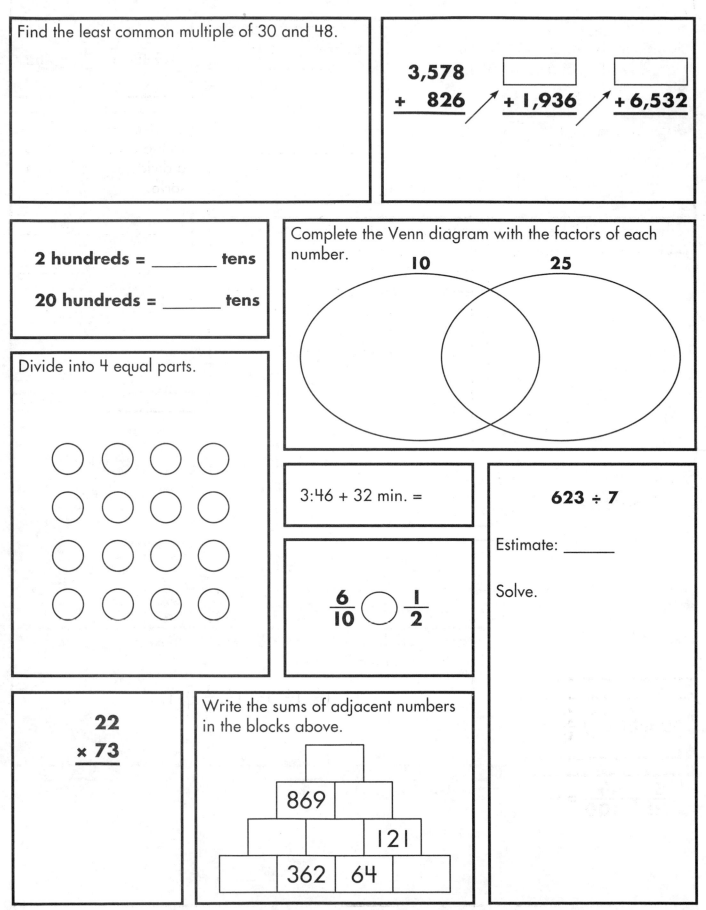

Divide into 4 equal parts.

3:46 + 32 min. =

$$\frac{6}{10} \bigcirc \frac{1}{2}$$

623 ÷ 7

Estimate: _____

Solve.

$$22$$
$$\times 73$$

Write the sums of adjacent numbers in the blocks above.

869	
	121
362	64

Jon read a book for $\frac{3}{4}$ of an hour. He started reading at 5:30. When did he finish?

Inches	Feet
12	1
24	
	3

3.5 lb. = _____ oz.

Write a word problem with a divisor of 3 and a dividend of 36. Then, solve.

_____

_____

_____

What time will it be 43 minutes from now?

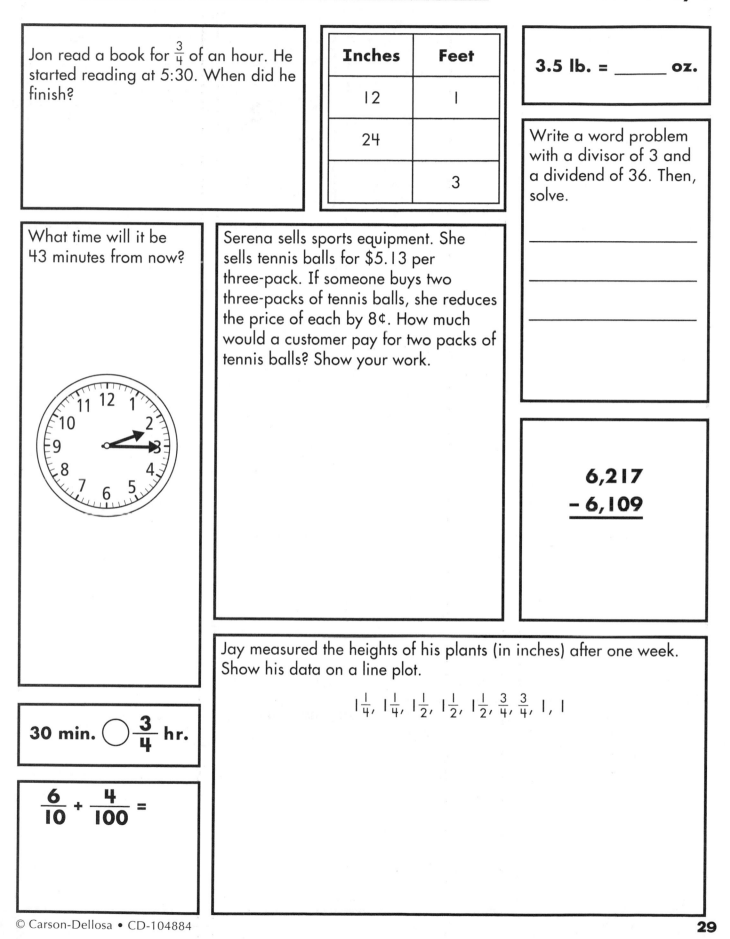

Serena sells sports equipment. She sells tennis balls for $5.13 per three-pack. If someone buys two three-packs of tennis balls, she reduces the price of each by 8¢. How much would a customer pay for two packs of tennis balls? Show your work.

6,217
− 6,109

30 min. $\bigcirc$ $\frac{3}{4}$ hr.

$\frac{6}{10} + \frac{4}{100} =$

Jay measured the heights of his plants (in inches) after one week. Show his data on a line plot.

$1\frac{1}{4}$, $1\frac{1}{4}$, $1\frac{1}{2}$, $1\frac{1}{2}$, $1\frac{1}{2}$, $\frac{3}{4}$, $\frac{3}{4}$, 1, 1

Order the numbers from least to greatest.

5,129   9,125   5,921

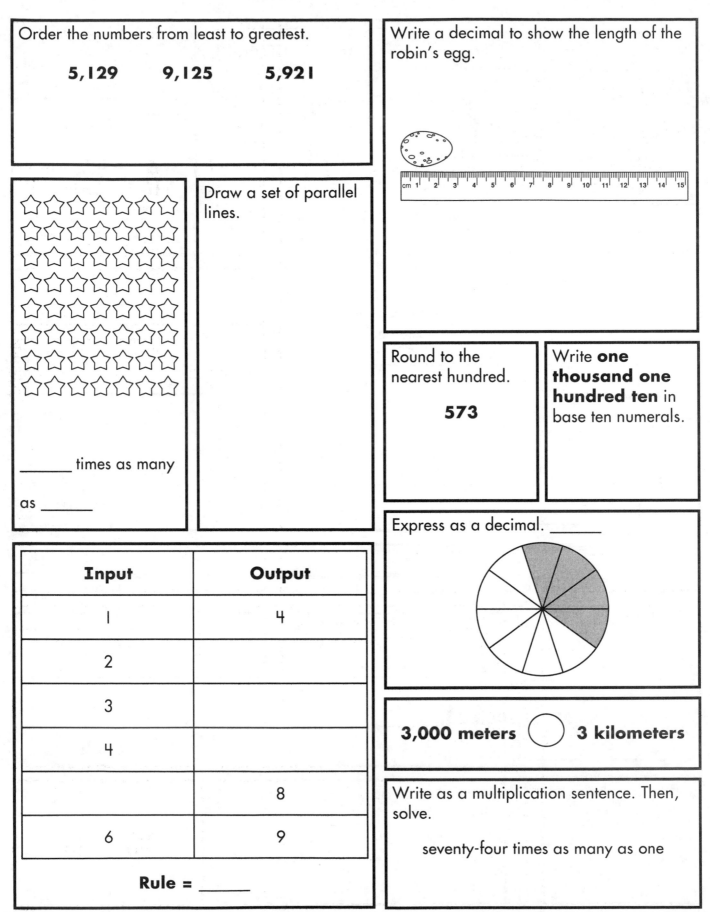

Write a decimal to show the length of the robin's egg.

_____ times as many

as _____

Draw a set of parallel lines.

Round to the nearest hundred.

573

Write **one thousand one hundred ten** in base ten numerals.

Express as a decimal. _____

3,000 meters ◯ **3 kilometers**

Input	Output
1	4
2	
3	
4	
	8
6	9

Rule = _____

Write as a multiplication sentence. Then, solve.

seventy-four times as many as one

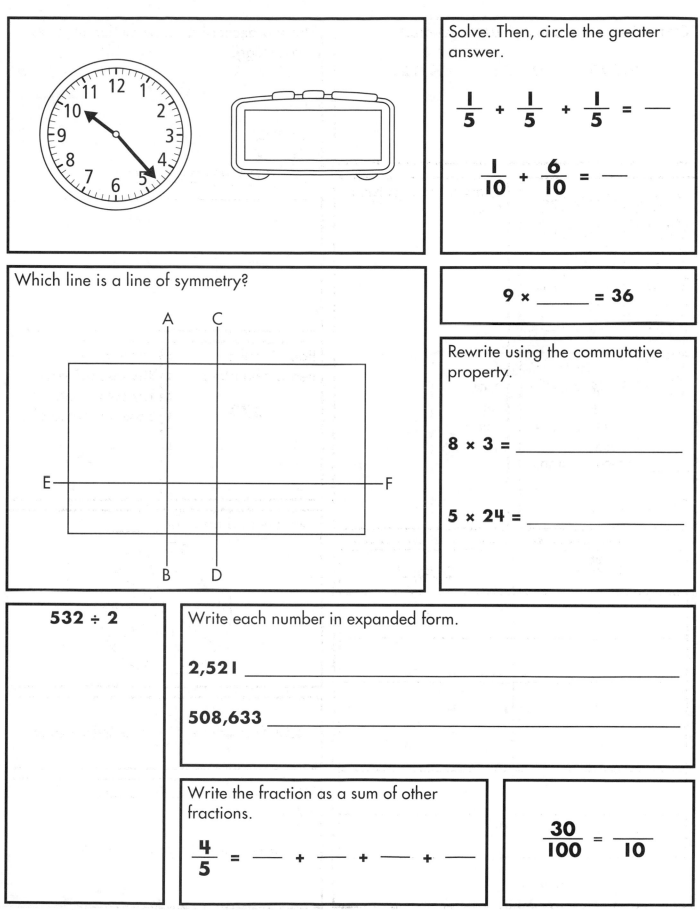

Solve. Then, circle the greater answer.

$$\frac{1}{5} + \frac{1}{5} + \frac{1}{5} = \underline{\quad}$$

$$\frac{1}{10} + \frac{6}{10} = \underline{\quad}$$

Which line is a line of symmetry?

$9 \times \underline{\quad} = 36$

Rewrite using the commutative property.

$8 \times 3 = $ _____

$5 \times 24 = $ _____

$532 \div 2$

Write each number in expanded form.

2,521 _____

508,633 _____

Write the fraction as a sum of other fractions.

$$\frac{4}{5} = \underline{\ } + \underline{\ } + \underline{\ } + \underline{\ }$$

$$\frac{30}{100} = \frac{\underline{\ }}{10}$$

Locate 0.5 on the number line.

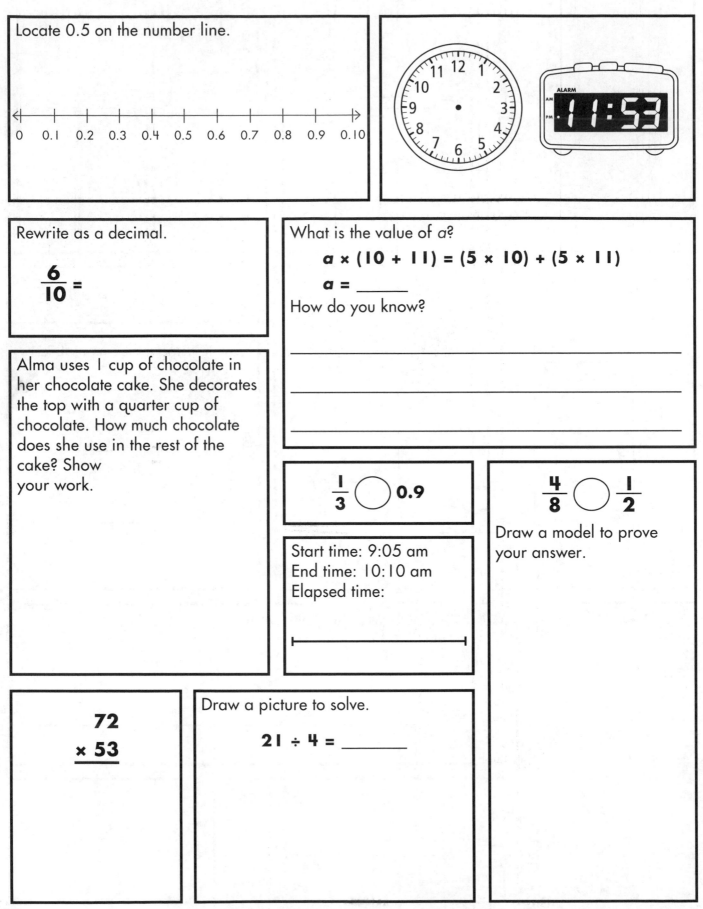

0   0.1   0.2   0.3   0.4   0.5   0.6   0.7   0.8   0.9   0.10

Rewrite as a decimal.

$$\frac{6}{10} =$$

Alma uses 1 cup of chocolate in her chocolate cake. She decorates the top with a quarter cup of chocolate. How much chocolate does she use in the rest of the cake? Show your work.

What is the value of *a*?

$$a \times (10 + 11) = (5 \times 10) + (5 \times 11)$$

$$a = \_\_\_\_\_$$

How do you know?

_____

_____

_____

$$\frac{1}{3} \bigcirc 0.9$$

Start time: 9:05 am
End time: 10:10 am
Elapsed time:

$\vdash$———————$\dashv$

$$\frac{4}{8} \bigcirc \frac{1}{2}$$

Draw a model to prove your answer.

$$\begin{array}{r} 72 \\ \times\ 53 \\ \hline \end{array}$$

Draw a picture to solve.

$$21 \div 4 = \_\_\_\_\_$$

Express as a decimal.

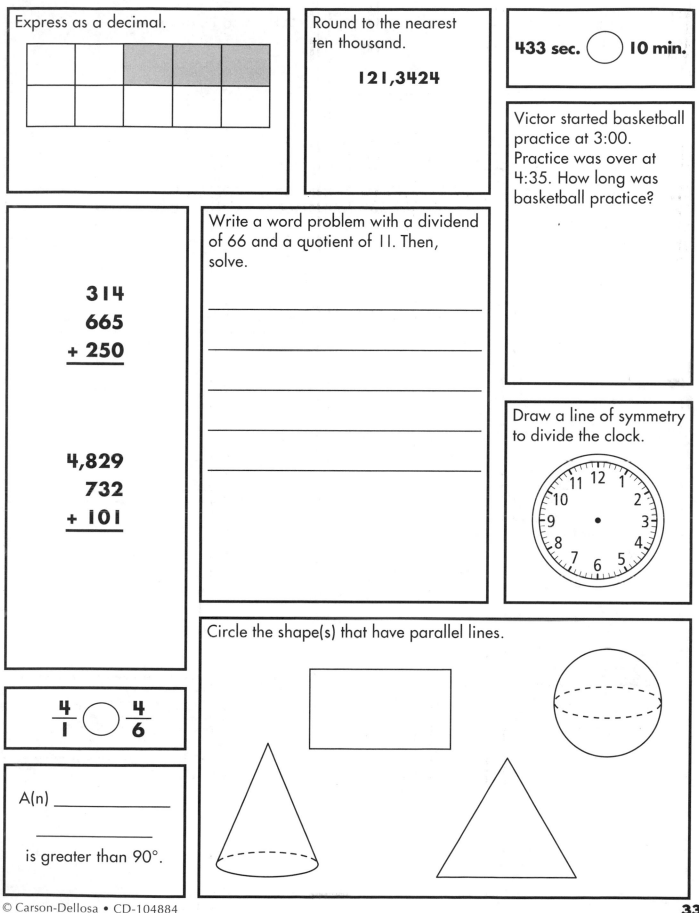

Round to the nearest ten thousand.

121,3424

433 sec. ◯ **10 min.**

Victor started basketball practice at 3:00. Practice was over at 4:35. How long was basketball practice?

314
665
+ 250

4,829
732
+ 101

Write a word problem with a dividend of 66 and a quotient of 11. Then, solve.

_____

_____

_____

_____

_____

Draw a line of symmetry to divide the clock.

$\frac{4}{1}$ ◯ $\frac{4}{6}$

Circle the shape(s) that have parallel lines.

A(n) _____

_____

is greater than 90°.

In 674,757, what is the value of the **4**? _____
How do you know?

_____

_____

Is **27** composite or prime?

_____

Prove your answer.

Color the sections greater than the fraction blue. Color the sections less than the fraction yellow.

$$\frac{2}{5}$$

$\frac{1}{3}$	$\frac{4}{6}$
$\frac{2}{4}$	$\frac{3}{8}$
$\frac{5}{8}$	$\frac{2}{3}$
$\frac{3}{10}$	$\frac{1}{4}$

_____ : _____

What time was it 30 minutes ago?

_____ : _____

Estimate the sum using front-end estimation.

13,371 + 42,590

Express as a decimal.

9,804
- 7,627

A bag of apples costs $2.99. A bunch of bananas costs $2.19. Albert has $5. Does he have enough money to buy the apples and the bananas?

Why or why not?

_____

_____

_____

202,597 ◯ **203,903**

Use the digits on the star to complete the division problem.

13711

_____ ÷ _____ = **9**

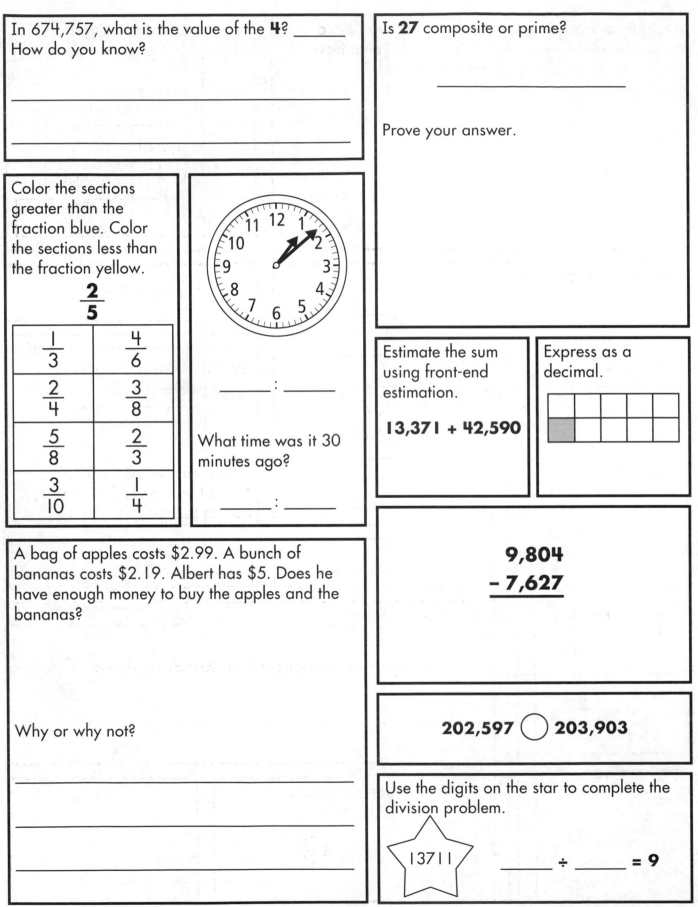

Maya practices guitar for 30 minutes on two days a week. It takes her 2 hours to learn a new song. How many new songs can she learn in four weeks?

Write the sums of adjacent numbers in the blocks above.

3,008
1,921
689
1,146

Draw the next term of the pattern.

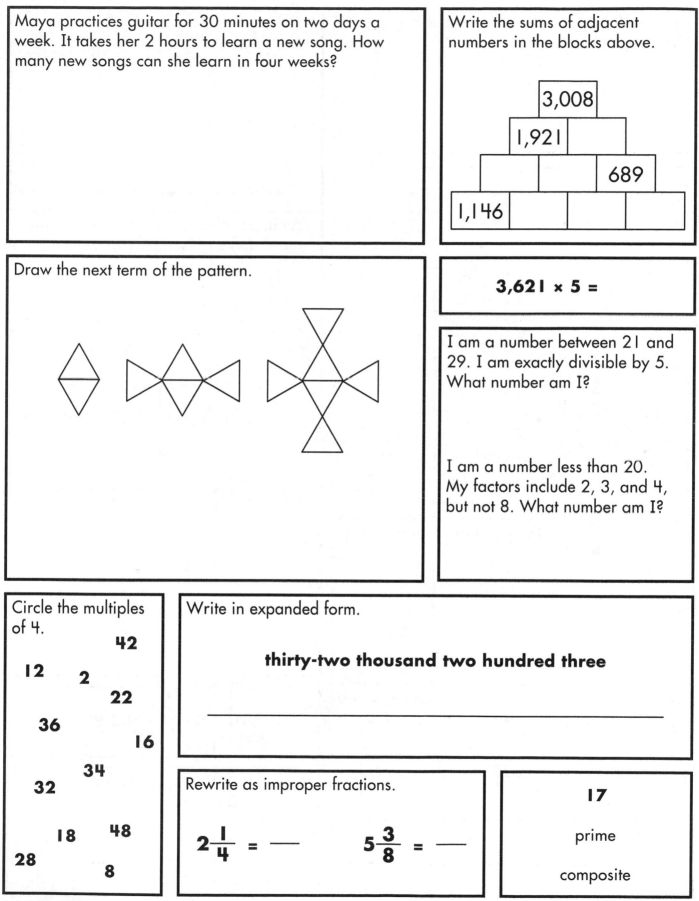

3,621 × 5 =

I am a number between 21 and 29. I am exactly divisible by 5. What number am I?

I am a number less than 20. My factors include 2, 3, and 4, but not 8. What number am I?

Circle the multiples of 4.

42

12   2

22

36

16

34

32

18   48

28

8

Write in expanded form.

thirty-two thousand two hundred three

_____

Rewrite as improper fractions.

$2\frac{1}{4}$ = —— $5\frac{3}{8}$ = ——

17

prime

composite

Write as a multiplication sentence. Then, solve.

eighty-two times as many as eighty-one

What is the value of *a*?

$$4(1 + 4) = (a \times 1) + (a \times 4)$$

3 thousands = _____ hundreds

Mr. Green's class has 36 students. If 12 of them are boys, how many times more girls are there than boys?

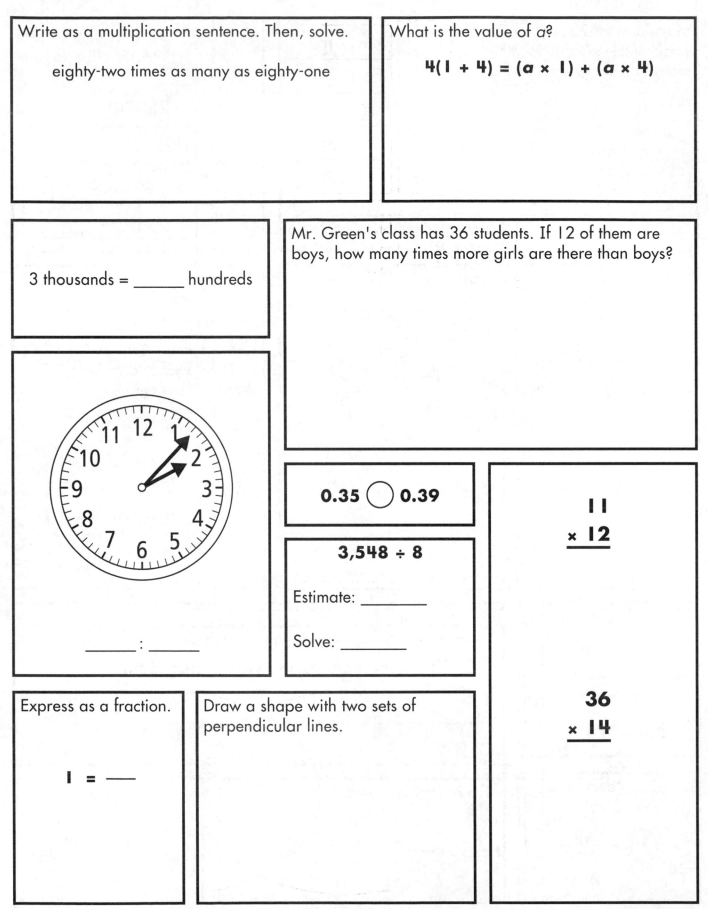

_____ : _____

0.35 ◯ 0.39

3,548 ÷ 8

Estimate: _____

Solve: _____

11
× 12

Express as a fraction.

1 = —

Draw a shape with two sets of perpendicular lines.

36
× 14

Start time: 11:22 pm
End time: 1:19 pm
Elapsed time:

|———————————————————|

km	m	cm
1		100,000
1.5	1,500	
2	2,000	
	3,000	

1,848 ◯ 1,448

Draw the clock hands to show the time it will be 3 hours from 10:55.

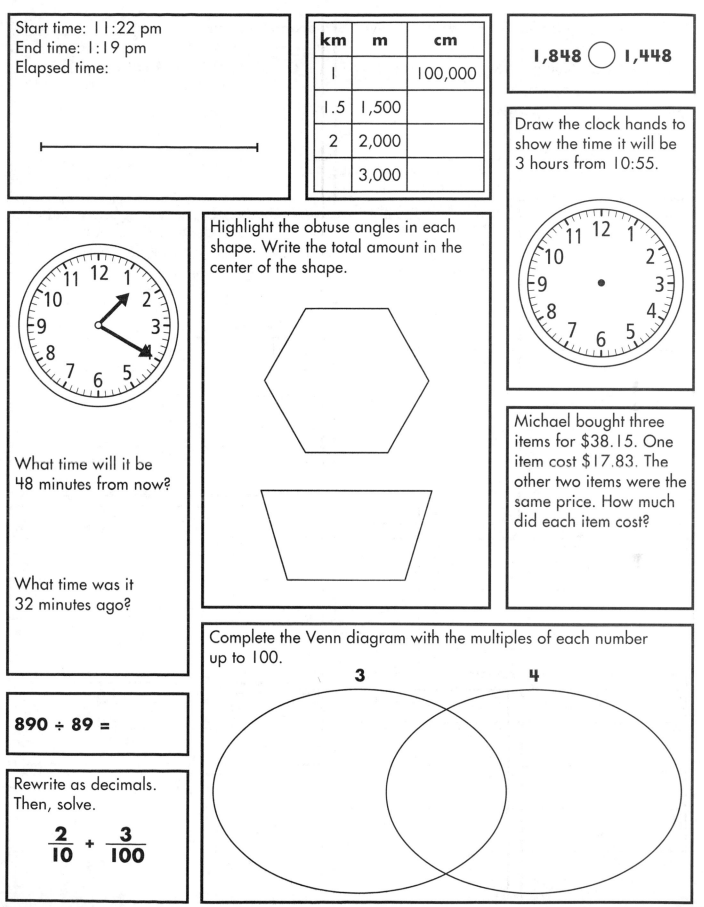

What time will it be 48 minutes from now?

What time was it 32 minutes ago?

Highlight the obtuse angles in each shape. Write the total amount in the center of the shape.

Michael bought three items for $38.15. One item cost $17.83. The other two items were the same price. How much did each item cost?

890 ÷ 89 =

Rewrite as decimals. Then, solve.

$$\frac{2}{10} + \frac{3}{100}$$

Complete the Venn diagram with the multiples of each number up to 100.

3   4

135,811

What is the value of the **3**? _____

What is the value of the **8**? _____

5)27

7)61

It takes three scoops
of ice cream to make
a triple-dip cone.
How many scoops are
needed to make
11 triple-dip cones?

Six balls can fit in the bag.

**The bag is (less than, equal to,
more than) half full.**

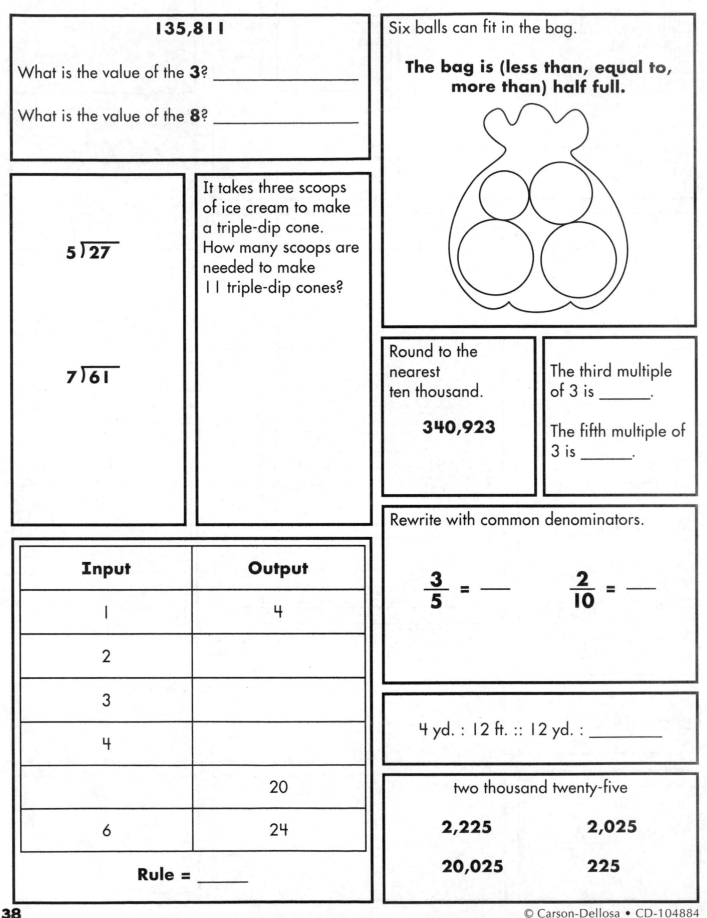

Round to the
nearest
ten thousand.

340,923

The third multiple
of 3 is _____.

The fifth multiple of
3 is _____.

Rewrite with common denominators.

$\dfrac{3}{5}$ = — $\dfrac{2}{10}$ = —

4 yd. : 12 ft. :: 12 yd. : _____

Input	Output
1	4
2	
3	
4	
	20
6	24

Rule = _____

two thousand twenty-five

2,225   **2,025**

20,025   **225**

Find the multiples of each number up to 200.

25 _____

50 _____

75 _____

$$\frac{3}{8} + \frac{2}{8} + \frac{1}{8} = —$$

Draw a model to show the addition.

These fractions (are, are not) equivalent.

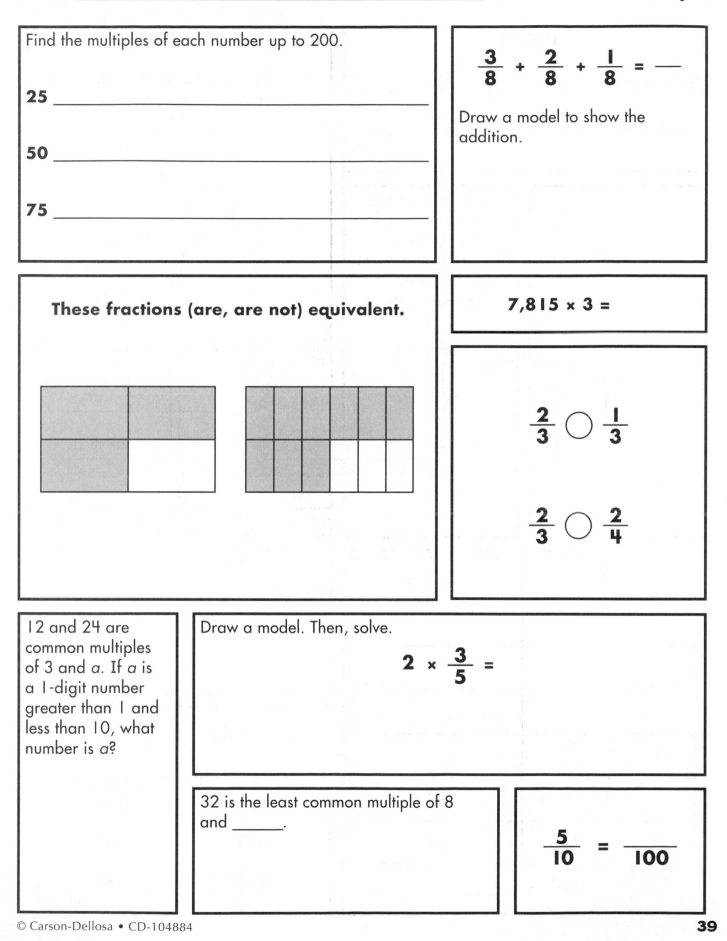

$$7,815 \times 3 =$$

$$\frac{2}{3} \bigcirc \frac{1}{3}$$

$$\frac{2}{3} \bigcirc \frac{2}{4}$$

12 and 24 are common multiples of 3 and a. If a is a 1-digit number greater than 1 and less than 10, what number is a?

Draw a model. Then, solve.

$$2 \times \frac{3}{5} =$$

32 is the least common multiple of 8 and _____.

$$\frac{5}{10} = \frac{}{100}$$

Locate 0.25 on the number line.

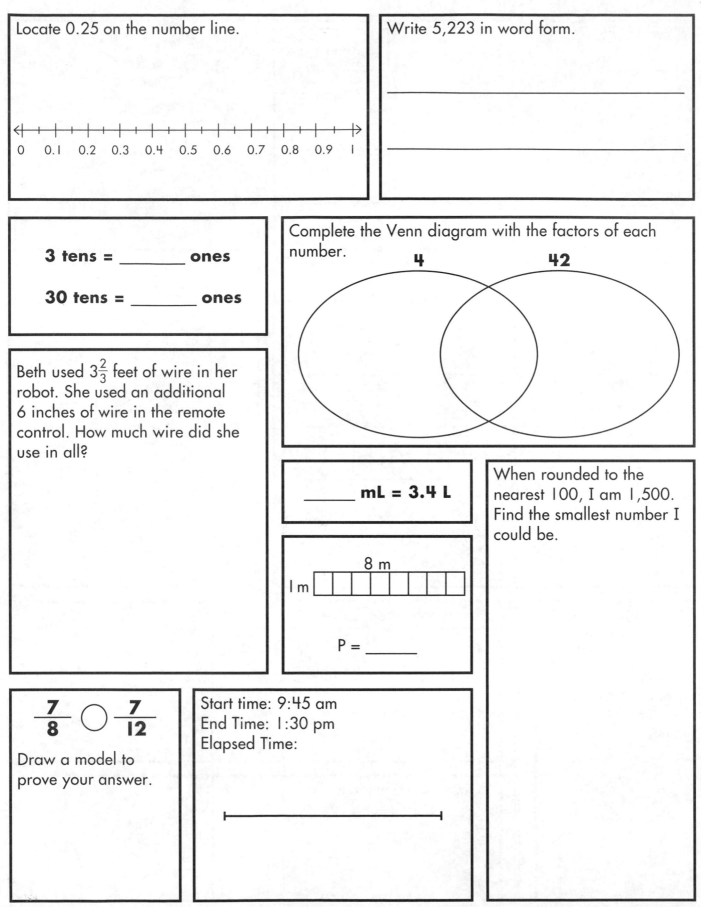

```
⟨——+——+——+——+——+——+——+——+——+——+——⟩
  0   0.1  0.2  0.3  0.4  0.5  0.6  0.7  0.8  0.9   1
```

Write 5,223 in word form.

_____

_____

3 tens = _____ ones

30 tens = _____ ones

Complete the Venn diagram with the factors of each number.

4   **42**

Beth used $3\frac{2}{3}$ feet of wire in her robot. She used an additional 6 inches of wire in the remote control. How much wire did she use in all?

_____ mL = 3.4 L

When rounded to the nearest 100, I am 1,500. Find the smallest number I could be.

8 m

1 m

P = _____

$\frac{7}{8}$ ◯ $\frac{7}{12}$

Draw a model to prove your answer.

Start time: 9:45 am
End Time: 1:30 pm
Elapsed Time:

├———————————————————————┤

Express as a decimal.

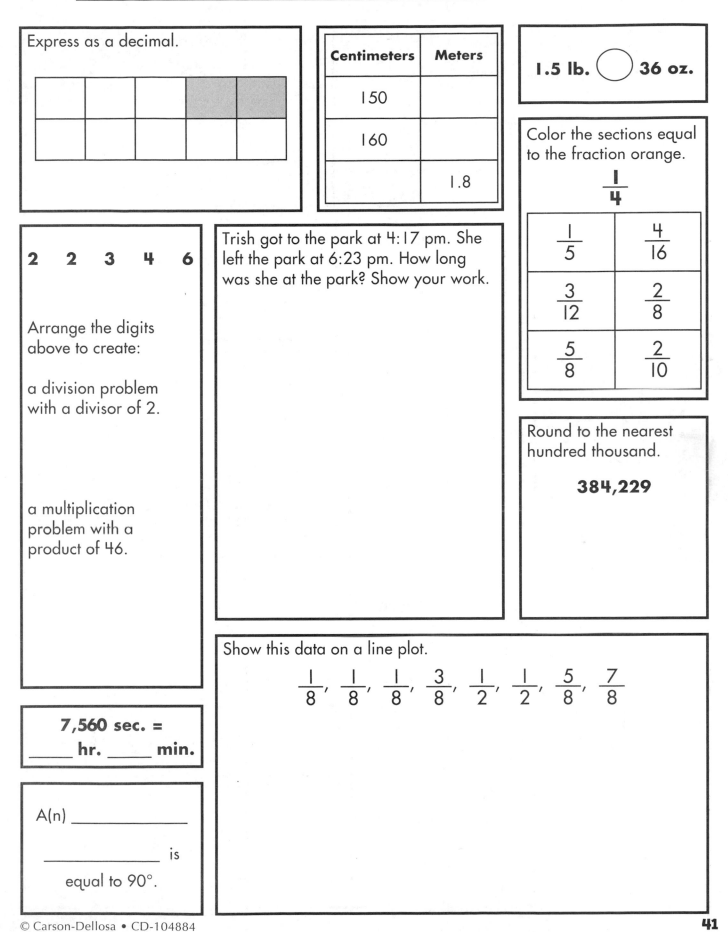

Centimeters	Meters
150	
160	
	1.8

1.5 lb. ◯ 36 oz.

Color the sections equal to the fraction orange.

$$\frac{1}{4}$$

$\frac{1}{5}$	$\frac{4}{16}$
$\frac{3}{12}$	$\frac{2}{8}$
$\frac{5}{8}$	$\frac{2}{10}$

2   2   3   4   6

Arrange the digits above to create:

a division problem with a divisor of 2.

a multiplication problem with a product of 46.

Trish got to the park at 4:17 pm. She left the park at 6:23 pm. How long was she at the park? Show your work.

Round to the nearest hundred thousand.

384,229

7,560 sec. =
_____ hr. _____ min.

A(n) _____

_____ is
equal to 90°.

Show this data on a line plot.

$$\frac{1}{8}, \frac{1}{8}, \frac{1}{8}, \frac{3}{8}, \frac{1}{2}, \frac{1}{2}, \frac{5}{8}, \frac{7}{8}$$

What number is 9 times as many as 5? _____

What number is 7 times as many as 8? _____

Write a decimal to show the length of a chicken's egg. _____

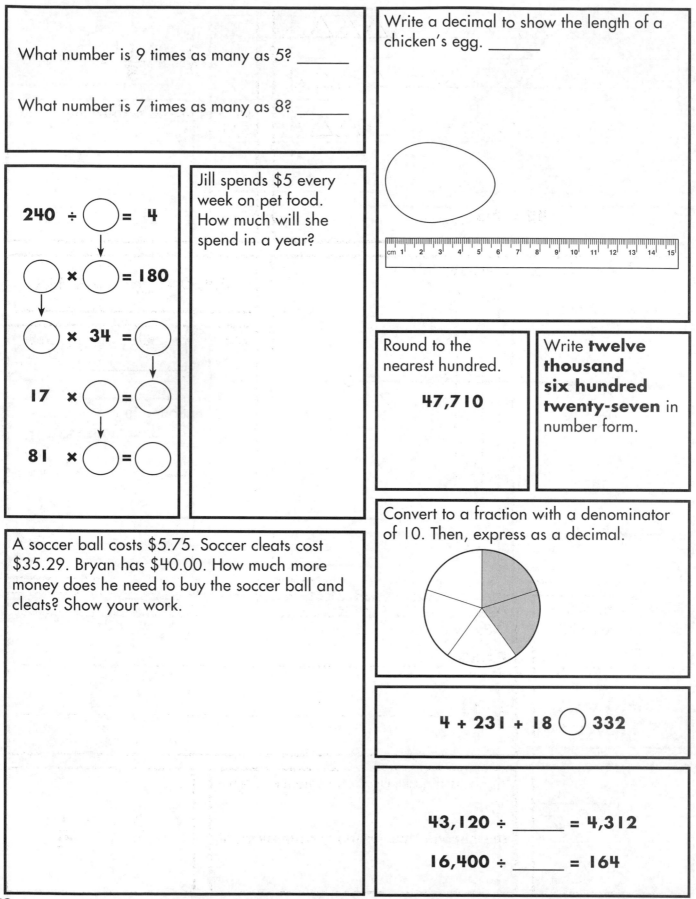

$240 \div \bigcirc = 4$

$\bigcirc \times \bigcirc = 180$

$\bigcirc \times 34 = \bigcirc$

$17 \times \bigcirc = \bigcirc$

$81 \times \bigcirc = \bigcirc$

Jill spends $5 every week on pet food. How much will she spend in a year?

Round to the nearest hundred.

47,710

Write **twelve thousand six hundred twenty-seven** in number form.

Convert to a fraction with a denominator of 10. Then, express as a decimal.

A soccer ball costs $5.75. Soccer cleats cost $35.29. Bryan has $40.00. How much more money does he need to buy the soccer ball and cleats? Show your work.

$4 + 231 + 18 \bigcirc 332$

$43,120 \div \underline{\quad} = 4,312$

$16,400 \div \underline{\quad} = 164$

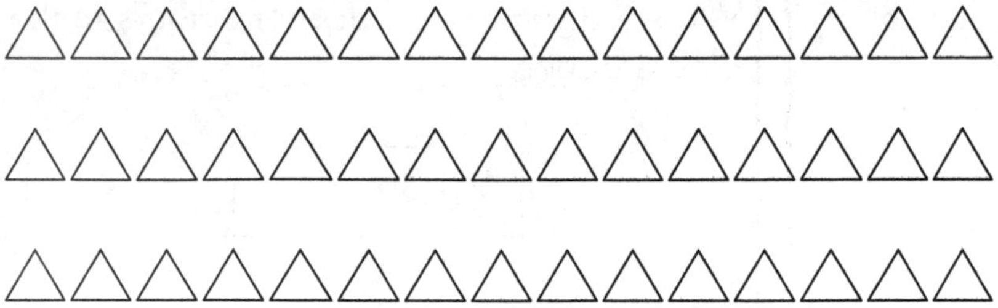

△△△△△△△△△△△△△△△
△△△△△△△△△△△△△△△
△△△△△△△△△△△△△△△

45 = 3 × _____

$$\frac{3}{4} - \frac{1}{4} = \underline{\quad}$$

Draw a model to show the subtraction.

Which line is a line of symmetry?

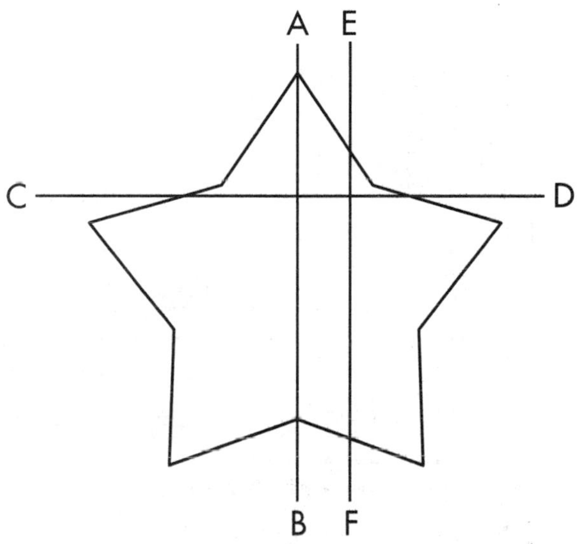

A   E

C ———————————— D

B   F

3,820 + _____ = 4,194

What is the area of the square?

8 yd.

Find four multiples of 5 between 120 and 150.

Write in expanded form.

7,063 _____

2,411 _____

Write as a multiplication sentence. Then, solve.

seventy-one times as many as thirty-eight

$$\frac{7}{8} \bigcirc \frac{1}{2}$$

Find the least common multiple of 24 and 18.

Write the sums of adjacent numbers in the blocks above.

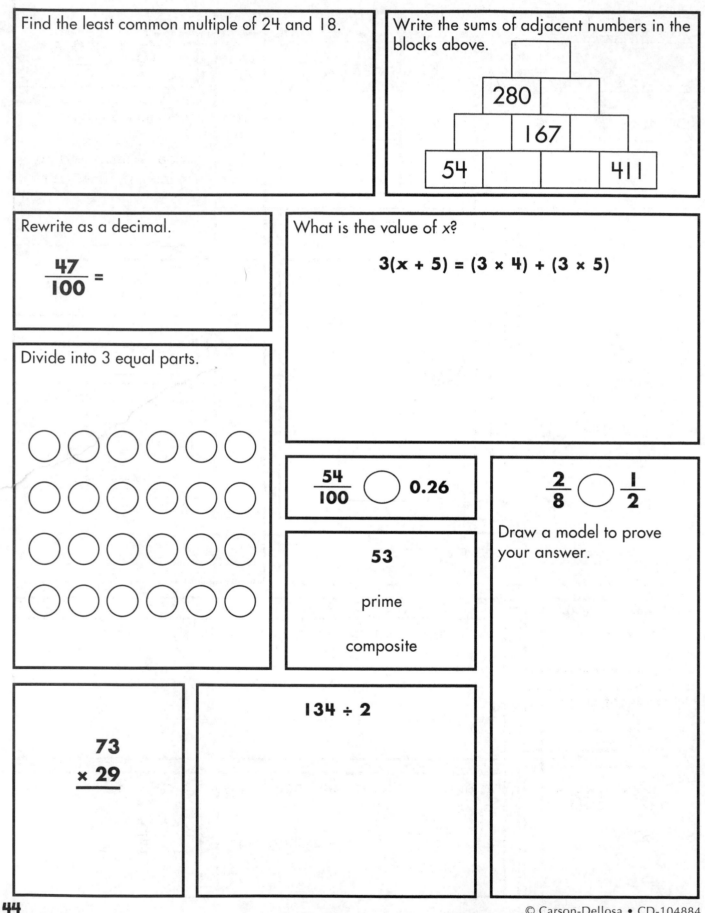

Rewrite as a decimal.

$$\frac{47}{100} =$$

What is the value of x?

$$3(x + 5) = (3 \times 4) + (3 \times 5)$$

Divide into 3 equal parts.

$\frac{54}{100}$ ◯ 0.26

$\frac{2}{8}$ ◯ $\frac{1}{2}$

Draw a model to prove your answer.

53

prime

composite

73
× 29

134 ÷ 2

A house is 21 feet tall. How many inches tall is the house? Show your work.

1.65 L = _____ mL

13.65 L = _____ mL

$\dfrac{7}{10}$ ◯ 0.6

A picture frame is 3 feet high by 2 feet wide. What is its area in inches? Show your work.

What time will it be 17 minutes from now?

What time was it 30 minutes ago?

Draw a congruent shape.

Draw a line of symmetry.

straight angle

_____ °

$\dfrac{5}{10}$ + $\dfrac{1}{100}$ =

Circle the shape(s) that have perpendicular sides.

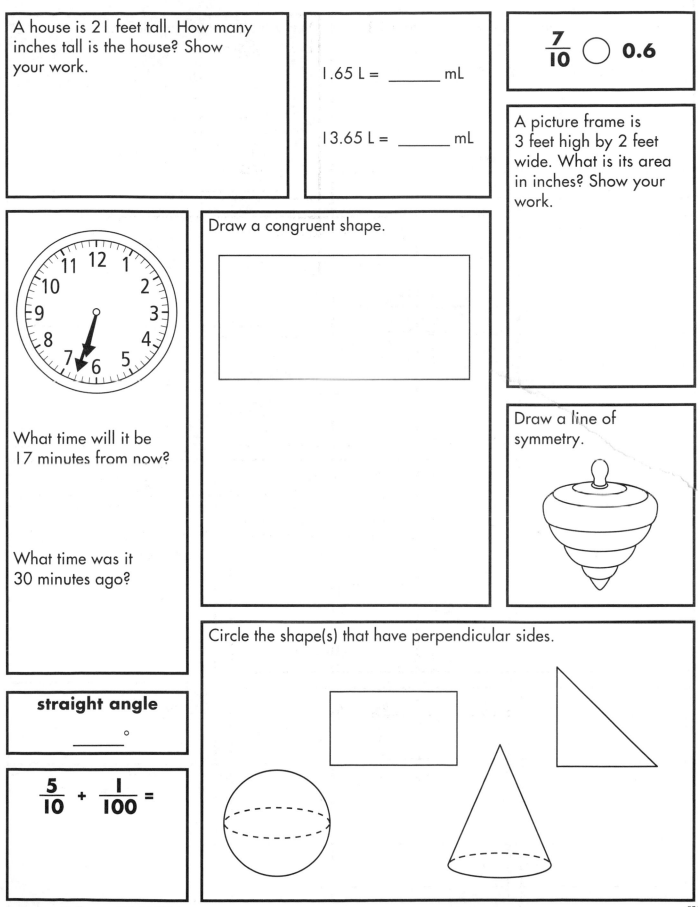

397,532

What is the value of the **7**? _____

What is the value of the **9**? _____

---

348 ÷ 3

505 ÷ 5

```
   ┌─────────┐
   │         │
   └─────────┘
 -     738
 ─────────
   2,734
```

Is **33** composite or prime?

_____

Prove your answer.

Round to the nearest hundred.

29,610

$$\frac{3}{8} + \frac{1}{8} =$$

45,733
- 13,682

Round **26,296** using front-end estimation.

Write as a multiplication sentence. Then, solve.

forty five times as many as sixty five

Rule = –2, ×2

Input	Output
10	16
12	
11	
	14
5	6
8	

Find the multiples of 2.

Find the multiples of 3.

Circle the common multiples.

Express as a decimal.

These fractions (are, are not) equivalent.

What composite number comes after 43?

$\dfrac{3}{4}$ ◯ $\dfrac{2}{4}$

$\dfrac{3}{4}$ ◯ $\dfrac{1}{2}$

2,384
4,629
+ 739

Rewrite as an improper fraction.

$3\dfrac{4}{6} =$

$4\dfrac{3}{5} =$

Write the fraction as a sum of other fractions.

$\dfrac{2}{8} =$

$\dfrac{60}{100} = \dfrac{}{10}$

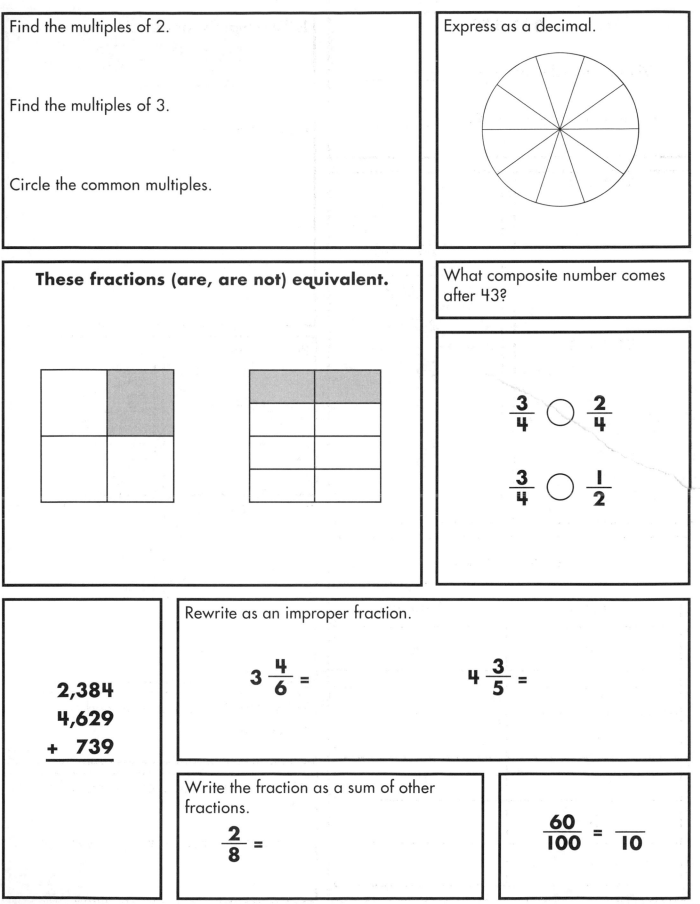

Locate 0.75 on the number line.

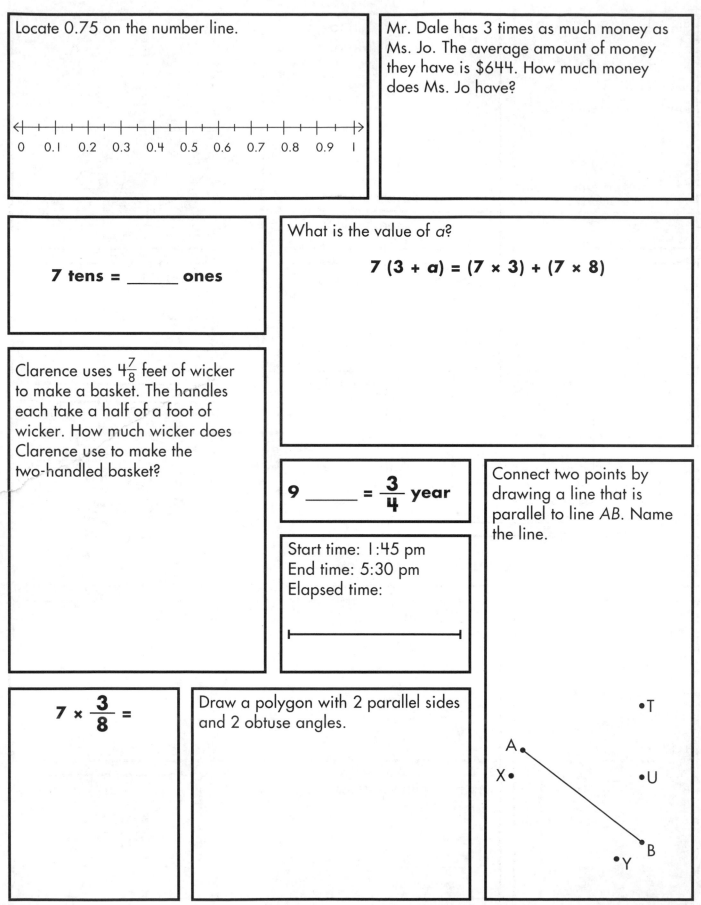

0   0.1   0.2   0.3   0.4   0.5   0.6   0.7   0.8   0.9   1

Mr. Dale has 3 times as much money as Ms. Jo. The average amount of money they have is $644. How much money does Ms. Jo have?

7 tens = _____ ones

What is the value of *a*?

7 (3 + a) = (7 × 3) + (7 × 8)

Clarence uses $4\frac{7}{8}$ feet of wicker to make a basket. The handles each take a half of a foot of wicker. How much wicker does Clarence use to make the two-handled basket?

9 _____ = $\frac{3}{4}$ year

Start time: 1:45 pm
End time: 5:30 pm
Elapsed time:

Connect two points by drawing a line that is parallel to line *AB*. Name the line.

$7 \times \dfrac{3}{8} =$

Draw a polygon with 2 parallel sides and 2 obtuse angles.

•T

A•

X•   •U

•Y   B

Name _____

Start time: 12:02 pm
End time: 12:19 pm
Elapsed time:

|——————————————————————|

Round to the nearest hundred.

34,592

0.82 ◯ 0.91

Color the sections less than the fraction purple.

$$\frac{3}{8}$$

$\frac{1}{3}$	$\frac{3}{6}$
$\frac{4}{10}$	$\frac{2}{3}$
$\frac{2}{7}$	$\frac{1}{5}$

3 4 4 6 8 9

Arrange the digits above to create:

a division problem with a divisor of 4.

a multiplication problem with a factor of 96.

Sven went to see a movie. The movie started at 5:10 pm. It was 1 hour and 50 minutes long. What time did the movie end? Show your work.

Sally had $13.42. She found 3 quarters. How much money does she have now?

$$\frac{7}{10} + \frac{3}{100} =$$

? – 5,293 = 7,384

Circle the shape(s) that have acute angles.

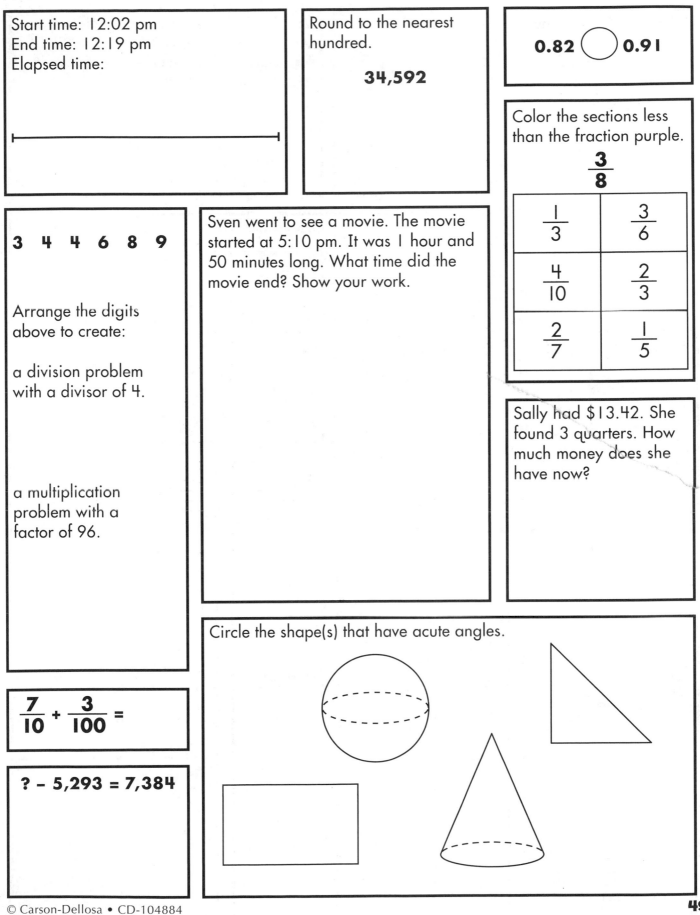

237,581

What is the value of the **2**? _____

What is the value of the **1**? _____

$81 \div 9 = \bigcirc$

$\bigcirc \div 4 = \bigcirc$

$\bigcirc \div \bigcirc = 3$

$48 \div \bigcirc = \bigcirc$

$\bigcirc \div 8 = \bigcirc$

Anne uses two scoops of raisins when she makes cinnamon raisin bread.

How many scoops are needed to make 15 loaves of bread?

Twenty-four books fit on the shelf.

This shelf is (less than, equal to, more than) $\frac{1}{2}$ full.

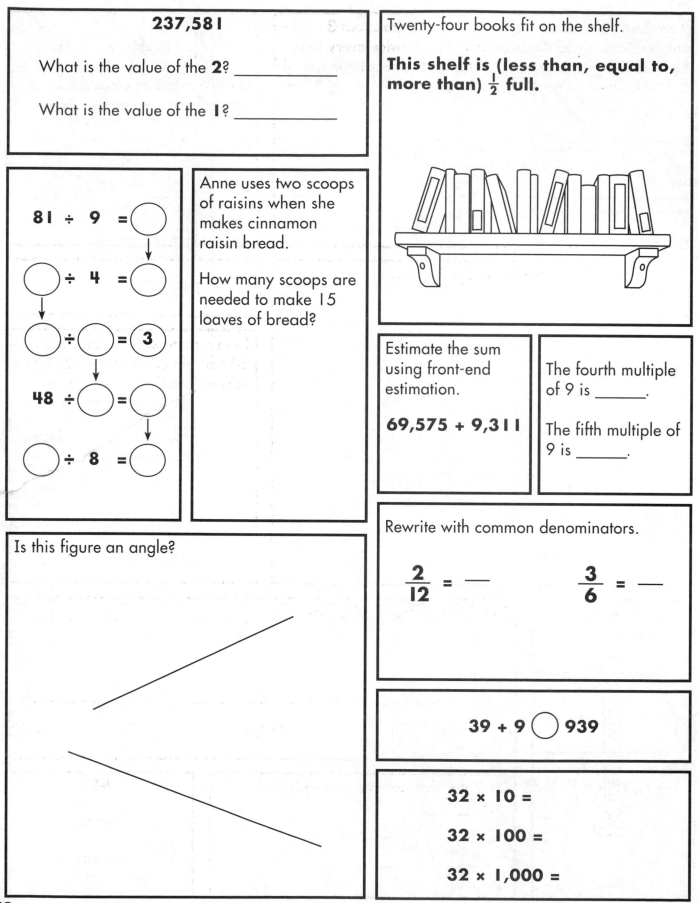

Estimate the sum using front-end estimation.

69,575 + 9,311

The fourth multiple of 9 is _____.

The fifth multiple of 9 is _____.

Rewrite with common denominators.

$\frac{2}{12} = \underline{\quad}$ $\frac{3}{6} = \underline{\quad}$

Is this figure an angle?

$39 + 9 \bigcirc 939$

$32 \times 10 =$

$32 \times 100 =$

$32 \times 1,000 =$

Tara played darts at the fair. It cost 50¢ to shoot 3 darts. She popped the balloons at least twice every time she played. If she spent $2, what is the fewest number of balloons that she popped? Show your work.

$$\frac{9}{12} - \frac{6}{12} =$$

Draw a model to show the subtraction.

The pattern rule is **increase by 2**. Draw the next term of the pattern.

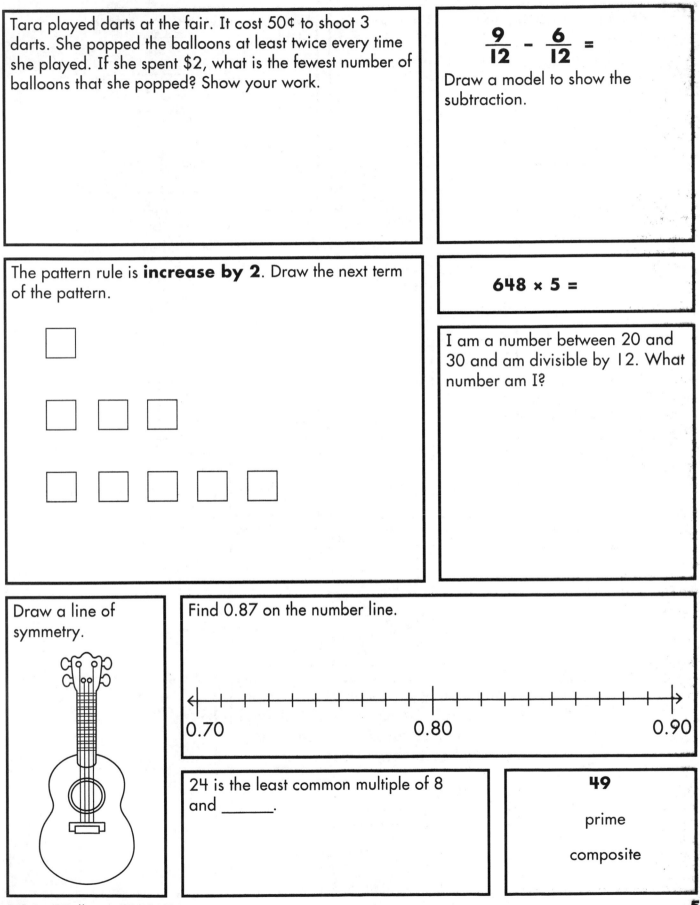

---

648 × 5 =

I am a number between 20 and 30 and am divisible by 12. What number am I?

Draw a line of symmetry.

Find 0.87 on the number line.

0.70   0.80   0.90

---

24 is the least common multiple of 8 and _____.

49

prime

composite

Write as a multiplication sentence. Then, solve.

eighty-three times as many as seventy-six

Write the sums of adjacent numbers in the blocks above.

	440	
211		
	36	64

9 hundreds = _____ tens

Han is saving money to buy a new book. Last month, he saved $2. This month he saved three times as much. How much did he save this month?

A room measures 18 feet by 16 feet. Martin wants to buy a rug. He wants to leave 2 feet all of the way around the rug. What is the area of the rug that he buys? Show your work.

90 sec. = _____ min.

$\frac{1}{8} \bigcirc \frac{1}{2}$

Draw a model to prove your answer.

943 ÷ 5

Estimate: _____

Solve: _____

2,147 ÷ 5

There are 53 baseballs. Coach Leslie wants to put 7 baseballs in each bag. How many bags does he need? How many baseballs will be left over?

Express as a decimal.

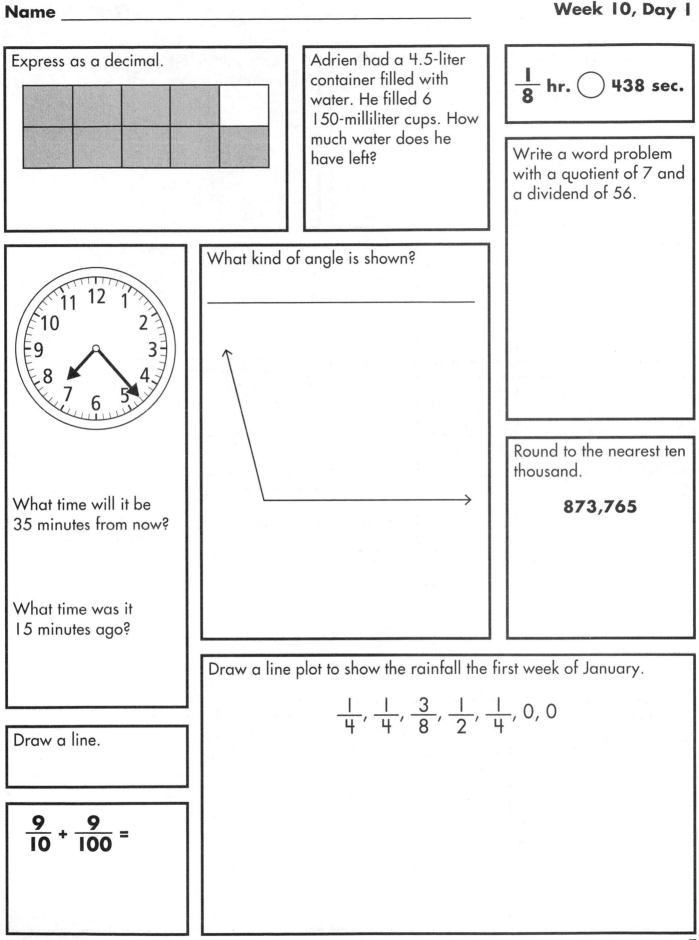

Adrien had a 4.5-liter container filled with water. He filled 6 150-milliliter cups. How much water does he have left?

$\frac{1}{8}$ hr. ◯ 438 sec.

Write a word problem with a quotient of 7 and a dividend of 56.

What time will it be 35 minutes from now?

What time was it 15 minutes ago?

What kind of angle is shown?

_____

Round to the nearest ten thousand.

873,765

Draw a line.

$\frac{9}{10} + \frac{9}{100} =$

Draw a line plot to show the rainfall the first week of January.

$\frac{1}{4}, \frac{1}{4}, \frac{3}{8}, \frac{1}{2}, \frac{1}{4}, 0, 0$

What number is 5 times as many as 5? _____

What number is 12 times as many as 12? _____

237 ÷ 4

563 ÷ 5

Ian saves $25 each month. He started saving in July. How much will he have in December?

Write a decimal to show the length of the hummingbird's egg.

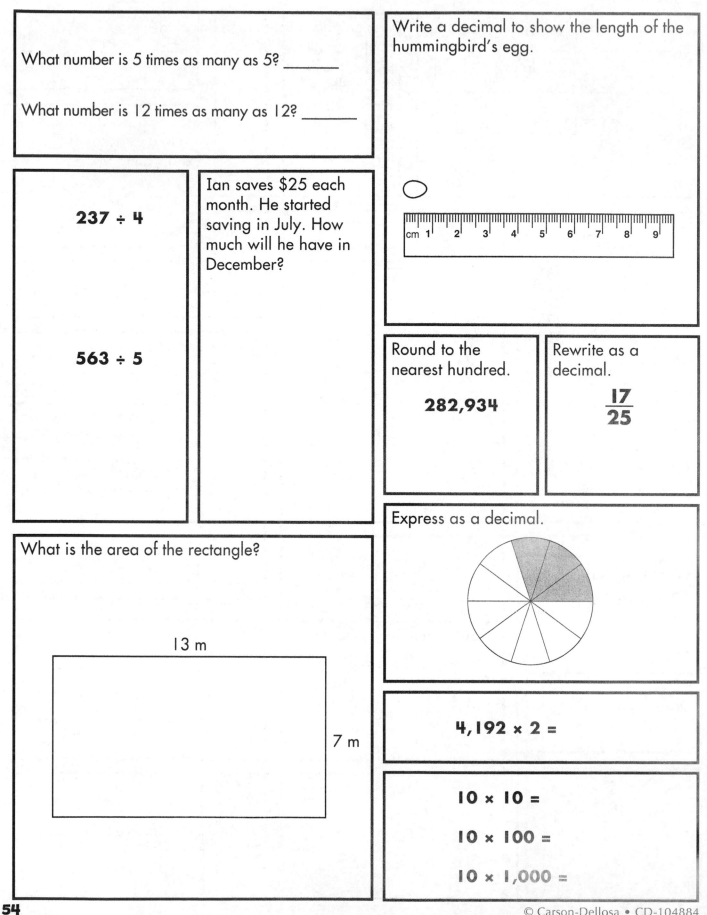

Round to the nearest hundred.

282,934

Rewrite as a decimal.

$\dfrac{17}{25}$

Express as a decimal.

What is the area of the rectangle?

13 m

7 m

4,192 × 2 =

10 × 10 =

10 × 100 =

10 × 1,000 =

Find the multiples of each number up to 70.

5 _____

8 _____

12 _____

Express as a decimal.

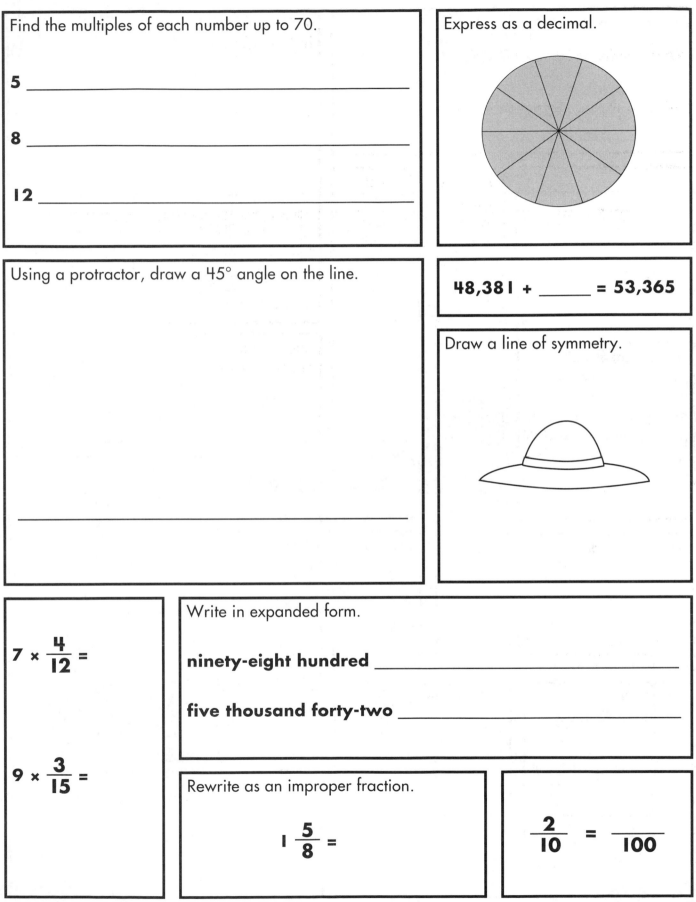

Using a protractor, draw a 45° angle on the line.

_____

48,381 + _____ = 53,365

Draw a line of symmetry.

$7 \times \dfrac{4}{12} =$

$9 \times \dfrac{3}{15} =$

Write in expanded form.

ninety-eight hundred _____

five thousand forty-two _____

Rewrite as an improper fraction.

$1\dfrac{5}{8} =$

$\dfrac{2}{10} = \dfrac{}{100}$

Find the least common multiple of 4 and 10.

Write 239,972 in word form.

_____

_____

Rewrite as a decimal.

$$\frac{2}{5} =$$

Complete the Venn diagram with the factors of each number.

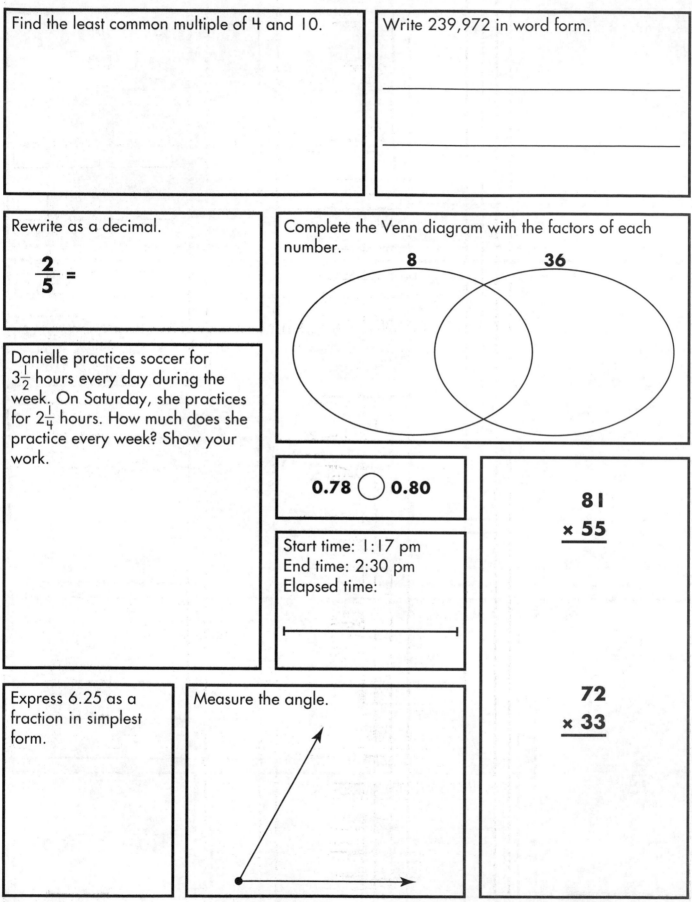

8   36

Danielle practices soccer for $3\frac{1}{2}$ hours every day during the week. On Saturday, she practices for $2\frac{1}{4}$ hours. How much does she practice every week? Show your work.

0.78 ◯ 0.80

Start time: 1:17 pm
End time: 2:30 pm
Elapsed time:

$$\begin{array}{r} 81 \\ \times\ 55 \\ \hline \end{array}$$

Express 6.25 as a fraction in simplest form.

Measure the angle.

$$\begin{array}{r} 72 \\ \times\ 33 \\ \hline \end{array}$$

It started raining at 9:23 in the morning. It didn't stop until 1:50 in the afternoon. How long did it rain?

2 hr. = _____ min.

2 hr. = _____ sec.

$$\frac{7}{10} + \frac{7}{100} =$$

Seconds	Minutes
30	
60	
90	
	2

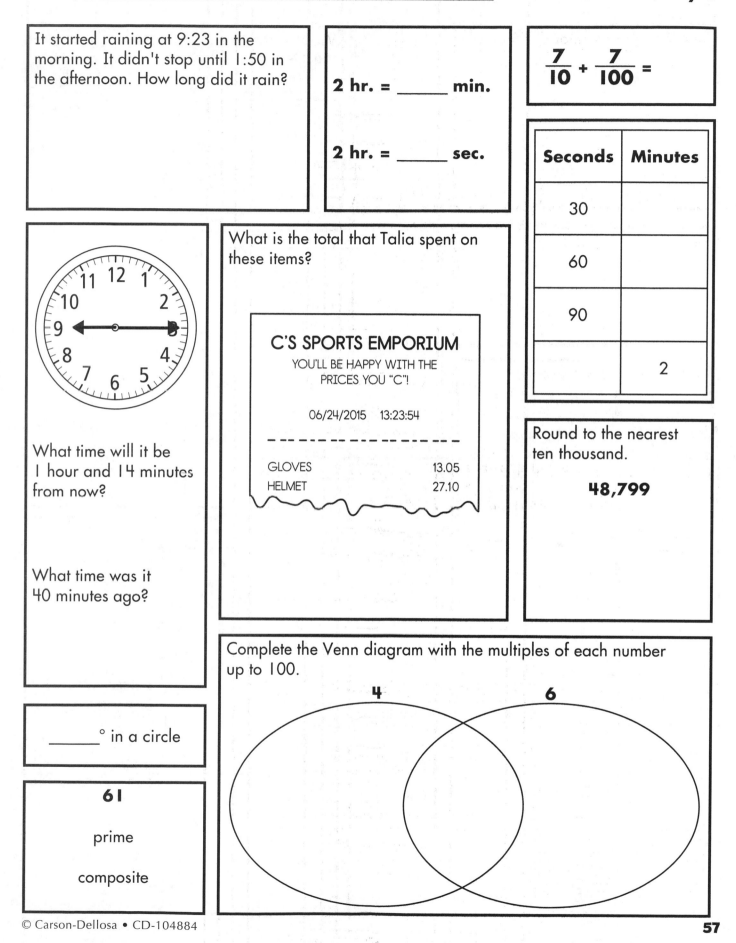

What time will it be 1 hour and 14 minutes from now?

What time was it 40 minutes ago?

What is the total that Talia spent on these items?

C'S SPORTS EMPORIUM
YOU'LL BE HAPPY WITH THE
PRICES YOU "C"!

06/24/2015   13:23:54
- - - - - - - - - - - - - - - -
GLOVES   13.05
HELMET   27.10

Round to the nearest ten thousand.

48,799

_____° in a circle

61

prime

composite

Complete the Venn diagram with the multiples of each number up to 100.

4

6

29,752

What is the value of the **5**? _____

What is the value of the **7**? _____

Complete the pattern.

4,850

4,855

4,860

_____

_____

2,837
7,379
+ 384

2,336
4,522
+ 474

Write a decimal to show the length of the duck's egg.

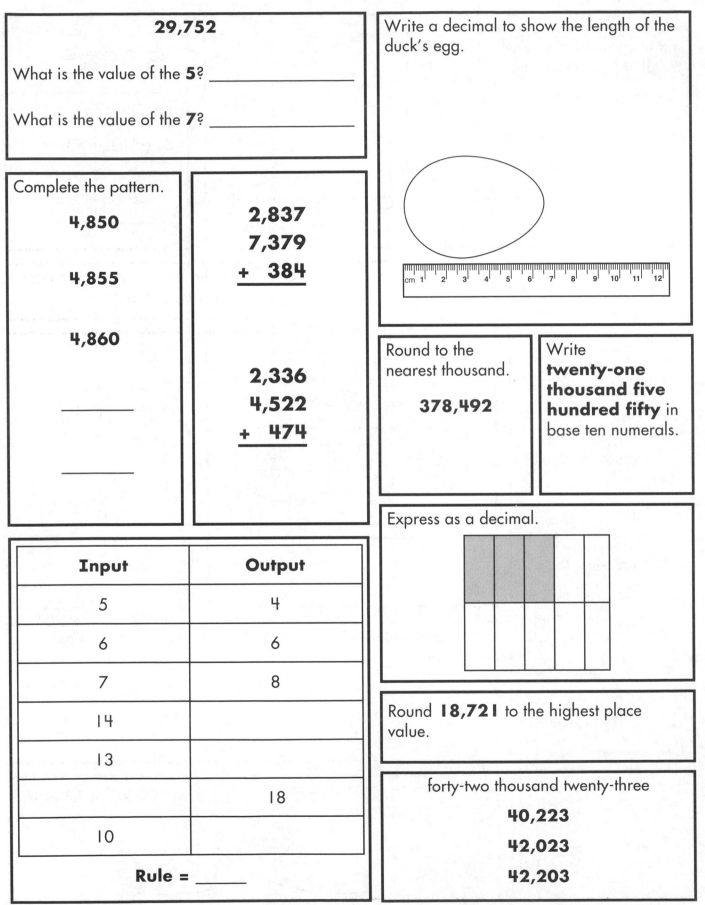

Round to the nearest thousand.

378,492

Write **twenty-one thousand five hundred fifty** in base ten numerals.

Express as a decimal.

Round **18,721** to the highest place value.

forty-two thousand twenty-three

40,223

42,023

42,203

Input	Output
5	4
6	6
7	8
14	
13	
	18
10	

Rule = _____

Name _____

Name the marked angle.

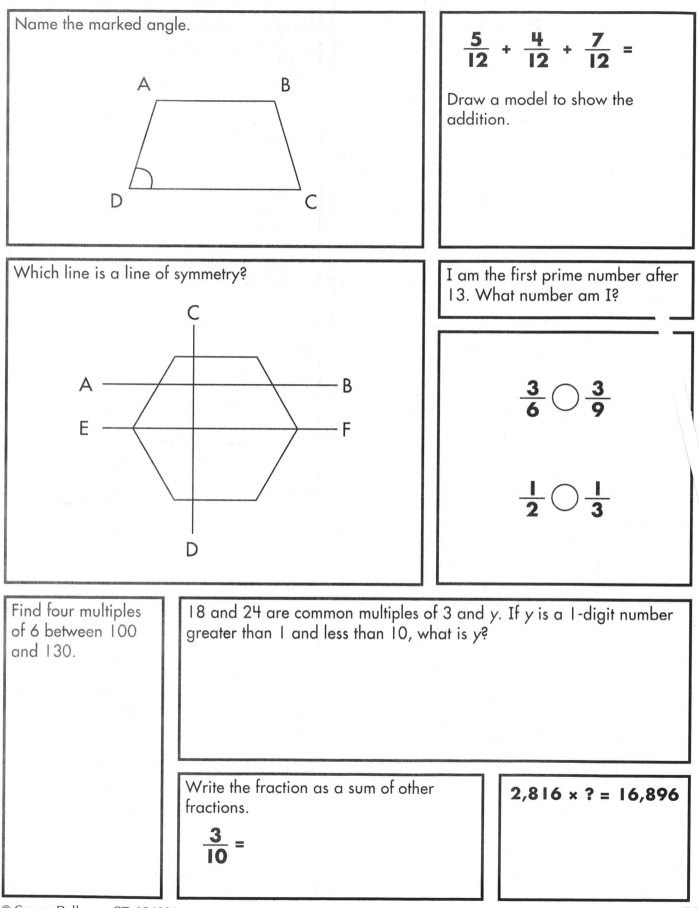

$$\frac{5}{12} + \frac{4}{12} + \frac{7}{12} =$$

Draw a model to show the addition.

Which line is a line of symmetry?

I am the first prime number after 13. What number am I?

$$\frac{3}{6} \bigcirc \frac{3}{9}$$

$$\frac{1}{2} \bigcirc \frac{1}{3}$$

Find four multiples of 6 between 100 and 130.

18 and 24 are common multiples of 3 and y. If y is a 1-digit number greater than 1 and less than 10, what is y?

Write the fraction as a sum of other fractions.

$$\frac{3}{10} =$$

$$2,816 \times ? = 16,896$$

Locate 0.95 on the number line.

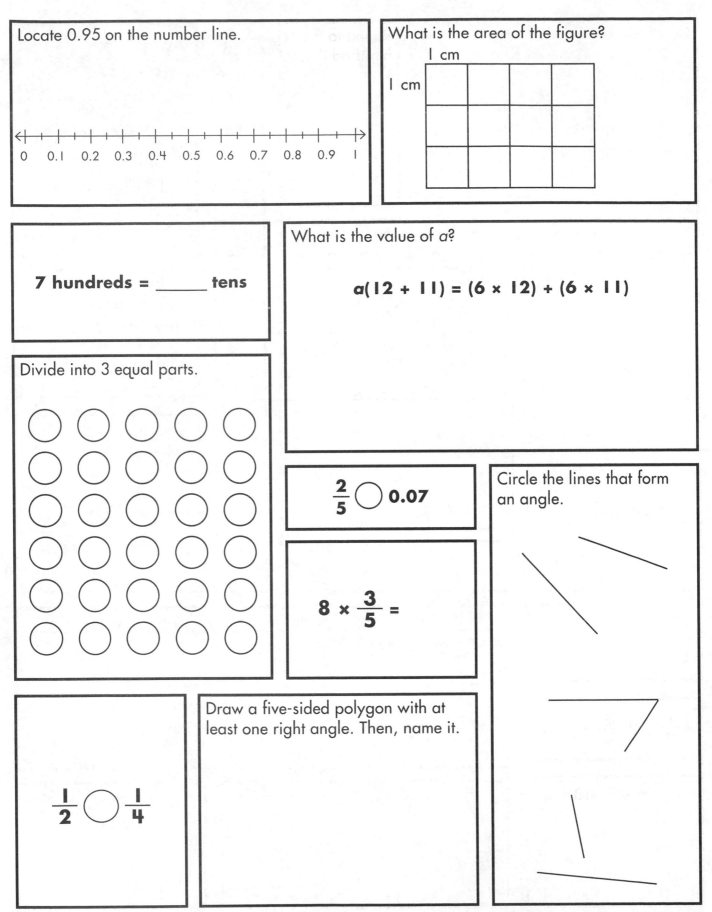

What is the area of the figure?

1 cm

1 cm

---

7 hundreds = _____ tens

What is the value of *a*?

$$a(12 + 11) = (6 \times 12) + (6 \times 11)$$

Divide into 3 equal parts.

$\dfrac{2}{5} \bigcirc 0.07$

$8 \times \dfrac{3}{5} =$

Circle the lines that form an angle.

$\dfrac{1}{2} \bigcirc \dfrac{1}{4}$

Draw a five-sided polygon with at least one right angle. Then, name it.

Start time: 2:02 pm
End time: 4:17 pm
Elapsed time:

Round to the nearest hundred thousand.

349,287

$\frac{3}{5}$ ◯ **0.15**

ABCD is a rectangle.
Angle *CAD* is 32°.

Find angle *BAC*.

_____°

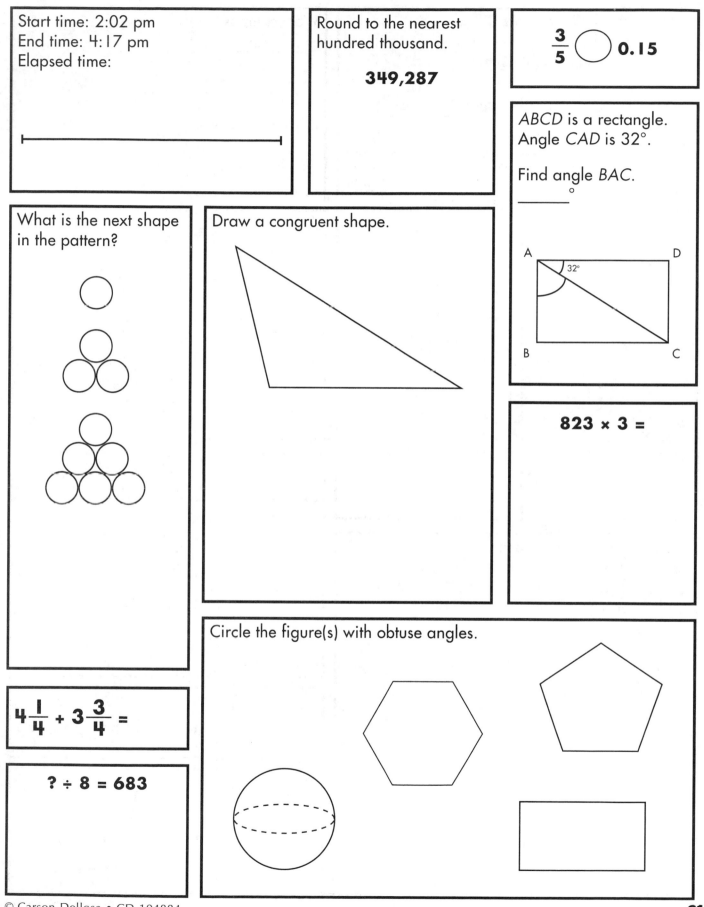

What is the next shape in the pattern?

Draw a congruent shape.

823 × 3 =

Circle the figure(s) with obtuse angles.

$4\frac{1}{4} + 3\frac{3}{4} =$

? ÷ 8 = 683

62,789

What is the value of the **2**? _____

What is the value of the **8**? _____

Is **54** composite or prime?

_____

Prove your answer.

438 ÷ 2

264 ÷ 4

Draw a line *CD* that is parallel to line *AB*.

A

B

$4 \times \dfrac{3}{5} =$

The sixth multiple of 5 is _____.

The eighth multiple of 5 is _____.

Tickets to the concert cost $15.50 for adults and $9.75 for children. The Foster family has 2 adults and 3 children. How much will their total ticket cost be? Show your work.

371
+ 684

nine hundred thousand six ◯ 10,996

Write as a multiplication sentence. Then, solve.

seventy-four times as many as thirty-five

Carlos has an order for 150 cookies. He baked 2 dozen cookies yesterday. The day before, he baked twice as many. How many more cookies does he have to bake?

$$\frac{6}{8} - \frac{2}{8} = \text{—}$$

Draw a model to show the subtraction.

These fractions (are, are not) equivalent.

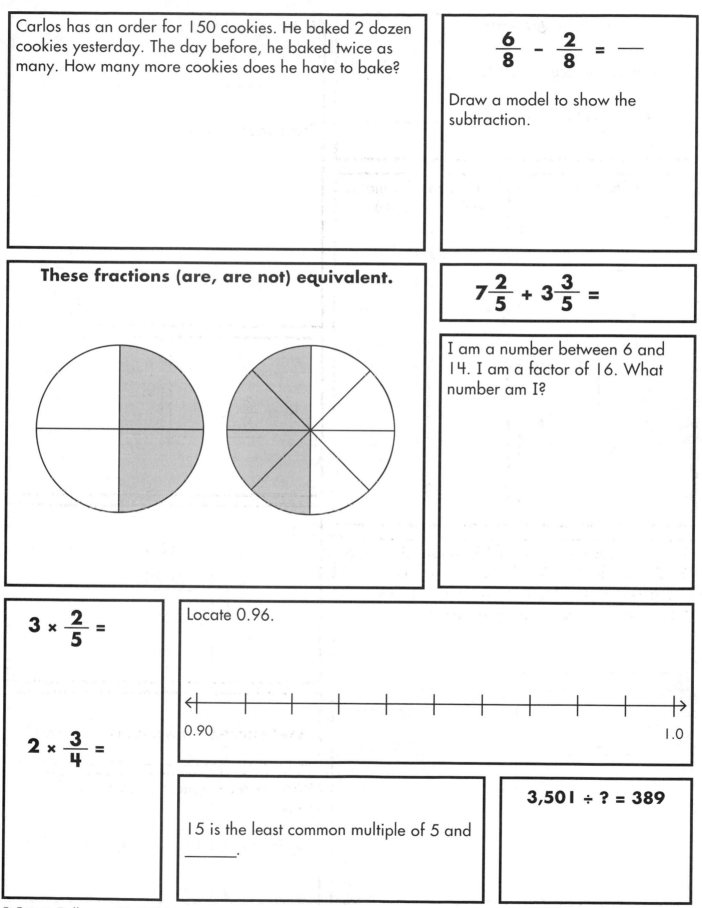

$$7\frac{2}{5} + 3\frac{3}{5} =$$

I am a number between 6 and 14. I am a factor of 16. What number am I?

$$3 \times \frac{2}{5} =$$

$$2 \times \frac{3}{4} =$$

Locate 0.96.

0.90   1.0

15 is the least common multiple of 5 and
_____ .

3,501 ÷ ? = 389

Find the least common multiple of 20 and 12.

If the rectangle is divided in half to make a triangle, what is the triangle's area?

6 in.

27 in.

---

99 × 32 =

Kim volunteers at the animal hospital. She volunteered 4 hours last week. This week, she only volunteered half that time. How much time did she volunteer this week?

Do these lines form an angle?

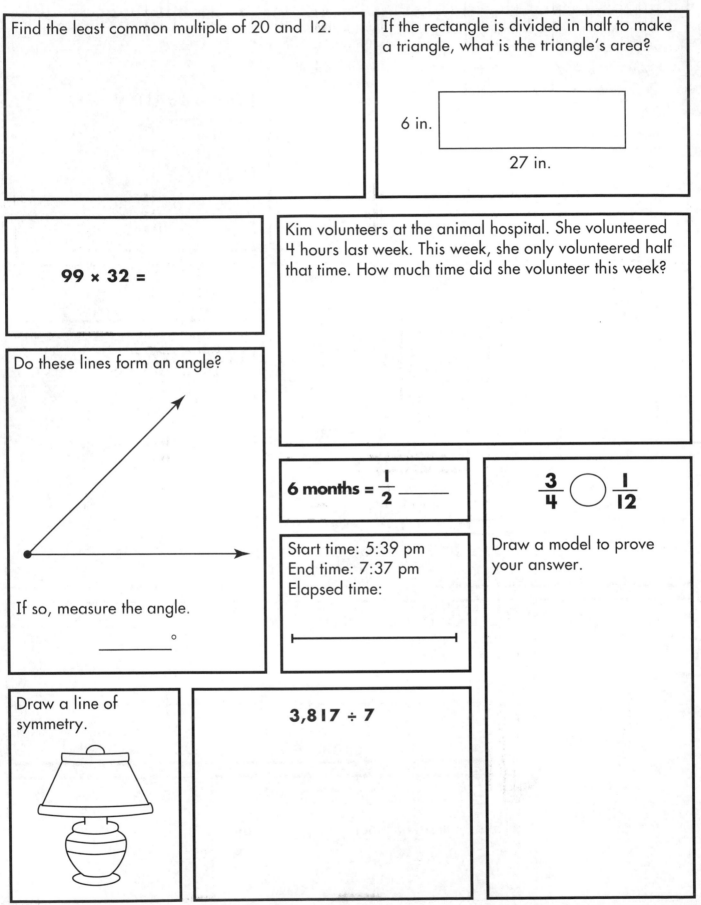

If so, measure the angle.

_____ °

---

6 months = $\frac{1}{2}$ _____

Start time: 5:39 pm
End time: 7:37 pm
Elapsed time:

⊢————————————⊣

$\frac{3}{4}$ ◯ $\frac{1}{12}$

Draw a model to prove your answer.

Draw a line of symmetry.

3,817 ÷ 7

Circle the two line segments that do not intersect.

0.5 kg ◯ 750 g

1 kg ◯ 750 g

Don is 5' 3" tall. Andy is 6' 1" tall. How much taller is Andy?

Use the digits on the star to complete the division problem.

2496

_____ ÷ 4 = _____

What time will it be 1 hour and 34 minutes from now?

What time was it 56 minutes ago?

Two items that Murray purchased are shown. How much did he spend on these items?

Fancy Fresh Foods
FEEDING FRESHNESS
11/20/2016   12:05:41

TURKEY   71.75
VEGETABLE TRAY   12.15

Darren had a box weighing 1.7 kilograms. He added three 300-gram items to the box. What does it weigh now?

$13 \times \dfrac{2}{6} =$

Measure the angle.

Circle the shape(s) that have only one set of parallel lines.

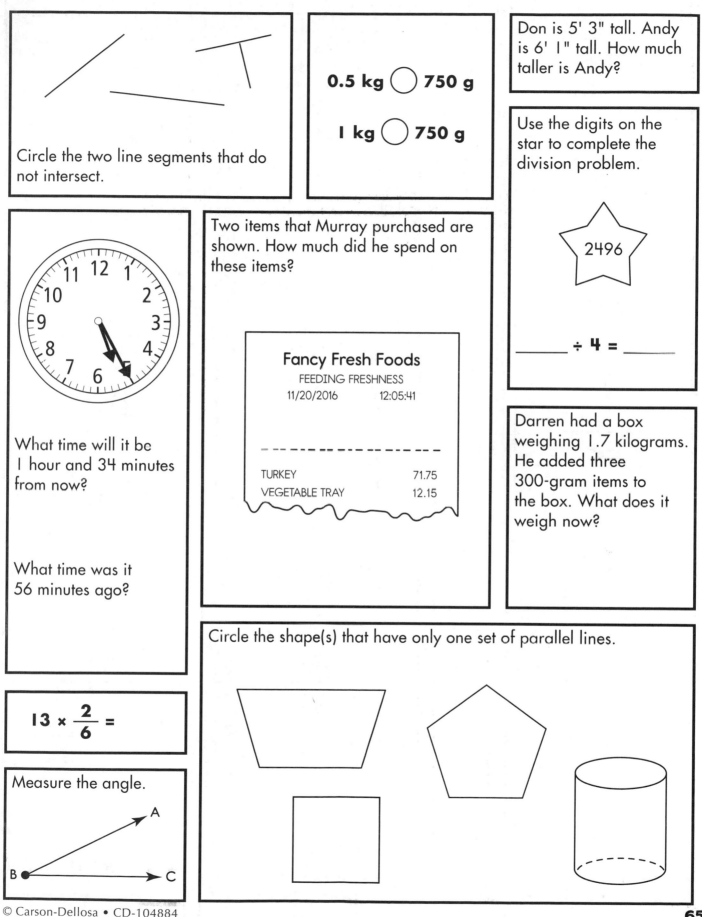

What number is 3 times as many as 8? _____

What number is 7 times as many as 17? _____

Complete the pattern.

632

633

634

_____

_____

Jerry adds 3 cherries to each milk shake. How many cherries are needed to make 12 milk shakes? Show your work.

Six parakeets fit in the cage.

This cage is (less than, equal to, more than) $\frac{1}{2}$ full.

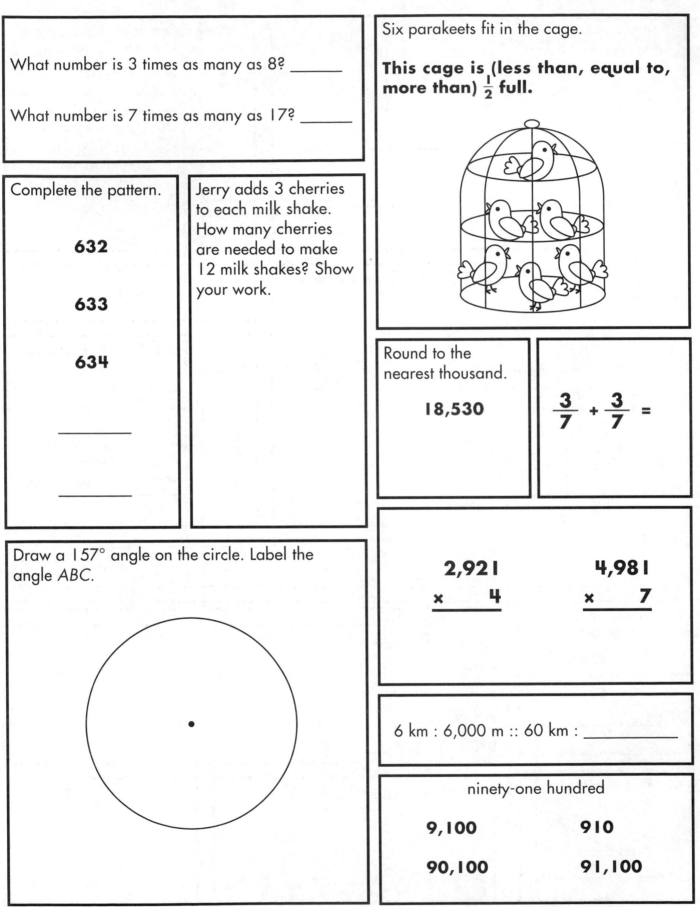

Round to the nearest thousand.

18,530

$$\frac{3}{7} + \frac{3}{7} =$$

Draw a 157° angle on the circle. Label the angle *ABC*.

$$\begin{array}{r} 2{,}921 \\ \times \quad 4 \\ \hline \end{array}$$

$$\begin{array}{r} 4{,}981 \\ \times \quad 7 \\ \hline \end{array}$$

6 km : 6,000 m :: 60 km : _____

ninety-one hundred

9,100   **910**

90,100   **91,100**

Find the multiples of each number up to 80.

7 _____

11 _____

13 _____

Express as a decimal.

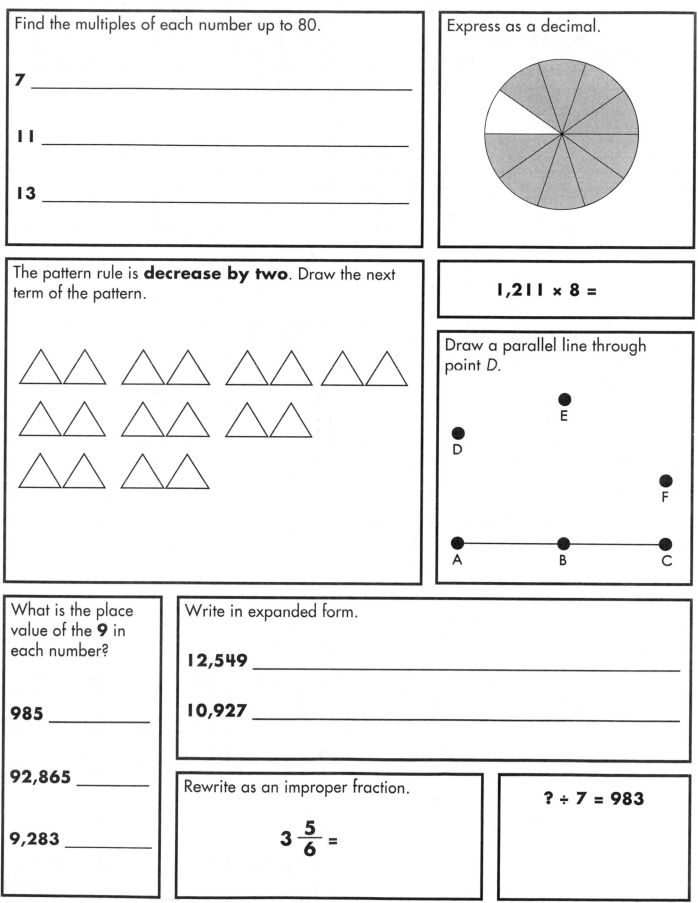

The pattern rule is **decrease by two**. Draw the next term of the pattern.

1,211 × 8 =

Draw a parallel line through point *D*.

What is the place value of the **9** in each number?

985 _____

92,865 _____

9,283 _____

Write in expanded form.

12,549 _____

10,927 _____

Rewrite as an improper fraction.

$3\frac{5}{6} =$

? ÷ 7 = 983

Locate $\frac{9}{10}$ on the number line.

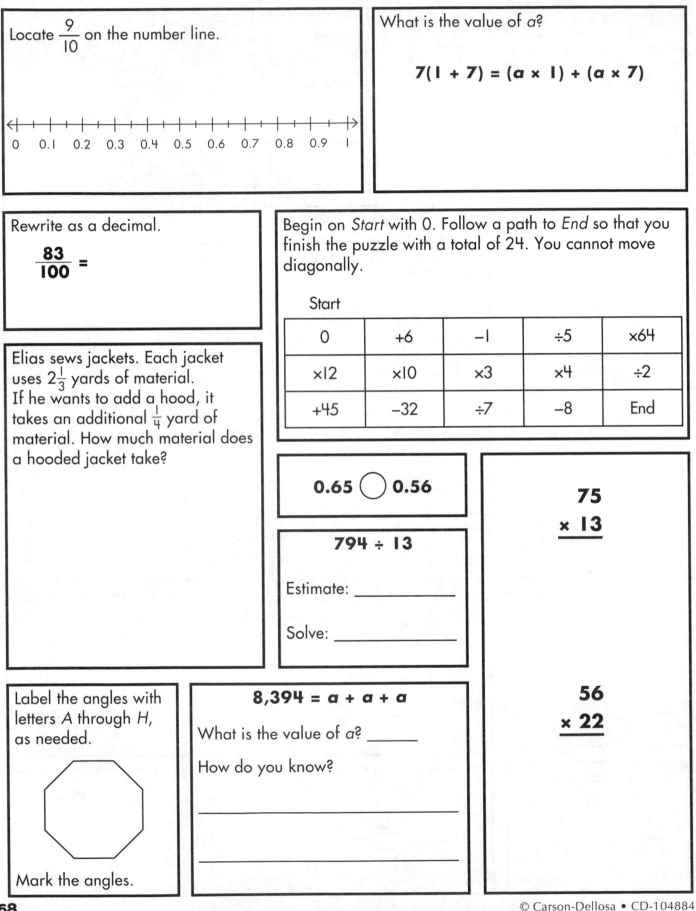

0   0.1   0.2   0.3   0.4   0.5   0.6   0.7   0.8   0.9   1

What is the value of *a*?

$$7(1 + 7) = (a \times 1) + (a \times 7)$$

Rewrite as a decimal.

$$\frac{83}{100} =$$

Elias sews jackets. Each jacket uses $2\frac{1}{3}$ yards of material.
If he wants to add a hood, it takes an additional $\frac{1}{4}$ yard of material. How much material does a hooded jacket take?

Begin on *Start* with 0. Follow a path to *End* so that you finish the puzzle with a total of 24. You cannot move diagonally.

Start

0	+6	−1	÷5	×64
×12	×10	×3	×4	÷2
+45	−32	÷7	−8	End

0.65 ◯ 0.56

794 ÷ 13

Estimate: _____

Solve: _____

75
× 13

Label the angles with letters *A* through *H*, as needed.

Mark the angles.

8,394 = *a* + *a* + *a*

What is the value of *a*? _____

How do you know?

_____

_____

56
× 22

Express as a decimal.

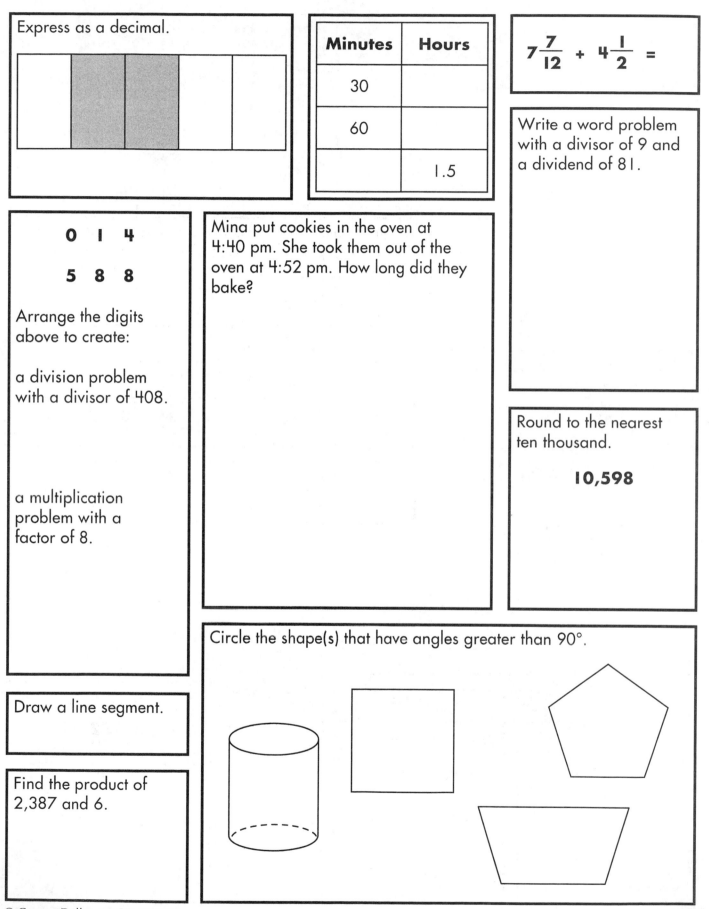

Minutes	Hours
30	
60	
	1.5

$7\dfrac{7}{12} + 4\dfrac{1}{2} =$

Write a word problem with a divisor of 9 and a dividend of 81.

0 1 4

5 8 8

Arrange the digits above to create:

a division problem with a divisor of 408.

a multiplication problem with a factor of 8.

Mina put cookies in the oven at 4:40 pm. She took them out of the oven at 4:52 pm. How long did they bake?

Round to the nearest ten thousand.

10,598

Draw a line segment.

Find the product of 2,387 and 6.

Circle the shape(s) that have angles greater than 90°.

42,466

What is the value of each **4**? _____

_____

4,238 ÷ 7

6,332 ÷ 5

Jan spends $1.75 each day on lunch at school. How much does she spend in a week? Show your work.

Write a decimal to show the length of the rope.

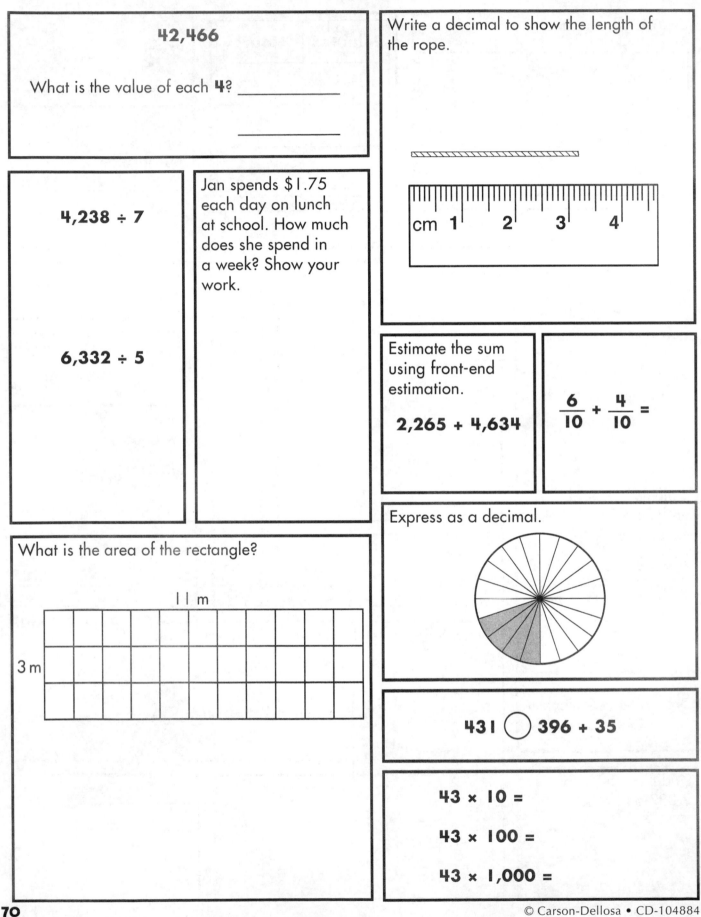

cm

Estimate the sum using front-end estimation.

2,265 + 4,634

$\frac{6}{10} + \frac{4}{10} =$

Express as a decimal.

What is the area of the rectangle?

11 m

3 m

431 ◯ 396 + 35

43 × 10 =

43 × 100 =

43 × 1,000 =

What would you use to measure the length of a bee?

centimeters   meters   hours

What would you use to measure the length of a car?

centimeters   meters   hours

Measure the angle.

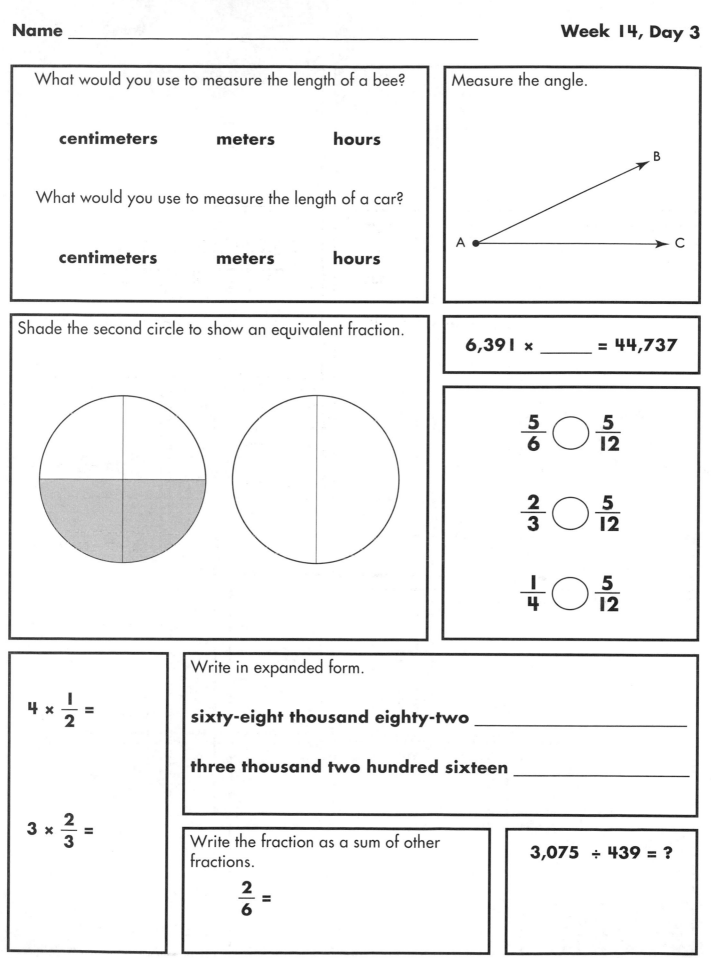

Shade the second circle to show an equivalent fraction.

6,391 × _____ = 44,737

$\frac{5}{6}$ ◯ $\frac{5}{12}$

$\frac{2}{3}$ ◯ $\frac{5}{12}$

$\frac{1}{4}$ ◯ $\frac{5}{12}$

$4 \times \frac{1}{2} =$

$3 \times \frac{2}{3} =$

Write in expanded form.

sixty-eight thousand eighty-two _____

three thousand two hundred sixteen _____

Write the fraction as a sum of other fractions.

$\frac{2}{6} =$

3,075 ÷ 439 = ?

Find the least common multiple of 5 and 12.

Write 63,210 in word form.

_____

_____

9 thousands = _____ hundreds

Complete the Venn diagram with the factors of each number.

14   **56**

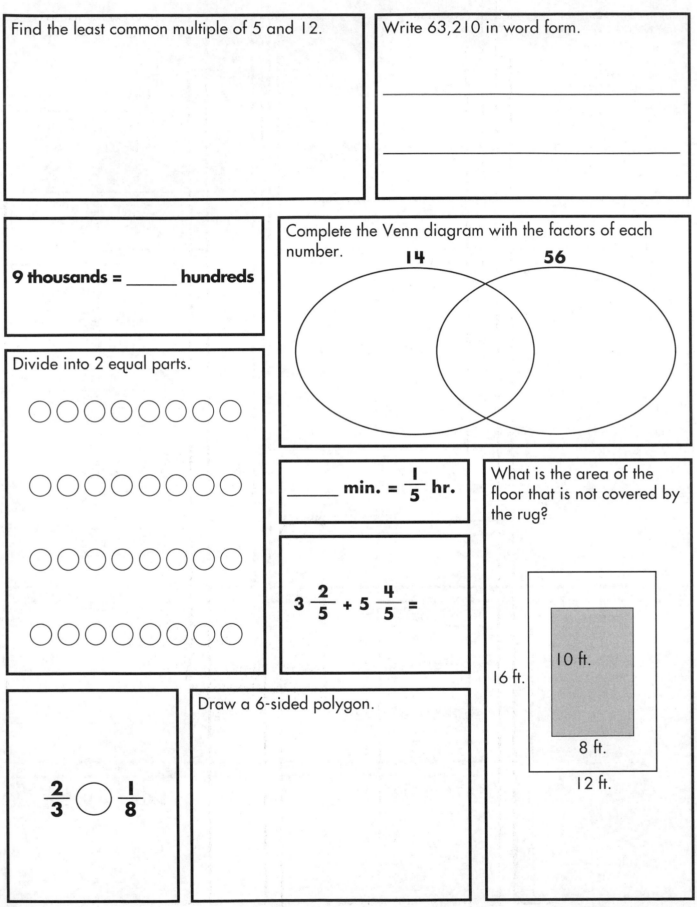

Divide into 2 equal parts.

○○○○○○○

○○○○○○○

○○○○○○○

○○○○○○○

_____ min. = $\frac{1}{5}$ hr.

$3\frac{2}{5} + 5\frac{4}{5} =$

What is the area of the floor that is not covered by the rug?

10 ft.

16 ft.

8 ft.

12 ft.

$\frac{2}{3}$ ◯ $\frac{1}{8}$

Draw a 6-sided polygon.

Draw a congruent shape.

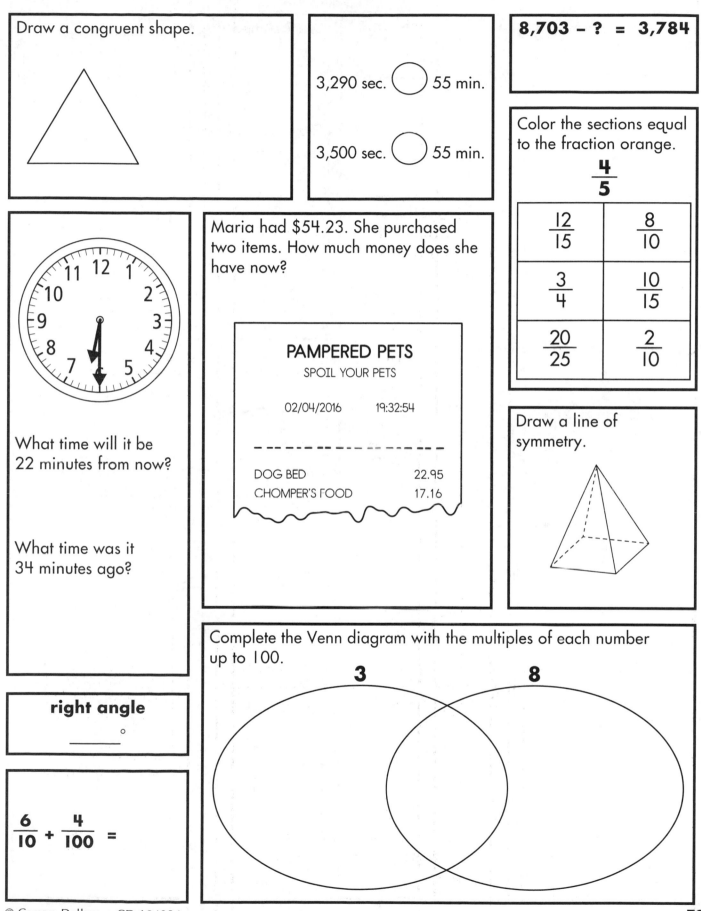

3,290 sec. ◯ 55 min.

3,500 sec. ◯ 55 min.

8,703 – ? = 3,784

Color the sections equal to the fraction orange.

$$\frac{4}{5}$$

$\frac{12}{15}$	$\frac{8}{10}$
$\frac{3}{4}$	$\frac{10}{15}$
$\frac{20}{25}$	$\frac{2}{10}$

What time will it be 22 minutes from now?

What time was it 34 minutes ago?

Maria had $54.23. She purchased two items. How much money does she have now?

PAMPERED PETS

SPOIL YOUR PETS

02/04/2016   19:32:54

DOG BED   22.95
CHOMPER'S FOOD   17.16

Draw a line of symmetry.

right angle

_____ °

$$\frac{6}{10} + \frac{4}{100} =$$

Complete the Venn diagram with the multiples of each number up to 100.

3   **8**

8,171

What is the value of each **1**? _____

_____

Is **19** composite or prime?

_____

Prove your answer.

9 × 12 = ◯

324 ÷ ◯ = ◯

◯ × ◯ = 42

◯ ÷ ◯ = 2

16 × ◯ = ◯

Draw a line of symmetry.

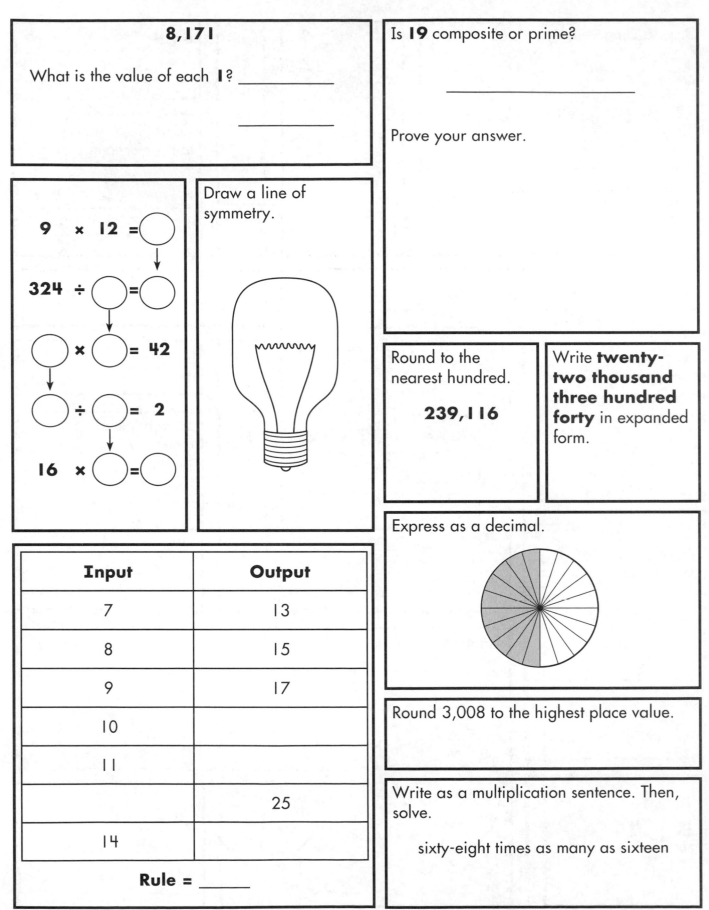

Round to the nearest hundred.

239,116

Write **twenty-two thousand three hundred forty** in expanded form.

Express as a decimal.

Round 3,008 to the highest place value.

Input	Output
7	13
8	15
9	17
10	
11	
	25
14	

Rule = _____

Write as a multiplication sentence. Then, solve.

sixty-eight times as many as sixteen

Find the first 9 multiples of 5.

Find the first 9 multiples of 7.

Circle the common multiples.

Express as a decimal.

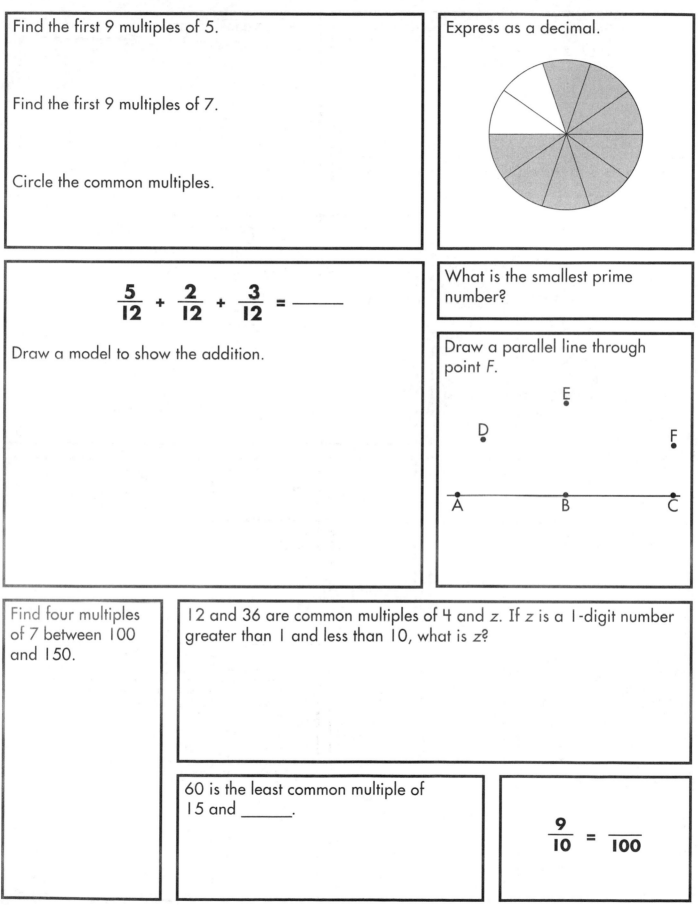

$$\frac{5}{12} + \frac{2}{12} + \frac{3}{12} = \underline{\hspace{1cm}}$$

Draw a model to show the addition.

What is the smallest prime number?

Draw a parallel line through point *F*.

E

D   F

A ────────── B ────────── C

Find four multiples of 7 between 100 and 150.

---

12 and 36 are common multiples of 4 and *z*. If *z* is a 1-digit number greater than 1 and less than 10, what is *z*?

60 is the least common multiple of 15 and _____.

$$\frac{9}{10} = \frac{}{100}$$

Find the least common multiple of 18 and 3.

The figure is a large square and 4 small congruent squares. The area of the figure is 80 square cm. What is the length of the side of a small square?

8 cm

**5 thousands
=
_____ hundreds**

Chantelle picked 12 ripe peppers after school today. Yesterday, she picked 3 times that many peppers. How many peppers did she pick yesterday? Show your work.

What is the value of *a*?

3 (a + 6) = (3 × 7) + (3 × 6)

$\frac{1}{5}$ ◯ **0.08**

1,882 ÷ 7

Estimate: _____

Solve: _____

$\frac{3}{8}$ ◯ $\frac{1}{3}$

Draw a model to prove your answer.

Anna has 14 cousins. Her friend Rebecca has 3 times as many. How many cousins does Rebecca have?

Circle the letter that has symmetry. Then, draw the line of symmetry.

A   F   Z

Start time: 2:02 am
End time: 3:59 am
Elapsed time:

|-----------------------------------|

Cents	Dollars
50	
75	
100	
	2

$\frac{3}{4}$ hr. ◯ 78 min.

What is the area of the figure?

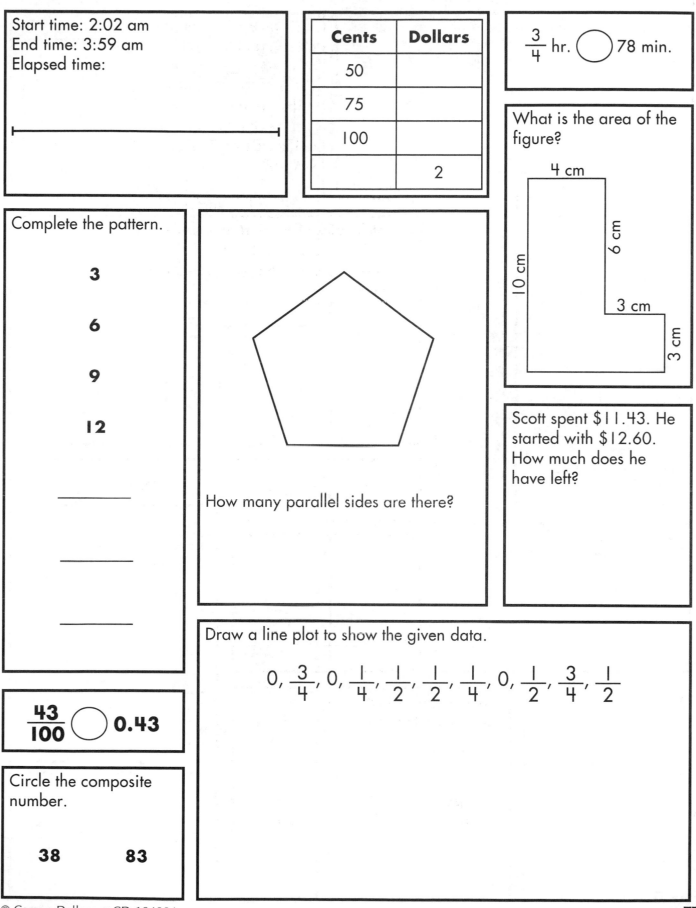

4 cm
10 cm
6 cm
3 cm
3 cm

Complete the pattern.

3

6

9

12

_____

_____

_____

How many parallel sides are there?

Scott spent $11.43. He started with $12.60. How much does he have left?

$\frac{43}{100}$ ◯ 0.43

Circle the composite number.

38   **83**

Draw a line plot to show the given data.

$$0, \frac{3}{4}, 0, \frac{1}{4}, \frac{1}{2}, \frac{1}{2}, \frac{1}{4}, 0, \frac{1}{2}, \frac{3}{4}, \frac{1}{2}$$

What number is 4 times as many as 6? _____

What number is 4 times as many as 18? _____

Complete the pattern.

6,242

5,242

4,242

_____

_____

Draw a model to show that $\frac{1}{8} = \frac{2}{16}$.

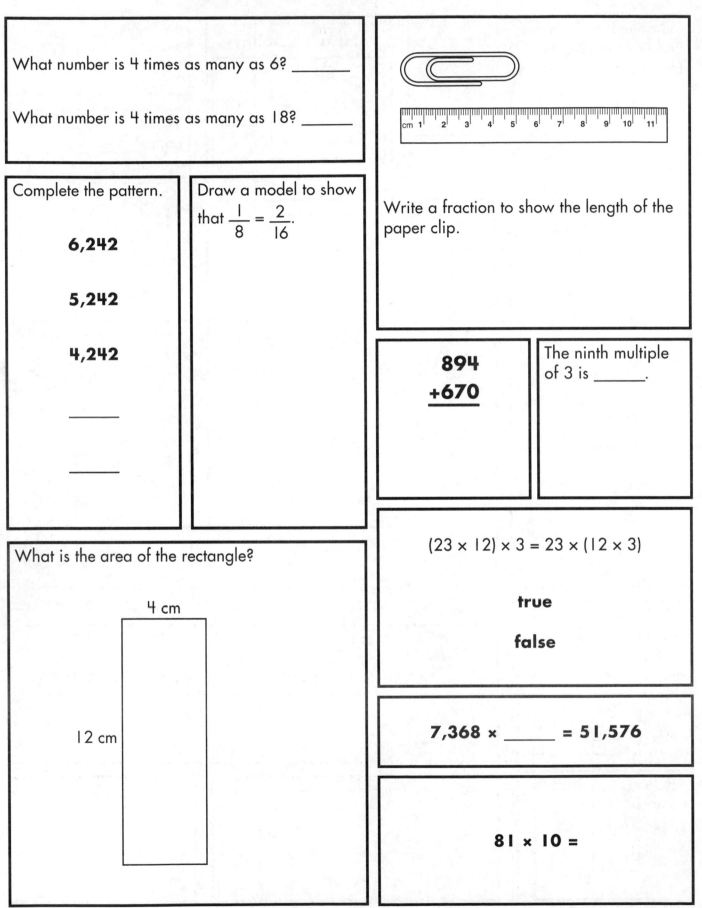

Write a fraction to show the length of the paper clip.

| 894 |
| +670 |

The ninth multiple of 3 is _____.

What is the area of the rectangle?

4 cm

12 cm

$(23 \times 12) \times 3 = 23 \times (12 \times 3)$

true

false

$7{,}368 \times$ _____ $= 51{,}576$

$81 \times 10 =$

What fraction is unshaded? Answer in simplest form.

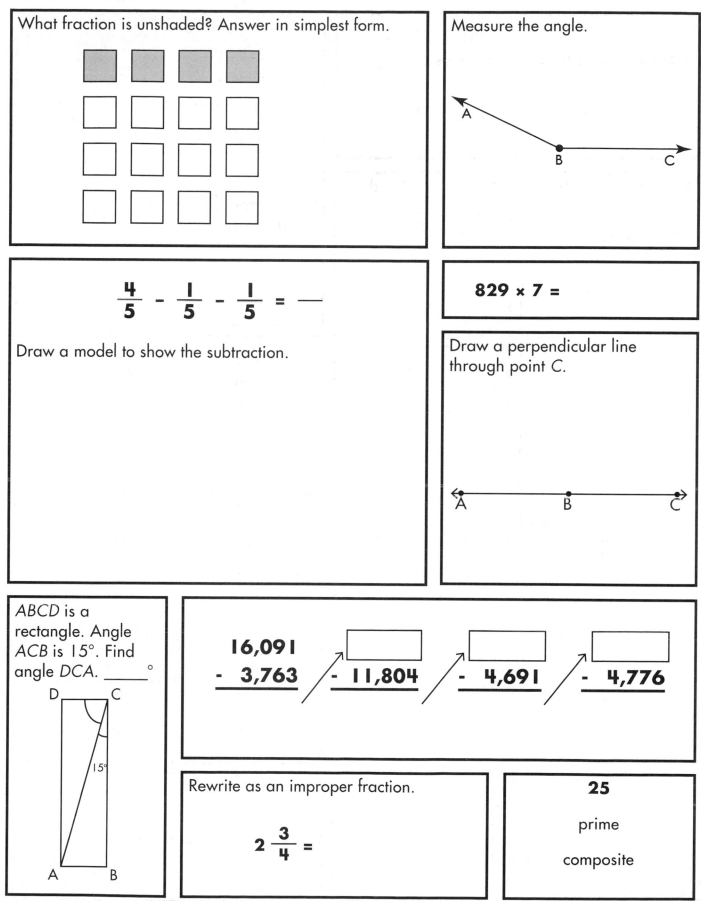

Measure the angle.

A

B   C

$$\frac{4}{5} - \frac{1}{5} - \frac{1}{5} = \underline{\quad}$$

Draw a model to show the subtraction.

829 × 7 =

Draw a perpendicular line through point C.

A   B   C

ABCD is a rectangle. Angle ACB is 15°. Find angle DCA. _____°

D   C

15°

A   B

| 16,091 | | | |
| - 3,763 | - 11,804 | - 4,691 | - 4,776 |

Rewrite as an improper fraction.

$$2\frac{3}{4} =$$

25

prime

composite

Find the least common multiple of 22 and 4.

What is the perimeter of the figure?

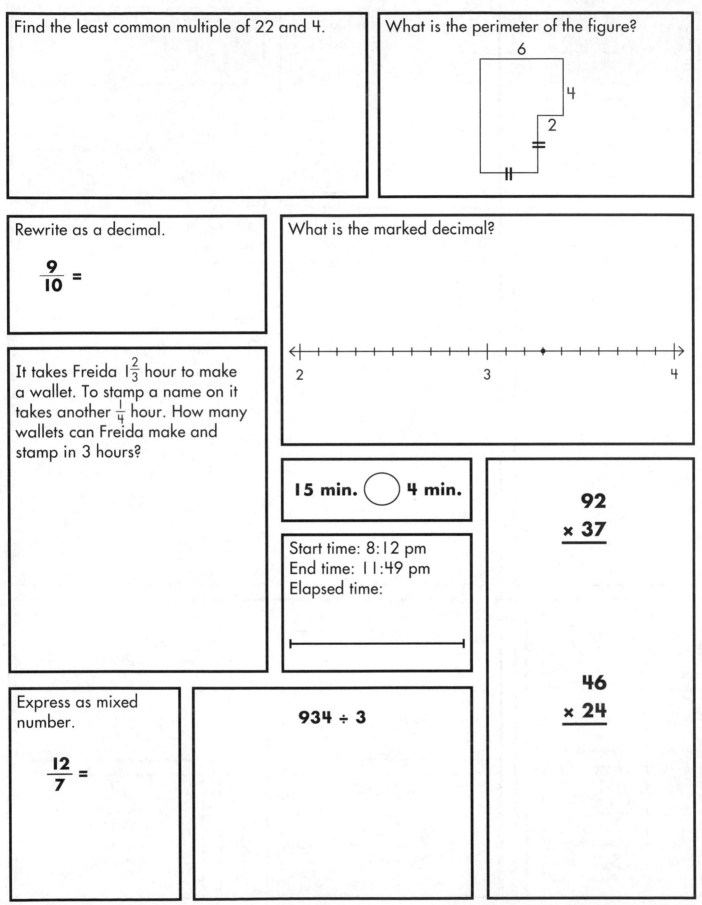

Rewrite as a decimal.

$$\frac{9}{10} =$$

What is the marked decimal?

It takes Freida $1\frac{2}{3}$ hour to make a wallet. To stamp a name on it takes another $\frac{1}{4}$ hour. How many wallets can Freida make and stamp in 3 hours?

15 min. ◯ **4 min.**

Start time: 8:12 pm
End time: 11:49 pm
Elapsed time:

$$\begin{array}{r} 92 \\ \times\ 37 \\ \hline \end{array}$$

Express as mixed number.

$$\frac{12}{7} =$$

934 ÷ 3

$$\begin{array}{r} 46 \\ \times\ 24 \\ \hline \end{array}$$

Start time: 3:22 pm
End time: 10:19 pm
Elapsed time:

Round to the nearest ten thousand.

123,498

Round **12,757** to the nearest ten.

Color the sections greater than the fraction yellow.
$$\frac{1}{6}$$

$\frac{1}{5}$	$\frac{4}{6}$
$\frac{5}{12}$	$\frac{2}{4}$
$\frac{1}{8}$	$\frac{3}{10}$

What is the next term in the pattern?

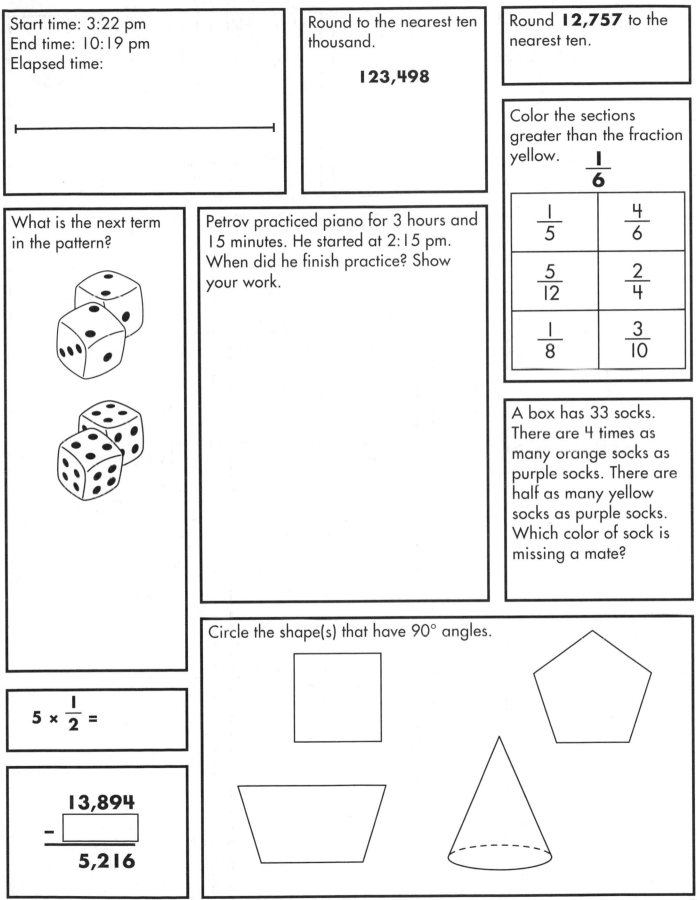

Petrov practiced piano for 3 hours and 15 minutes. He started at 2:15 pm. When did he finish practice? Show your work.

A box has 33 socks. There are 4 times as many orange socks as purple socks. There are half as many yellow socks as purple socks. Which color of sock is missing a mate?

$5 \times \dfrac{1}{2} =$

$$\begin{array}{r} 13,894 \\ -\boxed{} \\ \hline 5,216 \end{array}$$

Circle the shape(s) that have 90° angles.

19,880

What is the value of the **0**? _____

What is the value of the **9**? _____

Find the product of 2,874 and 7.

Find the product of 3,115 and 9.

572 ÷ 9

638 ÷ 3

Juan saves $15 each month. In February, he had $75. How much will he have in October? Show your work.

Round to the nearest ten thousand.

61,913

$\frac{1}{5} + \frac{3}{5} =$

Express as a decimal.

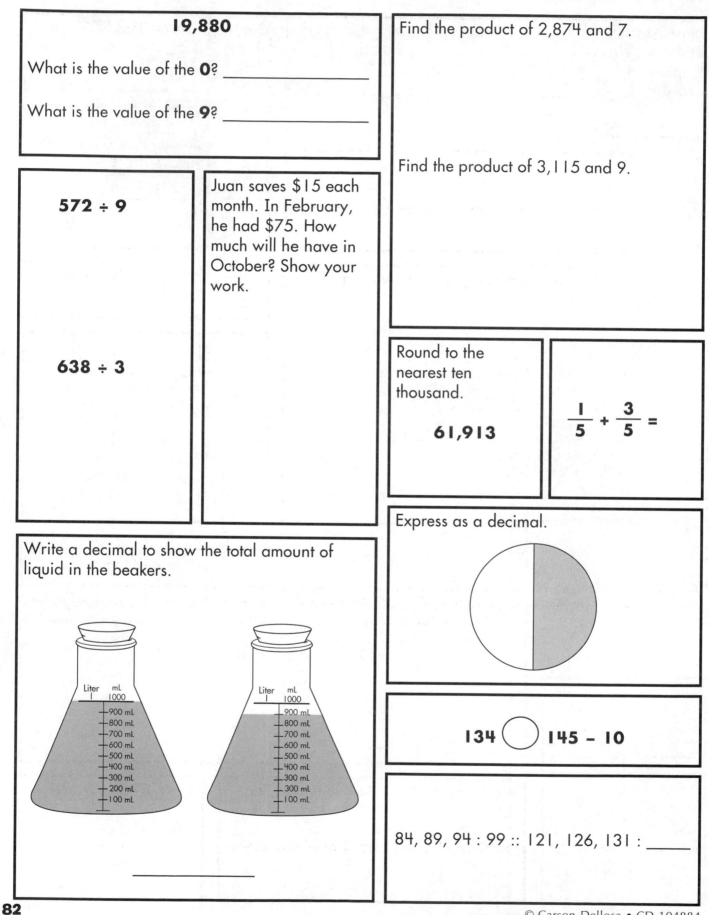

Write a decimal to show the total amount of liquid in the beakers.

_____

134 ◯ 145 – 10

84, 89, 94 : 99 :: 121, 126, 131 : _____

Find the multiples of each number up to 150.

16 _____

31 _____

35 _____

Express as a decimal.

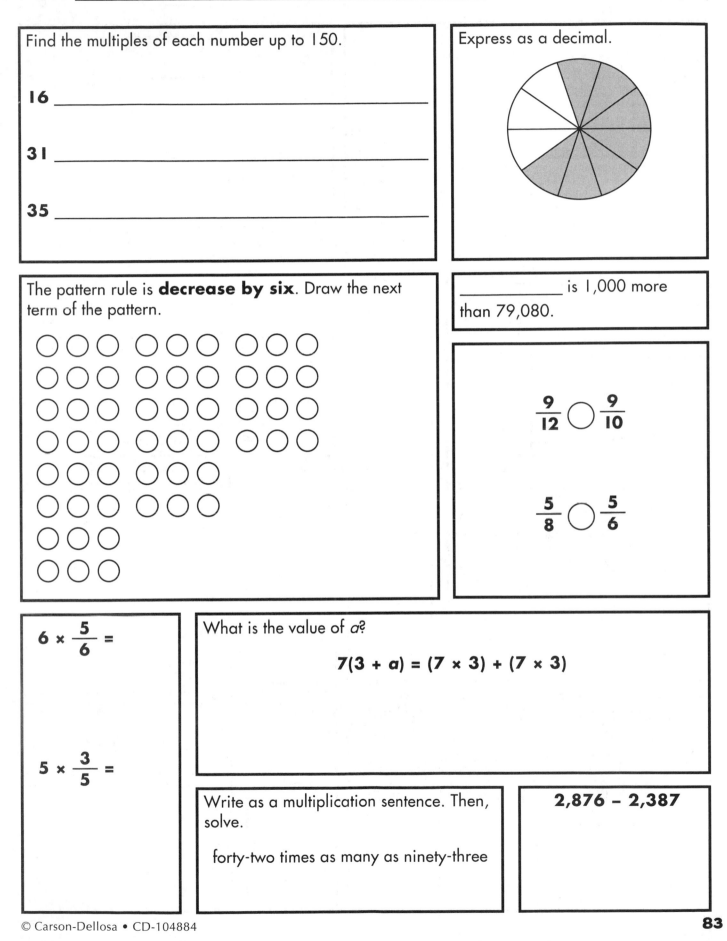

The pattern rule is **decrease by six**. Draw the next term of the pattern.

_____ is 1,000 more than 79,080.

$\frac{9}{12} \bigcirc \frac{9}{10}$

$\frac{5}{8} \bigcirc \frac{5}{6}$

$6 \times \frac{5}{6} =$

$5 \times \frac{3}{5} =$

What is the value of *a*?

$$7(3 + a) = (7 \times 3) + (7 \times 3)$$

Write as a multiplication sentence. Then, solve.

forty-two times as many as ninety-three

2,876 – 2,387

Locate $\frac{25}{100}$ on the number line.

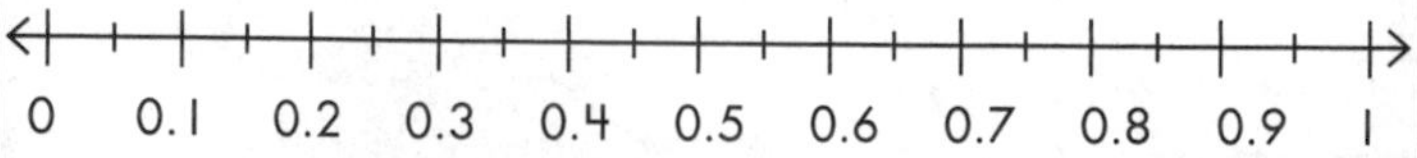

0   0.1   0.2   0.3   0.4   0.5   0.6   0.7   0.8   0.9   1

What is the area of the rectangle?

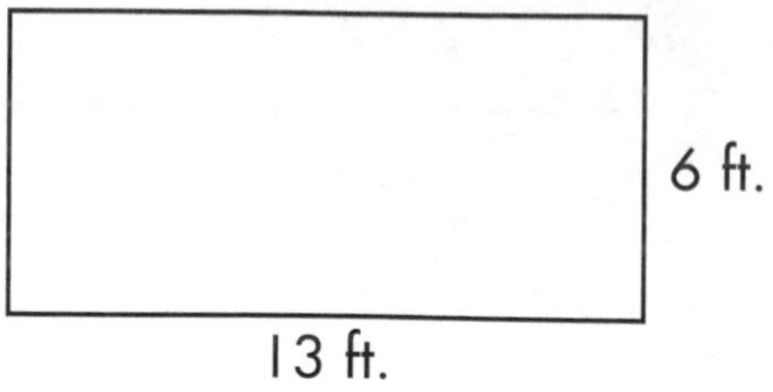

6 ft.

13 ft.

7 hundreds = _____ tens

Complete the Venn diagram with the factors of each number.

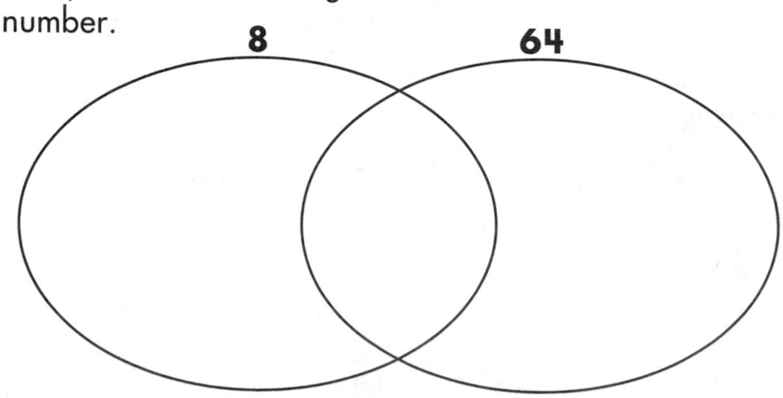

8   **64**

Divide into 3 equal parts.

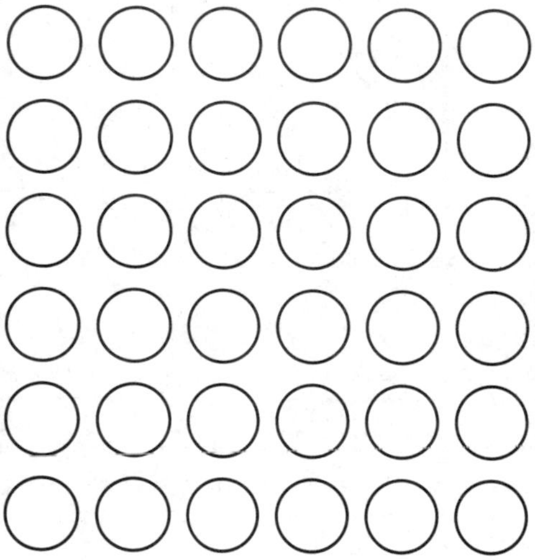

0.23 ◯ 0.39

8,797 + 881 =

Chuck has 5 times as many coins as Megan. They have 1,644 coins in all. How many coins does Megan have? Show your work.

_____ ÷ 8 = 384

Circle the letter that has symmetry. Then, draw the line of symmetry.

F   V   R

Express as a decimal.

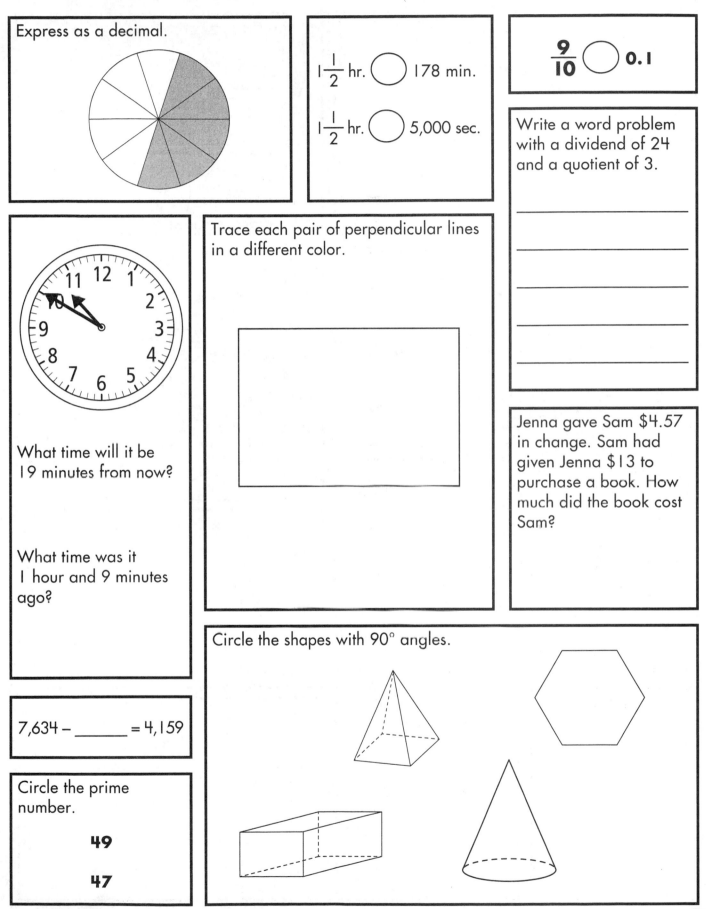

$1\frac{1}{2}$ hr. ◯ 178 min.

$1\frac{1}{2}$ hr. ◯ 5,000 sec.

$\dfrac{9}{10}$ ◯ 0.1

Write a word problem with a dividend of 24 and a quotient of 3.

_____

_____

_____

_____

_____

What time will it be 19 minutes from now?

What time was it 1 hour and 9 minutes ago?

Trace each pair of perpendicular lines in a different color.

Jenna gave Sam $4.57 in change. Sam had given Jenna $13 to purchase a book. How much did the book cost Sam?

$7{,}634 -$ _____ $= 4{,}159$

Circle the prime number.

49

47

Circle the shapes with 90° angles.

12,040

What is the value of the **4**? _____

What is the value of the **1**? _____

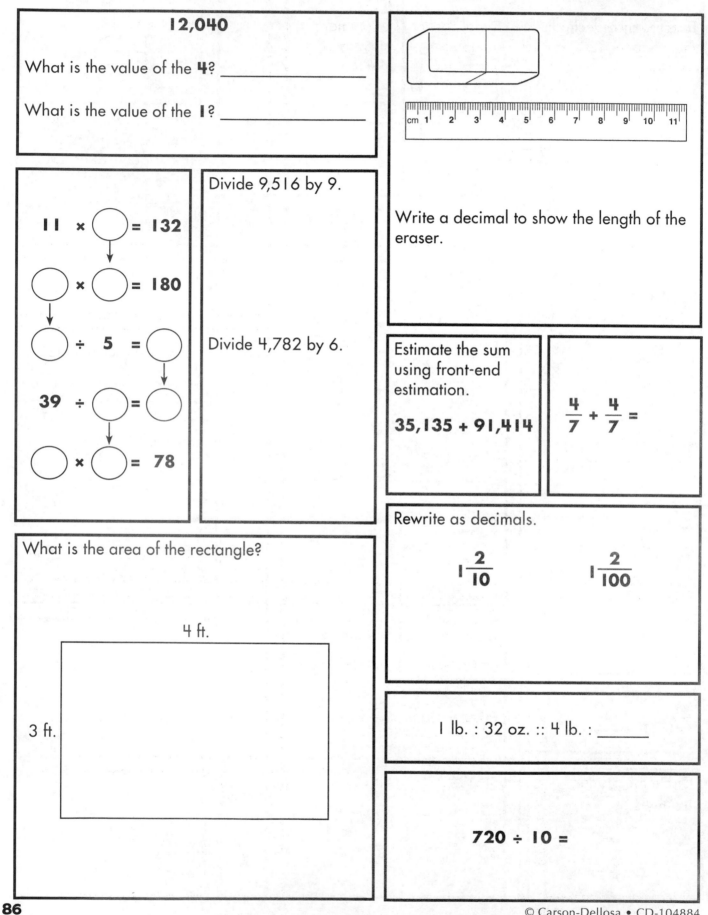

$11 \times \bigcirc = 132$

$\bigcirc \times \bigcirc = 180$

$\bigcirc \div 5 = \bigcirc$

$39 \div \bigcirc = \bigcirc$

$\bigcirc \times \bigcirc = 78$

Divide 9,516 by 9.

Divide 4,782 by 6.

Write a decimal to show the length of the eraser.

Estimate the sum using front-end estimation.

35,135 + 91,414

$\frac{4}{7} + \frac{4}{7} =$

Rewrite as decimals.

$1\frac{2}{10}$ $1\frac{2}{100}$

1 lb. : 32 oz. :: 4 lb. : _____

720 ÷ 10 =

What is the area of the rectangle?

4 ft.

3 ft.

Terrell donated $37 to the animal shelter. The animal shelter spends $3 per day on each dog. How many dogs can Terrell's donation take care of for one day? Show your work.

Measure the angle.

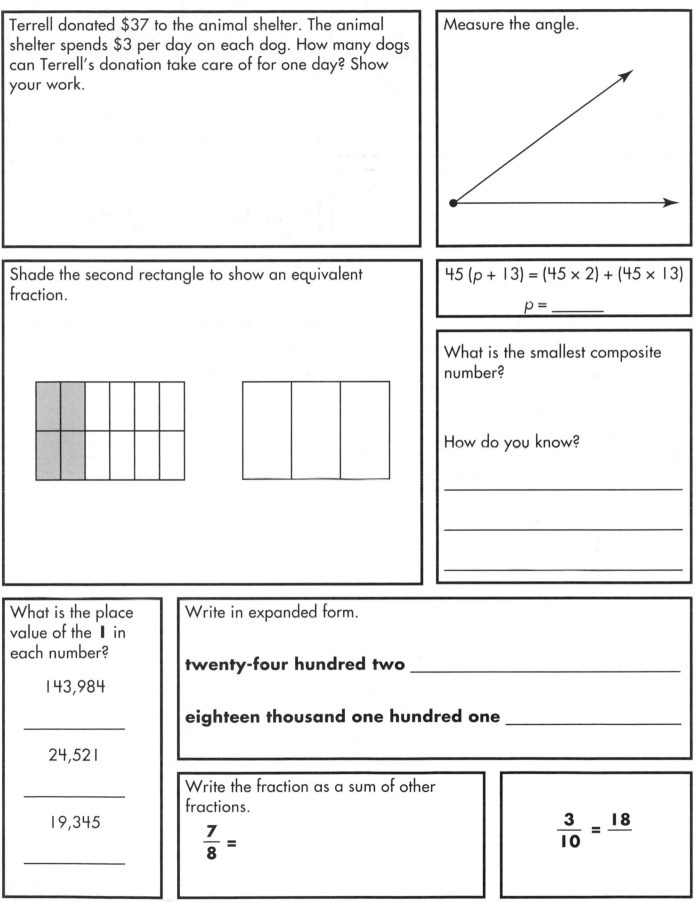

Shade the second rectangle to show an equivalent fraction.

$45 (p + 13) = (45 \times 2) + (45 \times 13)$

$p =$ _____

What is the smallest composite number?

How do you know?

_____

_____

_____

What is the place value of the **1** in each number?

143,984

_____

24,521

_____

19,345

_____

Write in expanded form.

twenty-four hundred two _____

eighteen thousand one hundred one _____

Write the fraction as a sum of other fractions.

$\dfrac{7}{8} =$

$\dfrac{3}{10} = \dfrac{18}{}$

Draw an obtuse angle.

Write the sums of adjacent numbers in the blocks above.

325		436
	172	218

Rewrite as a decimal.

$$\frac{110}{100} =$$

Deon made 3 toy tops yesterday. Today, he made 4 times as many. How many has he made in all? Show your work.

Gordon runs for $2\frac{1}{3}$ hours every afternoon. He warms up with a $\frac{1}{4}$ hour jog and cools down with a $\frac{1}{2}$ hour walk. How long does it take Gordon to warm up, run, and cool down every day? Show your work.

$\frac{1}{5}$ ◯ 0.17

Does this image have symmetry?

Draw a model to show that

$$\frac{1}{2} = \frac{2}{4}.$$

$\frac{7}{8}$ ◯ $\frac{1}{2}$

$$\begin{array}{r} 1,984 \\ - \boxed{} \\ \hline 1,199 \end{array}$$

Circle the obtuse angles.

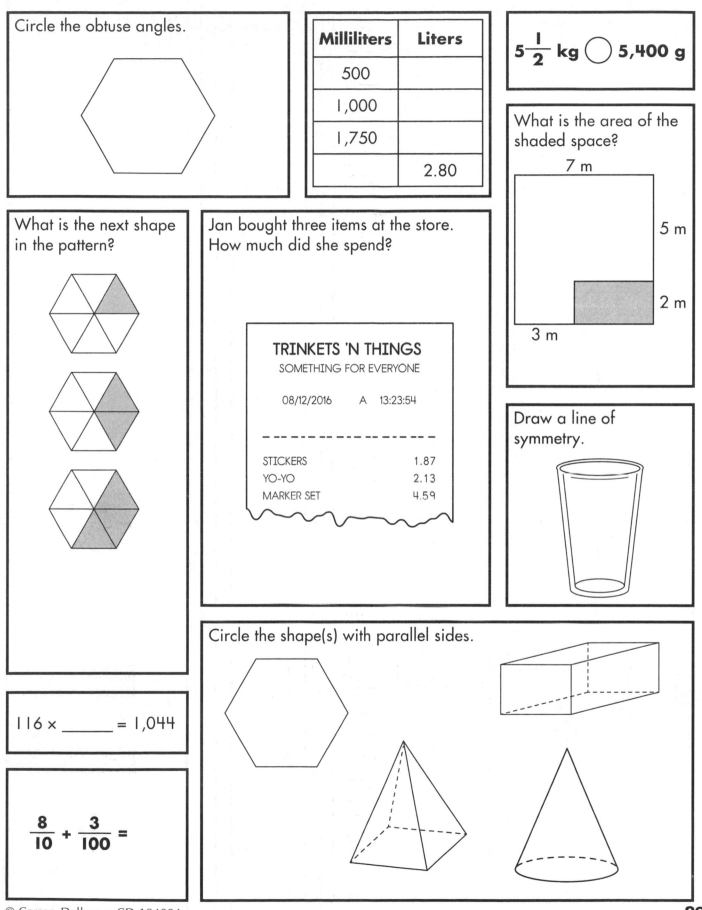

Milliliters	Liters
500	
1,000	
1,750	
	2.80

$5\frac{1}{2}$ kg ◯ 5,400 g

What is the area of the shaded space?

7 m

5 m

2 m

3 m

What is the next shape in the pattern?

Jan bought three items at the store. How much did she spend?

TRINKETS 'N THINGS

SOMETHING FOR EVERYONE

08/12/2016   A   13:23:54

STICKERS   1.87
YO-YO   2.13
MARKER SET   4.59

Draw a line of symmetry.

$116 \times$ _____ = 1,044

$\frac{8}{10} + \frac{3}{100} =$

Circle the shape(s) with parallel sides.

What number is 7 times as many as 6? _____

What number is 13 times as many as 9? _____

Is **23** composite or prime?

_____

Prove your answer.

What is the next shape in the pattern?

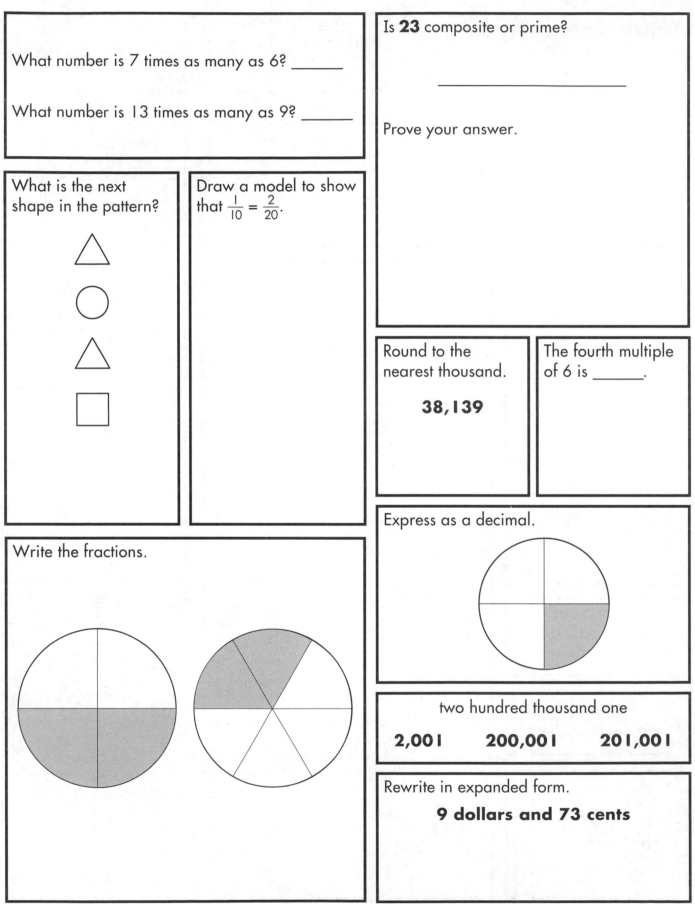

Draw a model to show that $\frac{1}{10} = \frac{2}{20}$.

Round to the nearest thousand.

38,139

The fourth multiple of 6 is _____.

Express as a decimal.

Write the fractions.

two hundred thousand one

2,001   200,001   201,001

Rewrite in expanded form.

9 dollars and 73 cents

Write the fractions. Compare them using **>**, **<**, or **=**.

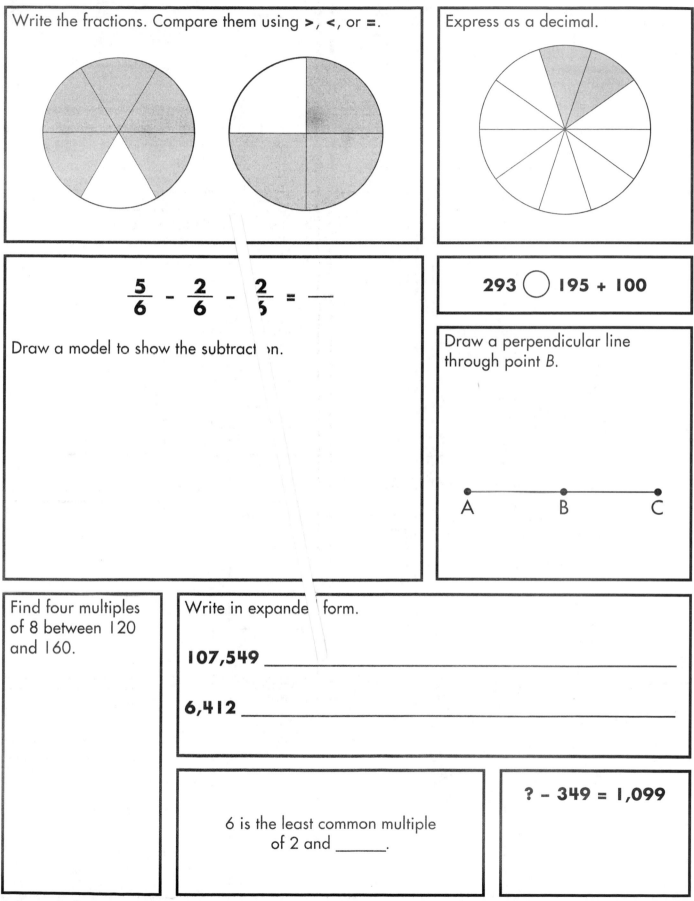

Express as a decimal.

$$\frac{5}{6} - \frac{2}{6} - \frac{2}{5} = \underline{\quad}$$

Draw a model to show the subtraction.

293 ◯ 195 + 100

Draw a perpendicular line through point *B*.

A   B   C

Find four multiples of 8 between 120 and 160.

Write in expanded form.

107,549 _____

6,412 _____

6 is the least common multiple of 2 and _____.

? – 349 = 1,099

Find the least common multiple of 3 and 32.

Write **73,996** in word form.

_____

_____

2 hundreds = _____ tens

Shade boxes to create rotational symmetry on this shape. Shade each possible position a different color.

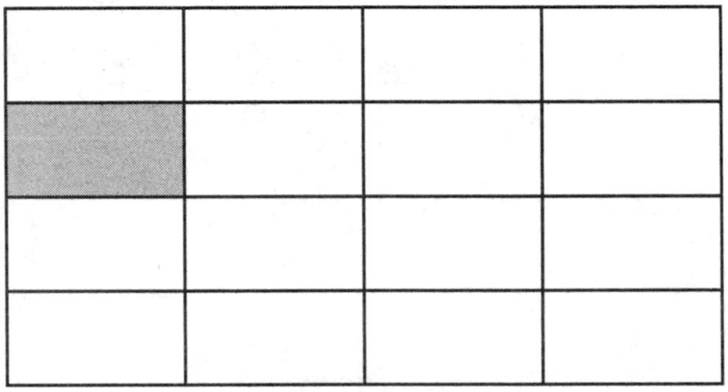

Divide into 6 equal parts.

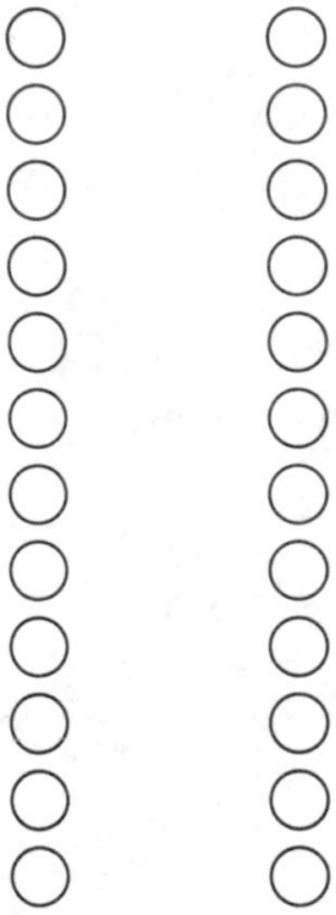

○ ○
○ ○
○ ○
○ ○
○ ○
○ ○
○ ○
○ ○
○ ○
○ ○
○ ○
○ ○
○ ○

37 min. ○ $\frac{1}{2}$ **hr.**

Start time: 10:28 pm
End time: 12:09 am
Elapsed time:

Draw a model to prove that

$$\frac{1}{6} = \frac{3}{18}.$$

527 × 3 =

Circle the letter that has symmetry. Then, draw the line of symmetry.

Q   D   L

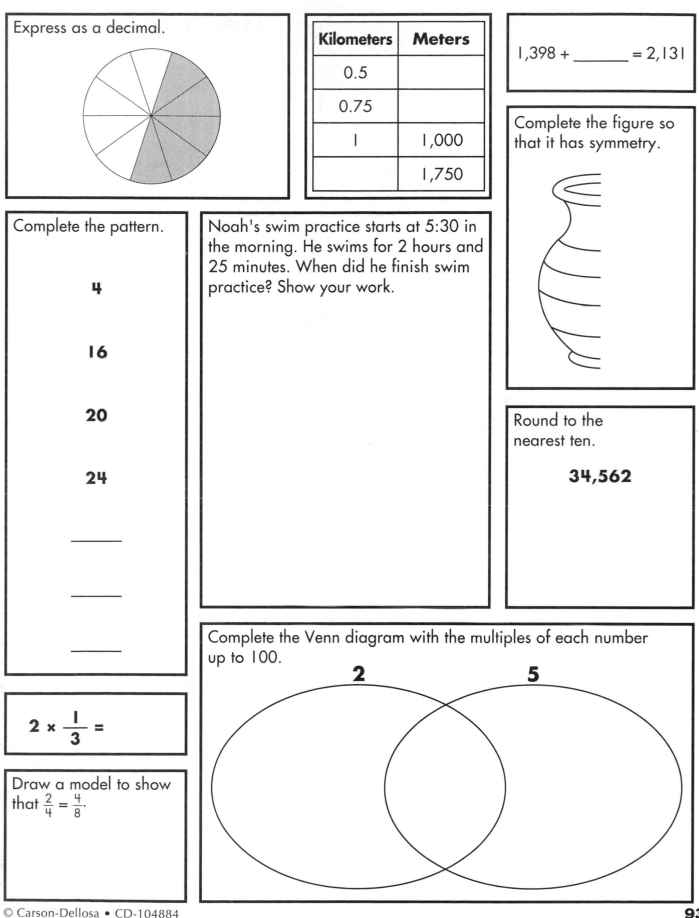

Express as a decimal.

Kilometers	Meters
0.5	
0.75	
1	1,000
	1,750

1,398 + _____ = 2,131

Complete the figure so that it has symmetry.

Complete the pattern.

4

16

20

24

_____

_____

_____

Noah's swim practice starts at 5:30 in the morning. He swims for 2 hours and 25 minutes. When did he finish swim practice? Show your work.

Round to the nearest ten.

34,562

$2 \times \dfrac{1}{3} =$

Draw a model to show that $\dfrac{2}{4} = \dfrac{4}{8}$.

Complete the Venn diagram with the multiples of each number up to 100.

2   **5**

42,082

What is the value of each **2**? _____

_____

Write a decimal to show the length of the grasshopper.

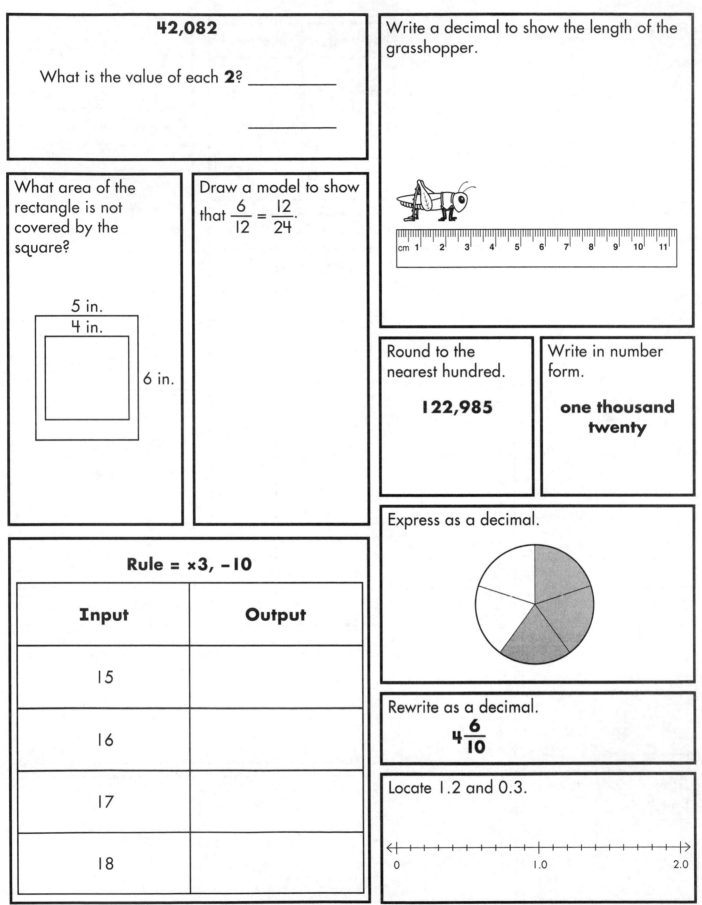

What area of the rectangle is not covered by the square?

5 in.
4 in.

6 in.

Draw a model to show that $\frac{6}{12} = \frac{12}{24}$.

Round to the nearest hundred.

122,985

Write in number form.

one thousand twenty

Express as a decimal.

Rewrite as a decimal.
$4\frac{6}{10}$

Locate 1.2 and 0.3.

0   1.0   2.0

Rule = ×3, −10

Input	Output
15	
16	
17	
18	

Find the multiples of each number up to 100.

14 _____

18 _____

22 _____

$$\frac{1}{5} + \frac{1}{5} + \frac{2}{5} = \text{—}$$

Draw a model to show the addition.

Shade the second rectangle to show an equivalent fraction.

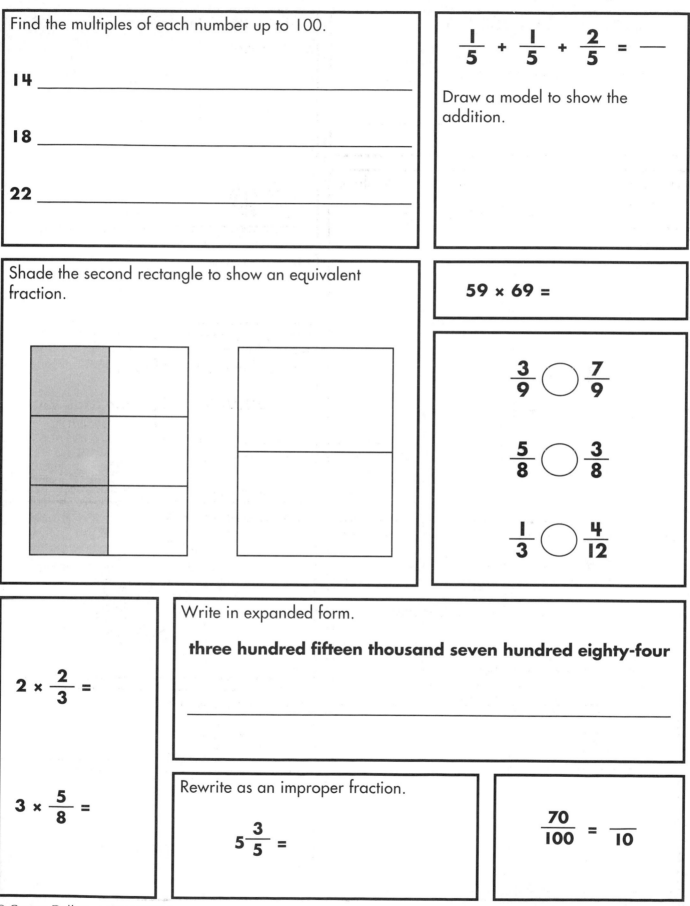

$59 \times 69 =$

$\frac{3}{9} \bigcirc \frac{7}{9}$

$\frac{5}{8} \bigcirc \frac{3}{8}$

$\frac{1}{3} \bigcirc \frac{4}{12}$

$2 \times \frac{2}{3} =$

$3 \times \frac{5}{8} =$

Write in expanded form.

three hundred fifteen thousand seven hundred eighty-four

_____

Rewrite as an improper fraction.

$5\frac{3}{5} =$

$\frac{70}{100} = \frac{}{10}$

Find the least common multiple of 30 and 9.

What is the perimeter of the rectangle?

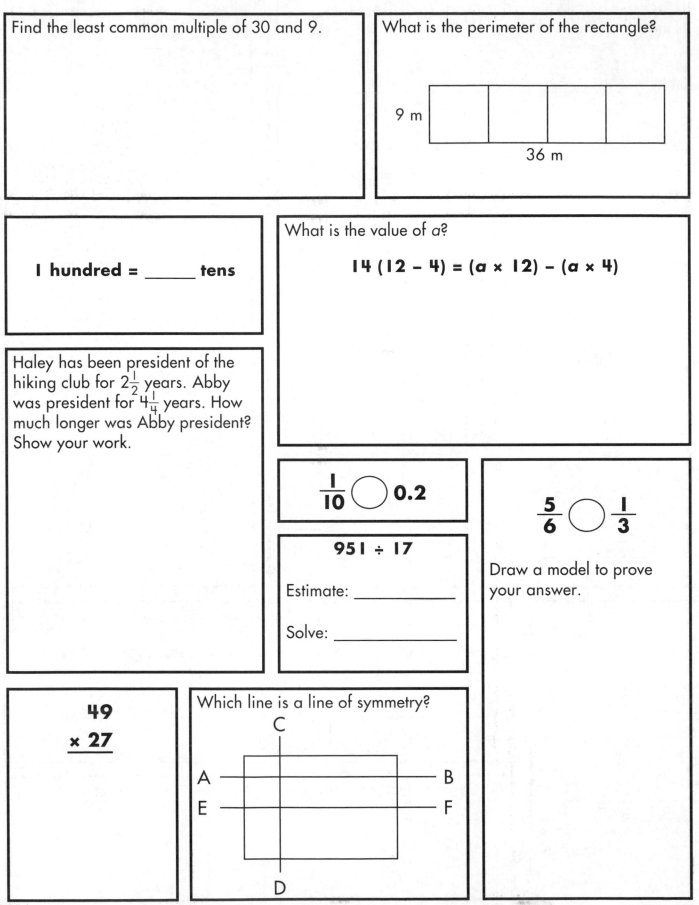

9 m

36 m

1 hundred = _____ tens

What is the value of *a*?

14 (12 – 4) = (a × 12) – (a × 4)

Haley has been president of the hiking club for $2\frac{1}{2}$ years. Abby was president for $4\frac{1}{4}$ years. How much longer was Abby president? Show your work.

$\frac{1}{10}$ ◯ **0.2**

$\frac{5}{6}$ ◯ $\frac{1}{3}$

Draw a model to prove your answer.

951 ÷ 17

Estimate: _____

Solve: _____

49
× 27

Which line is a line of symmetry?

C

A — — B

E — — F

D

Draw a similar shape.

Round to the nearest hundred thousand.

189,980

$13,928 + ? = 14,101$

What is the perimeter of the square?

4 cm

Jason purchased three items at the store. How much did he spend?

CONVENIENCE STOP

YOUR ONE-STOP SHOP

09/09/2014   13:23:54

- - - - - - - - - - - - - - - - - -

MAGAZINE   5.89
CHOCOLATE   4.19
GUMMY WORMS   3.99

What time will it be 53 minutes from now?

What time was it 29 minutes ago?

Richard purchased 4 items that were $11.31 each. He gave the clerk a $50 bill. How much should he get in return?

$10 \times \dfrac{1}{4} =$

Draw a model to show that $\dfrac{1}{2} = \dfrac{3}{6}$.

What is the value of c?

$$77(49 + 18) = (77 \times 49) + (77 \times c)$$

$$c = \underline{\hspace{2cm}}$$

$$24(13 + 34) = (24 \times 13) + (24 \times c)$$

$$c = \underline{\hspace{2cm}}$$

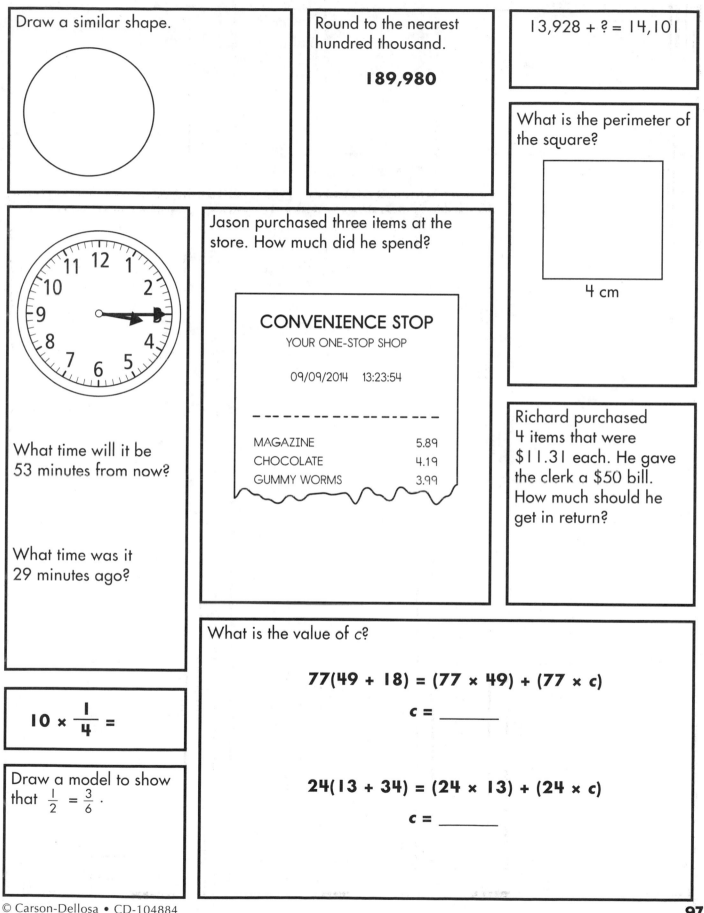

27,576

What is the value of the **5**? _____

What is the value of the **2**? _____

Complete the pattern.

3,609

3,659

3,709

_____

_____

Mr. Juarez has $3,218 in his savings account. Ms. Jackson saved $150 a month for 2 years. Who has saved more money?

Write a decimal to show the length of the turkey's egg.

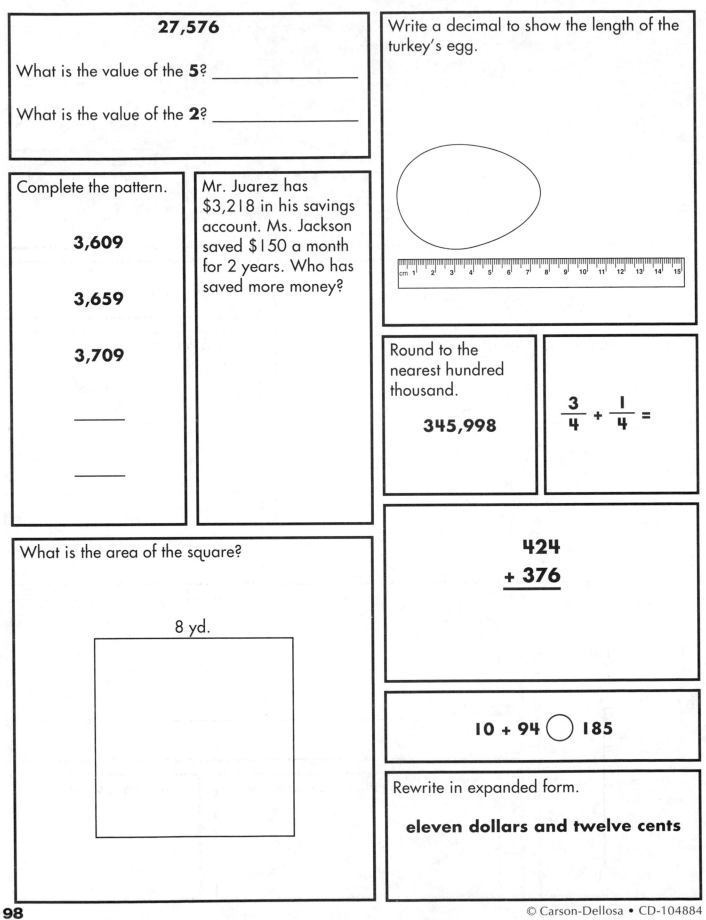

Round to the nearest hundred thousand.

345,998

$\frac{3}{4} + \frac{1}{4} =$

424
+ 376

$10 + 94 \bigcirc 185$

Rewrite in expanded form.

eleven dollars and twelve cents

What is the area of the square?

8 yd.

McKenzie picked 23 pineapples. Each pineapple filled 4 pint jars. She can preserve 9 pint jars at a time in her water bath canner. How many times will she have to fill the canner to preserve all of the pineapple? Show your work.

Measure the angle.

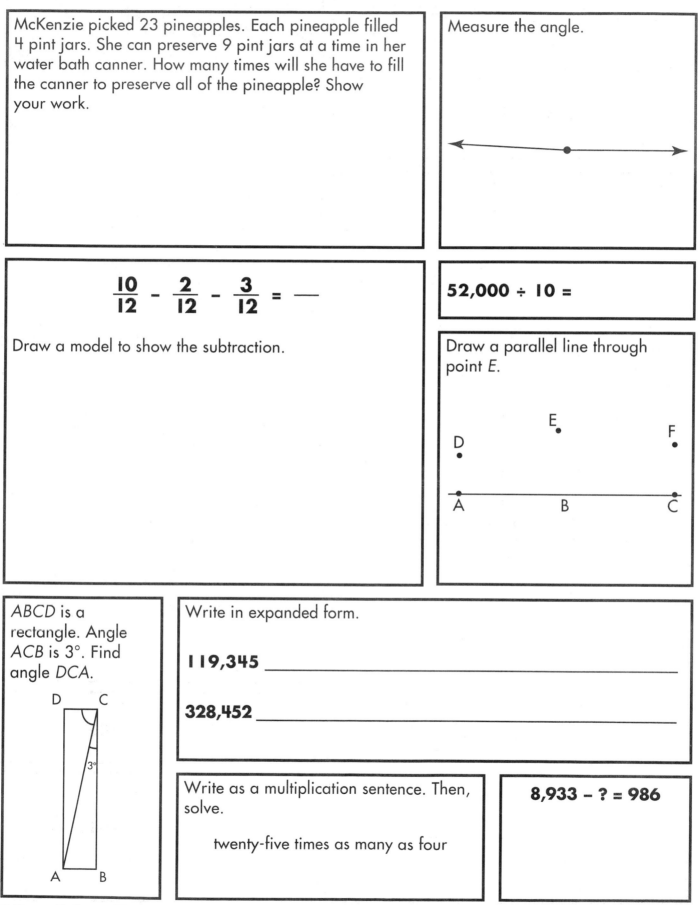

$\dfrac{10}{12} - \dfrac{2}{12} - \dfrac{3}{12} =$ ——

Draw a model to show the subtraction.

$52,000 \div 10 =$

Draw a parallel line through point *E*.

E
•
D   F
•   •

•_____•_____•
A   B   C

ABCD is a rectangle. Angle *ACB* is 3°. Find angle *DCA*.

D   C

3°

A   B

Write in expanded form.

119,345 _____

328,452 _____

Write as a multiplication sentence. Then, solve.

twenty-five times as many as four

8,933 – ? = 986

Locate $\frac{8}{10}$ on the number line.

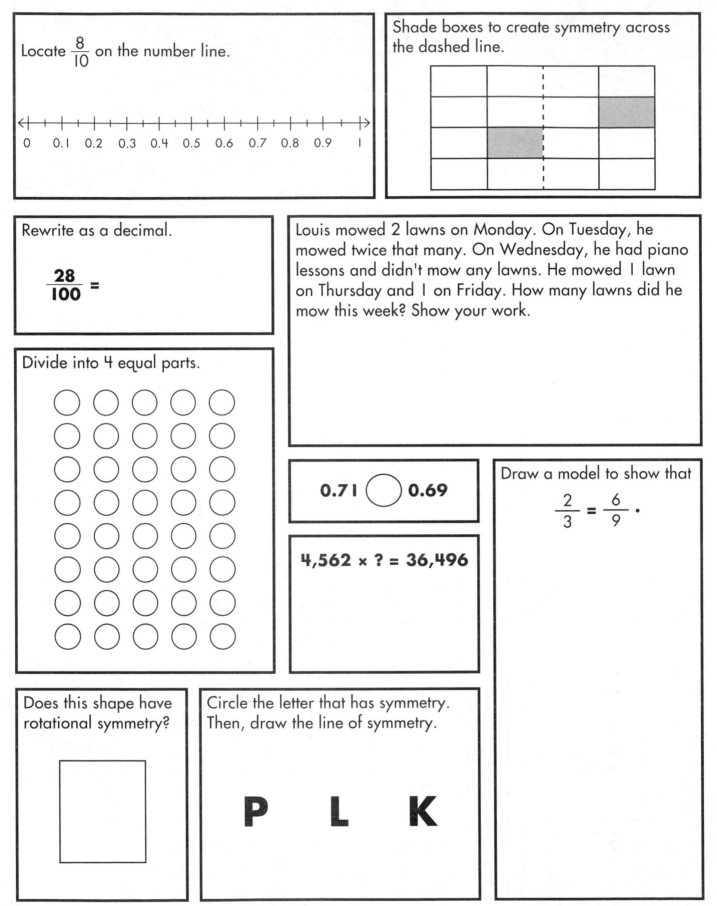

0   0.1   0.2   0.3   0.4   0.5   0.6   0.7   0.8   0.9   1

Shade boxes to create symmetry across the dashed line.

Rewrite as a decimal.

$$\frac{28}{100} =$$

Louis mowed 2 lawns on Monday. On Tuesday, he mowed twice that many. On Wednesday, he had piano lessons and didn't mow any lawns. He mowed 1 lawn on Thursday and 1 on Friday. How many lawns did he mow this week? Show your work.

Divide into 4 equal parts.

0.71 ◯ 0.69

4,562 × ? = 36,496

Draw a model to show that $\frac{2}{3} = \frac{6}{9}$.

Does this shape have rotational symmetry?

Circle the letter that has symmetry. Then, draw the line of symmetry.

P   L   K

Express as a decimal.

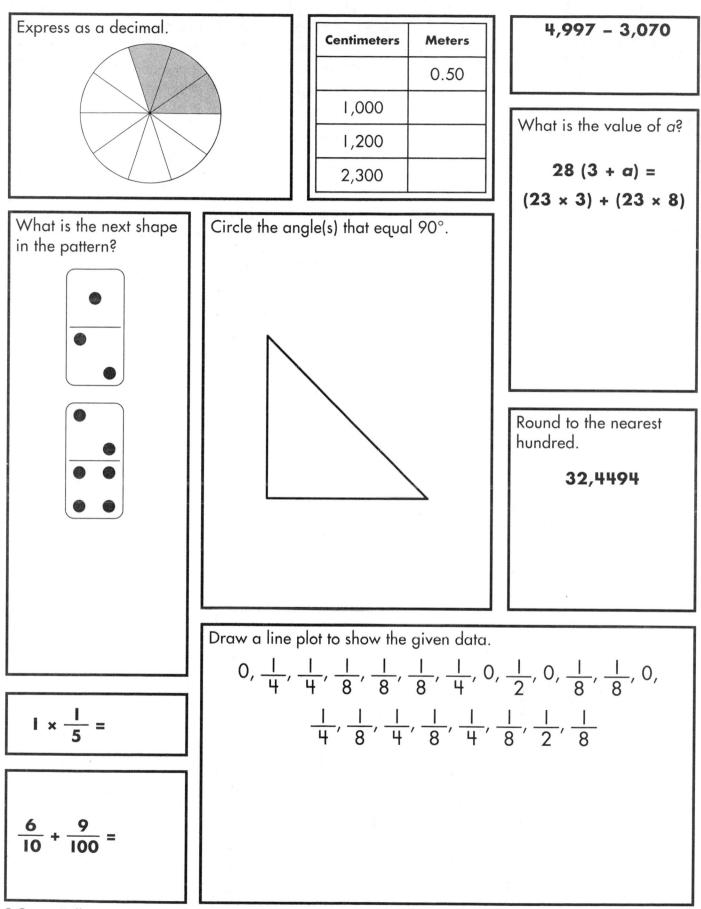

Centimeters	Meters
	0.50
1,000	
1,200	
2,300	

4,997 – 3,070

What is the value of *a*?

28 (3 + a) =

(23 × 3) + (23 × 8)

What is the next shape in the pattern?

Circle the angle(s) that equal 90°.

Round to the nearest hundred.

32,4494

$1 \times \dfrac{1}{5} =$

$\dfrac{6}{10} + \dfrac{9}{100} =$

Draw a line plot to show the given data.

$0, \dfrac{1}{4}, \dfrac{1}{4}, \dfrac{1}{8}, \dfrac{1}{8}, \dfrac{1}{8}, \dfrac{1}{4}, 0, \dfrac{1}{2}, 0, \dfrac{1}{8}, \dfrac{1}{8}, 0,$

$\dfrac{1}{4}, \dfrac{1}{8}, \dfrac{1}{4}, \dfrac{1}{8}, \dfrac{1}{4}, \dfrac{1}{8}, \dfrac{1}{2}, \dfrac{1}{8}$

What number is 9 times as many as 8? _____

What number is 15 times as many as 6? _____

Is this figure an angle? Why or why not?

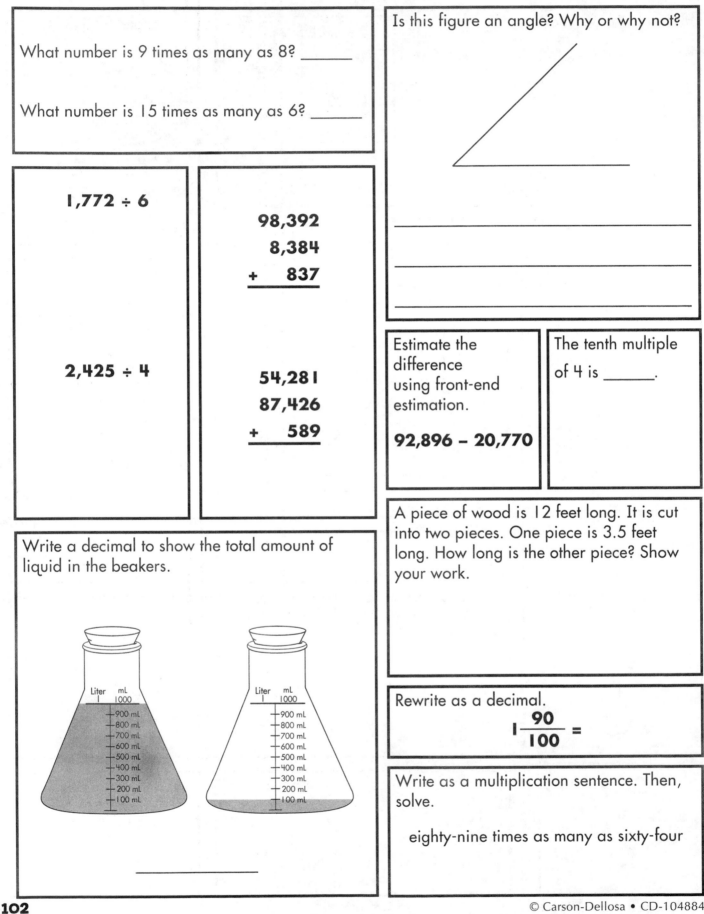

_____

_____

_____

1,772 ÷ 6

2,425 ÷ 4

98,392
8,384
+   837

54,281
87,426
+   589

Estimate the difference using front-end estimation.

92,896 − 20,770

The tenth multiple of 4 is _____.

A piece of wood is 12 feet long. It is cut into two pieces. One piece is 3.5 feet long. How long is the other piece? Show your work.

Write a decimal to show the total amount of liquid in the beakers.

_____

Rewrite as a decimal.

$1\dfrac{90}{100} =$

Write as a multiplication sentence. Then, solve.

eighty-nine times as many as sixty-four

What is the value of *a*?

$$4(a - 7) = (4 \times 4) - (4 \times 7)$$

Measure the angle.

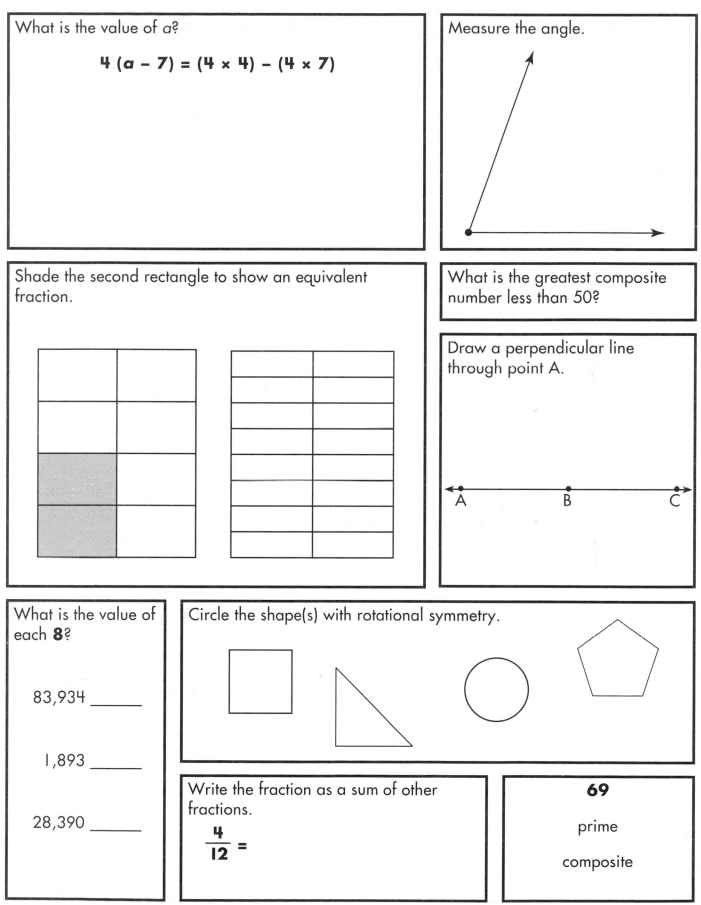

Shade the second rectangle to show an equivalent fraction.

What is the greatest composite number less than 50?

Draw a perpendicular line through point A.

A   B   C

What is the value of each **8**?

83,934 _____

1,893 _____

28,390 _____

Circle the shape(s) with rotational symmetry.

Write the fraction as a sum of other fractions.

$$\frac{4}{12} =$$

69

prime

composite

Draw an acute angle. Then, measure it.

Write the sums of adjacent numbers in the blocks above.

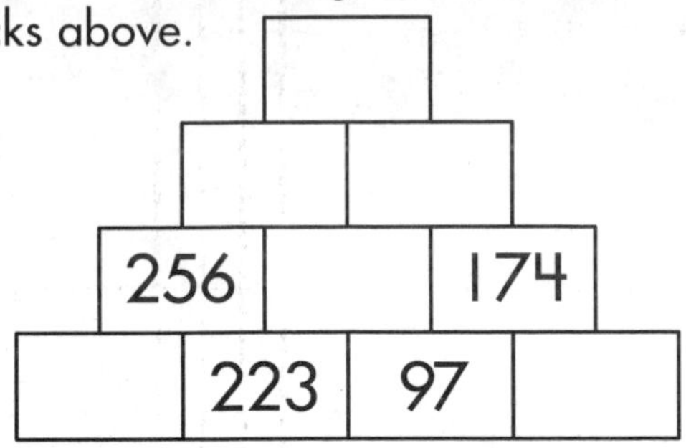

256   174

223 97

Draw a line with the point A.

Complete the Venn diagram with the factors of each number.

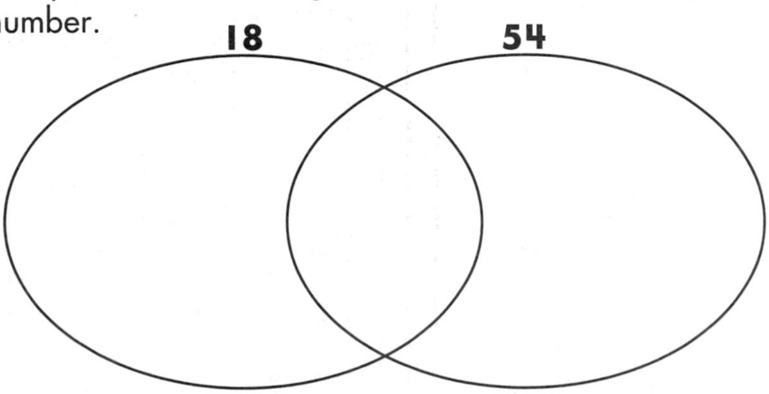

18   **54**

Ivan was on the phone for $5\frac{3}{4}$ hours at work. When he got home, he talked on the phone to his friend for 20 minutes. How long did Ivan spend on the phone altogether? Show your work.

$\frac{1}{10}$ ◯ 0.10

8,455 + 6,657

$\frac{4}{8}$ ◯ $\frac{1}{4}$

Draw a model to prove your answer.

3,448 ÷ 4

3,452
×   7

Start time: 7:43 pm
End time: 9:12 pm
Elapsed time:

|—————————————————————————|

Round to the nearest ten thousand.

11,983

50 L $\bigcirc$ 5,500 mL

Write a word problem with a quotient of 13 and a divisor of 3.

Complete the pattern.

3

9

15

21

_____

_____

Mr. McGregor started mowing the lawn at 4:50 pm. It takes him 45 minutes to mow it. When did he finish? Show your work.

A square has:

_____° angles.

_____ sides.

It is _____-dimensional.

$2 \times \dfrac{1}{16} =$

Draw a model to show that $\dfrac{1}{2} = \dfrac{4}{8}$.

Students measured the width of leaves from different trees in inches. Draw a line plot to show the given data.

$$\dfrac{7}{8}, \; 1\dfrac{1}{8}, \; \dfrac{4}{8}, \; \dfrac{5}{8}, \; 1\dfrac{2}{8}, \; 1\dfrac{2}{8}, \; \dfrac{6}{8}, \; 1\dfrac{3}{8}, \; \dfrac{4}{8}, \; \dfrac{6}{8}$$

8,936

What is the value of the **3**? _____

What is the value of the **9**? _____

Write a decimal to show the length of the turkey's egg.

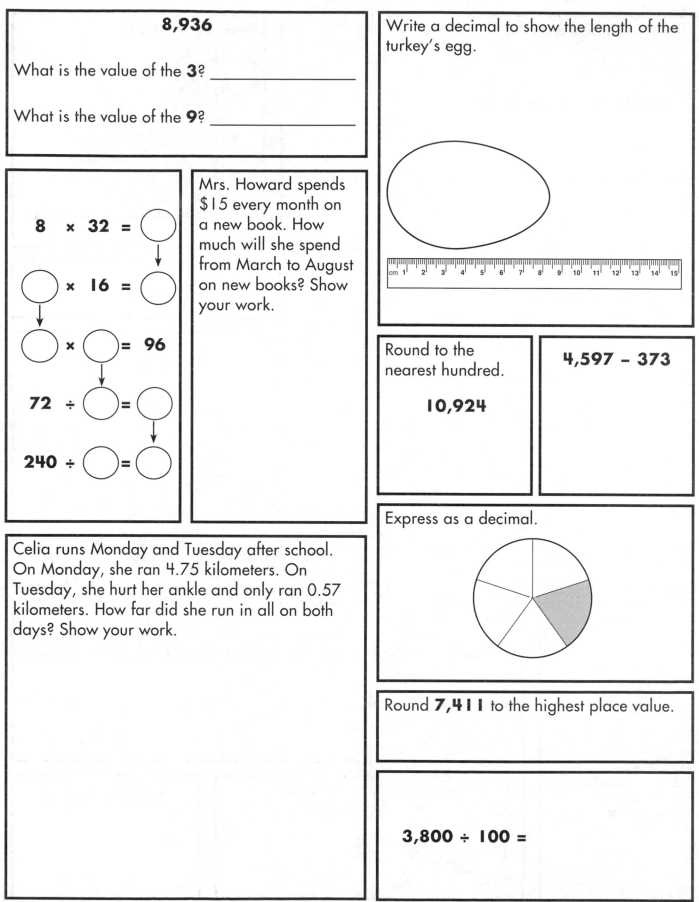

$8 \times 32 =$ ◯

◯ $\times 16 =$ ◯

◯ $\times$ ◯ $= 96$

$72 \div$ ◯ $=$ ◯

$240 \div$ ◯ $=$ ◯

Mrs. Howard spends $15 every month on a new book. How much will she spend from March to August on new books? Show your work.

Round to the nearest hundred.

10,924

4,597 – 373

Express as a decimal.

Round **7,411** to the highest place value.

Celia runs Monday and Tuesday after school. On Monday, she ran 4.75 kilometers. On Tuesday, she hurt her ankle and only ran 0.57 kilometers. How far did she run in all on both days? Show your work.

3,800 ÷ 100 =

Find the first nine multiples of 3.

Find the first nine multiples of 4.

Circle the common multiples.

Measure the angle.

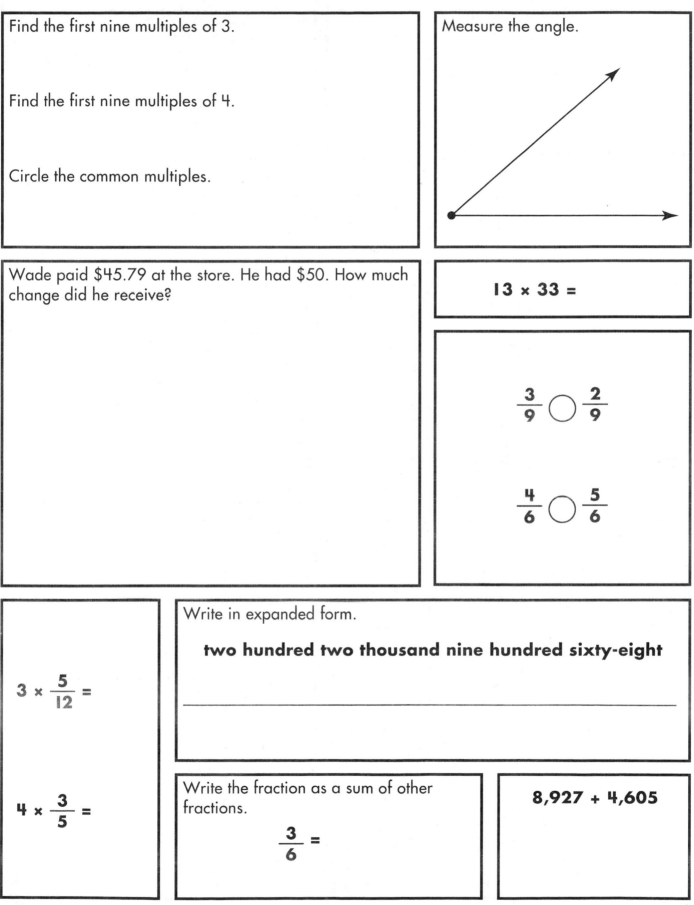

Wade paid $45.79 at the store. He had $50. How much change did he receive?

---

13 × 33 =

$\frac{3}{9}$ ◯ $\frac{2}{9}$

$\frac{4}{6}$ ◯ $\frac{5}{6}$

$3 \times \frac{5}{12} =$

$4 \times \frac{3}{5} =$

Write in expanded form.

two hundred two thousand nine hundred sixty-eight

_____

Write the fraction as a sum of other fractions.

$\frac{3}{6} =$

8,927 + 4,605

Find the least common multiple of 41 and 35.

What is the value of *a*?

$$7 (4 \times a) = (7 \times 4) \times (7 \times 6)$$

Rewrite as a decimal.

$$\frac{104}{100} =$$

Shade three boxes to create rotational symmetry on the shape.

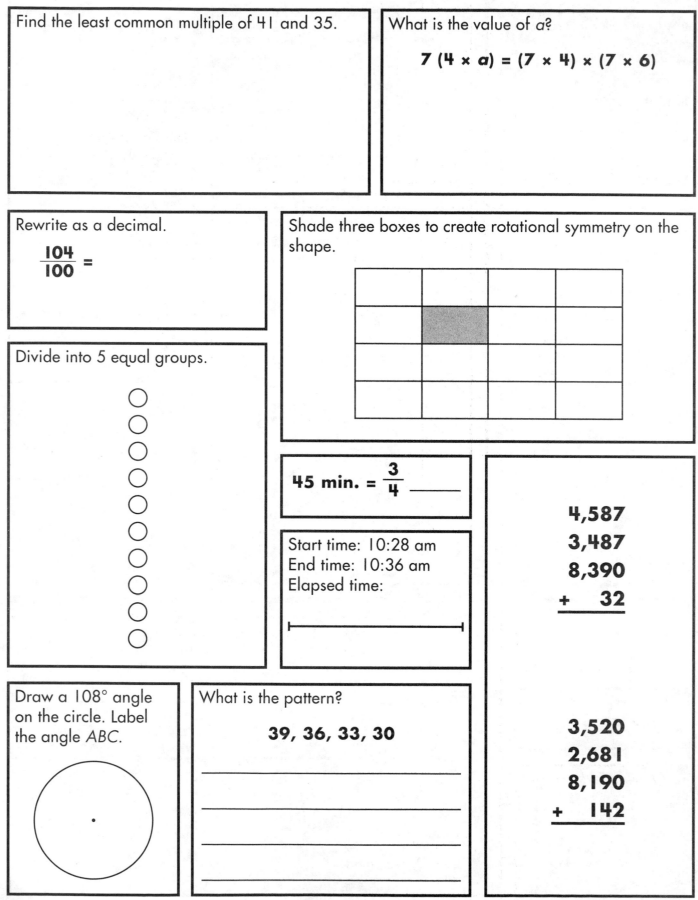

Divide into 5 equal groups.

○
○
○
○
○
○
○
○
○
○

$$45 \text{ min.} = \frac{3}{4} \_\_\_\_\_$$

Start time: 10:28 am
End time: 10:36 am
Elapsed time:

|———————————|

4,587
3,487
8,390
+   32
————

Draw a 108° angle on the circle. Label the angle *ABC*.

What is the pattern?

39, 36, 33, 30

_____

_____

_____

_____

3,520
2,681
8,190
+   142
————

Start time: 8:23 pm
End time: 10:57 pm
Elapsed time:

Grams	Kilograms
1,000	
12,000	
	38

$8,371 - 6,412$

Does this shape have rotational symmetry?

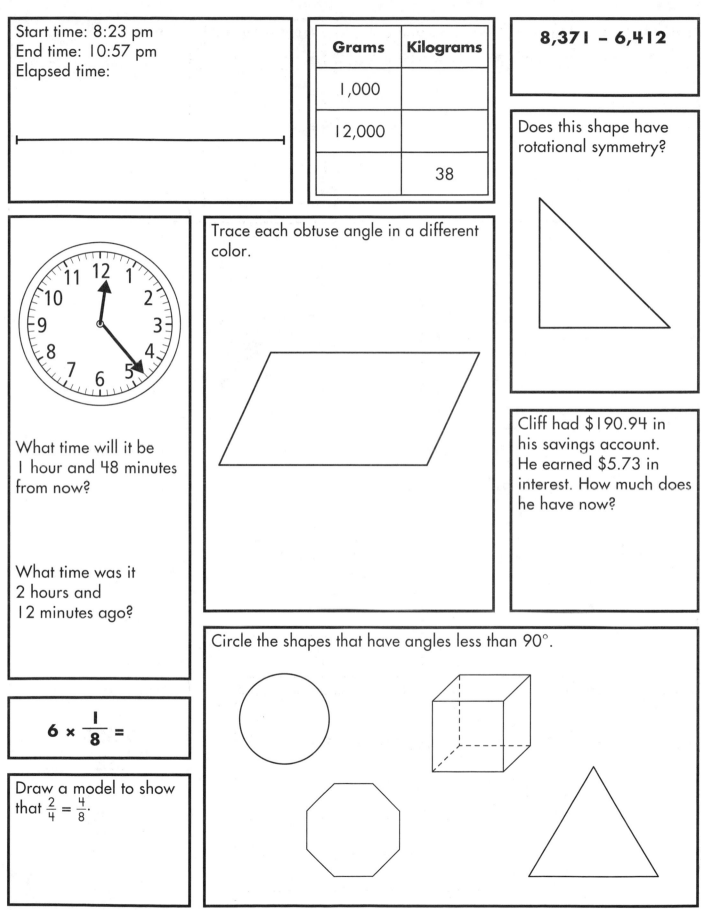

What time will it be 1 hour and 48 minutes from now?

What time was it 2 hours and 12 minutes ago?

Trace each obtuse angle in a different color.

Cliff had $190.94 in his savings account. He earned $5.73 in interest. How much does he have now?

$6 \times \dfrac{1}{8} =$

Draw a model to show that $\dfrac{2}{4} = \dfrac{4}{8}$.

Circle the shapes that have angles less than 90°.

What number is 13 times as many as 6? _____

What number is 123 times as many
as 3? _____

Is **37** composite or prime?

_____

Prove your answer.

Complete the pattern.

48

24

12

6

_____

_____

Draw a model to show
that $\frac{2}{5} = \frac{8}{20}$.

Round **981,393**
to the nearest ten
thousand.

7,426 + 3,618

Express as a decimal.

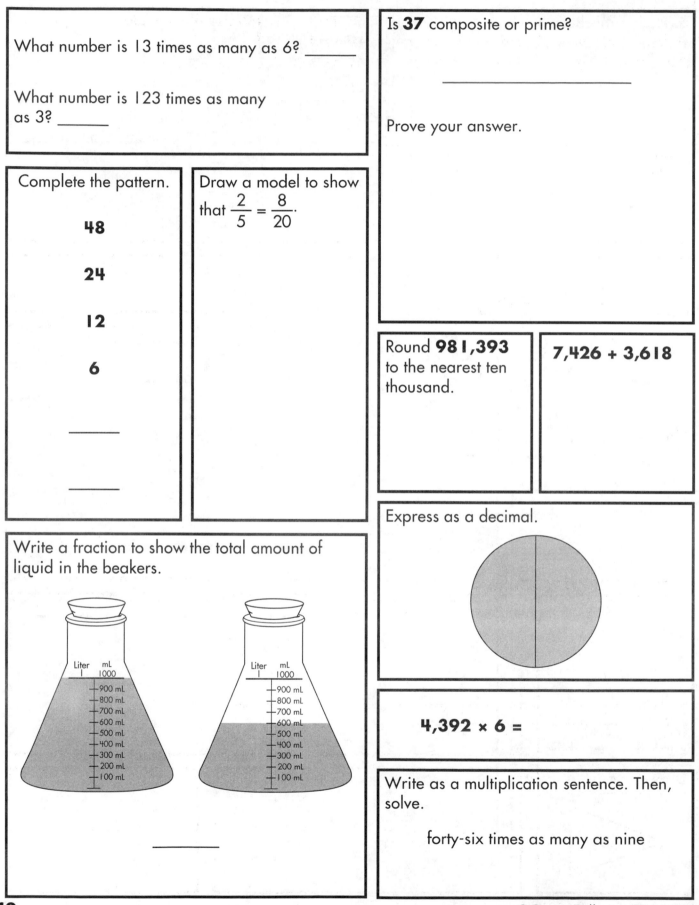

Write a fraction to show the total amount of
liquid in the beakers.

_____

4,392 × 6 =

Write as a multiplication sentence. Then,
solve.

forty-six times as many as nine

Tripp rides his horse three times a week. He rides for an hour every time. One week he was only able to ride twice. How long should he ride both times so that he still gets the same amount of practice? Show your work.

Measure the angle.

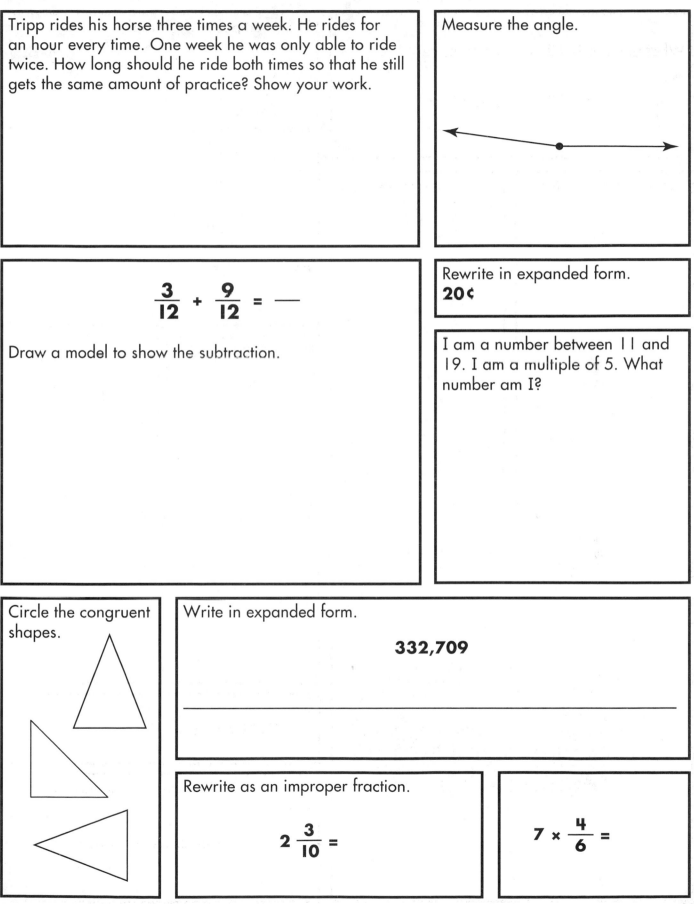

$$\frac{3}{12} + \frac{9}{12} = \underline{\quad}$$

Draw a model to show the subtraction.

Rewrite in expanded form.
20¢

I am a number between 11 and 19. I am a multiple of 5. What number am I?

Circle the congruent shapes.

Write in expanded form.

332,709

_____

Rewrite as an improper fraction.

$$2\frac{3}{10} = $$

$$7 \times \frac{4}{6} = $$

Locate $\frac{85}{100}$ on the number line.

<|---+--+--+--+--+--+--+--+--+--+--|>
0   0.1   0.2   0.3   0.4   0.5   0.6   0.7   0.8   0.9   1

Shade boxes to create symmetry across the dashed line.

Draw a line segment with the point G.

What would you use to measure the width of an eraser?

centimeters   inches   meters

What would you use to measure the width of a book?

centimeters   inches   meters

Janice practices guitar after school for $1\frac{3}{4}$ hours. She plays guitar in music class for 30 minutes. How long does Janice play guitar every school day? Show your work.

$\frac{1}{12} \bigcirc 0.3$

690 ÷ 8

Estimate: _____

Solve: _____

$\frac{3}{9} \bigcirc \frac{1}{3}$

Draw a model to prove your answer.

51
× 34

Circle the letter that has symmetry. Then, draw the line of symmetry.

U   G   P

Name _____

Express as a decimal.

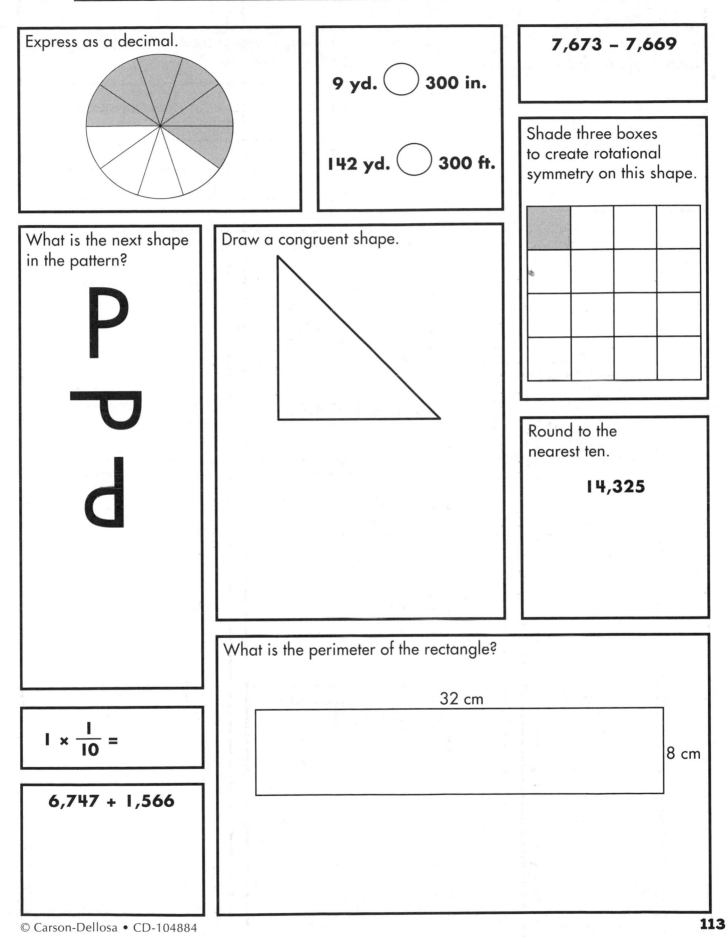

9 yd. ◯ 300 in.

142 yd. ◯ 300 ft.

7,673 – 7,669

Shade three boxes to create rotational symmetry on this shape.

What is the next shape in the pattern?

P P ꟼ

Draw a congruent shape.

Round to the nearest ten.

14,325

$1 \times \frac{1}{10} =$

6,747 + 1,566

What is the perimeter of the rectangle?

32 cm

8 cm

61,866

What is the value of the **1**? _____

What is the value of the **8**? _____

Write a decimal to show the length of the paper clip.

---

791 ÷ 3

684 ÷ 7

What is the next shape in the pattern?

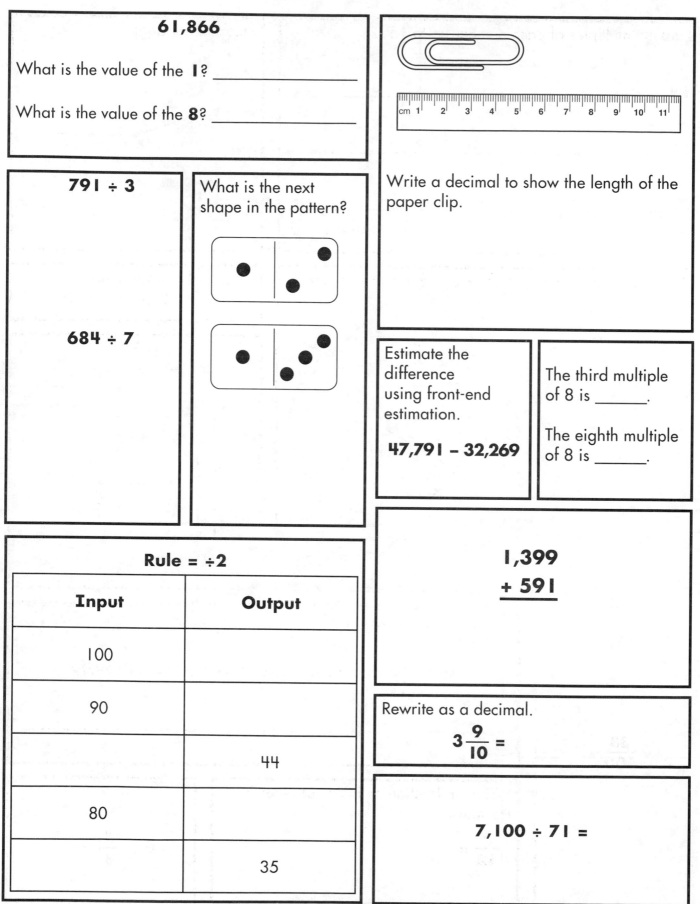

Estimate the difference using front-end estimation.

47,791 – 32,269

The third multiple of 8 is _____.

The eighth multiple of 8 is _____.

Rule = ÷2

Input	Output
100	
90	
	44
80	
	35

1,399
+ 591

Rewrite as a decimal.

$3\frac{9}{10} =$

7,100 ÷ 71 =

Find the multiples of each number up to 150.

19 _____

23 _____

29 _____

Measure the angle.

Shade the second circle to show an equivalent fraction.

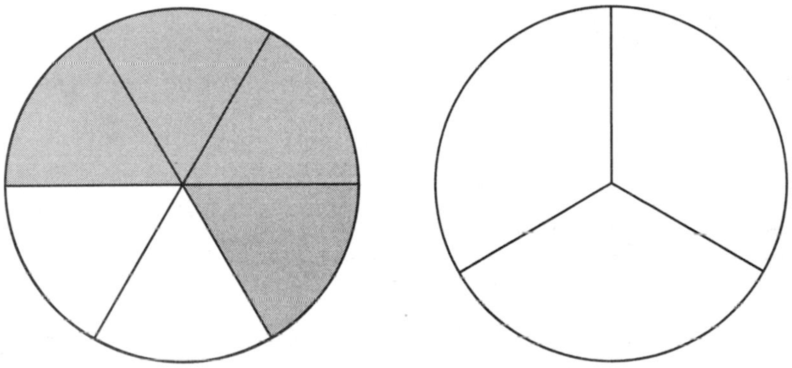

What is the greatest prime number less than 50?

$\dfrac{7}{10} \bigcirc \dfrac{7}{12}$

$\dfrac{5}{8} \bigcirc \dfrac{5}{6}$

$7 \times \dfrac{24}{100} =$

$3 \times \dfrac{38}{100} =$

Write in expanded form.

seventy-three thousand three hundred thirty

_____

Write the fraction as a sum of other fractions.

$\dfrac{3}{12} =$

$6 \times \dfrac{7}{8} =$

Draw a right angle on the line.

_____

Write **85,505** in word form.

_____

_____

Rewrite as a decimal.

$\frac{3}{100}$ =

Marcus read 3 books last month. His brother, Mikal, read twice as many. How many books did they read altogether? Show your work.

Divide into 5 equal parts.

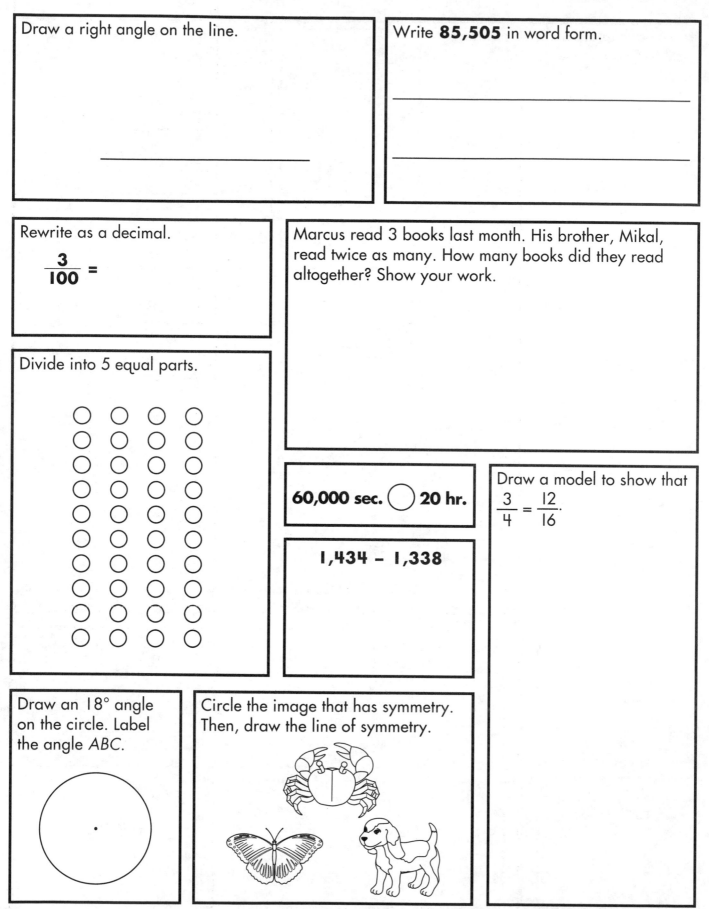

60,000 sec. ◯ 20 hr.

Draw a model to show that $\frac{3}{4} = \frac{12}{16}$.

1,434 – 1,338

Draw an 18° angle on the circle. Label the angle *ABC*.

Circle the image that has symmetry. Then, draw the line of symmetry.

Trace each acute angle in a different color.

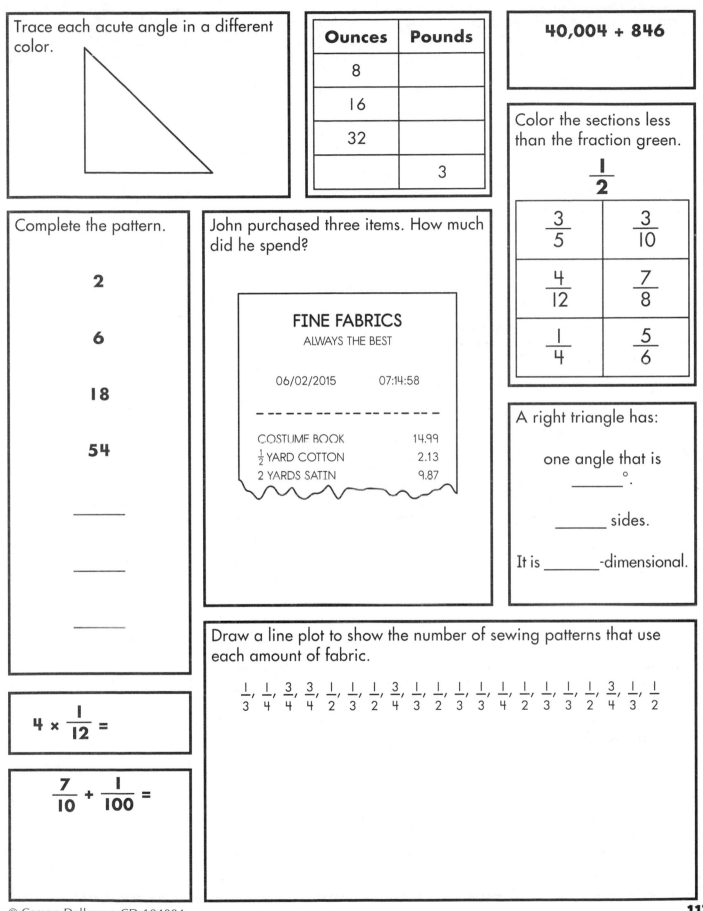

Ounces	Pounds
8	
16	
32	
	3

40,004 + 846

Color the sections less than the fraction green.

$\dfrac{1}{2}$

$\dfrac{3}{5}$	$\dfrac{3}{10}$
$\dfrac{4}{12}$	$\dfrac{7}{8}$
$\dfrac{1}{4}$	$\dfrac{5}{6}$

Complete the pattern.

2

6

18

54

_____

_____

_____

John purchased three items. How much did he spend?

FINE FABRICS

ALWAYS THE BEST

06/02/2015   07:14:58

- - - - - - - - - - - - - -

COSTUME BOOK   14.99
$\frac{1}{2}$ YARD COTTON   2.13
2 YARDS SATIN   9.87

A right triangle has:

one angle that is

_____°.

_____ sides.

It is _____-dimensional.

$4 \times \dfrac{1}{12} =$

$\dfrac{7}{10} + \dfrac{1}{100} =$

Draw a line plot to show the number of sewing patterns that use each amount of fabric.

$\dfrac{1}{3}, \dfrac{1}{4}, \dfrac{3}{4}, \dfrac{3}{4}, \dfrac{1}{2}, \dfrac{1}{3}, \dfrac{1}{2}, \dfrac{3}{4}, \dfrac{1}{3}, \dfrac{1}{2}, \dfrac{1}{3}, \dfrac{1}{3}, \dfrac{1}{4}, \dfrac{1}{2}, \dfrac{1}{3}, \dfrac{1}{3}, \dfrac{1}{2}, \dfrac{3}{4}, \dfrac{1}{3}, \dfrac{1}{2}$

Locate $\frac{5}{100}$ on the number line.

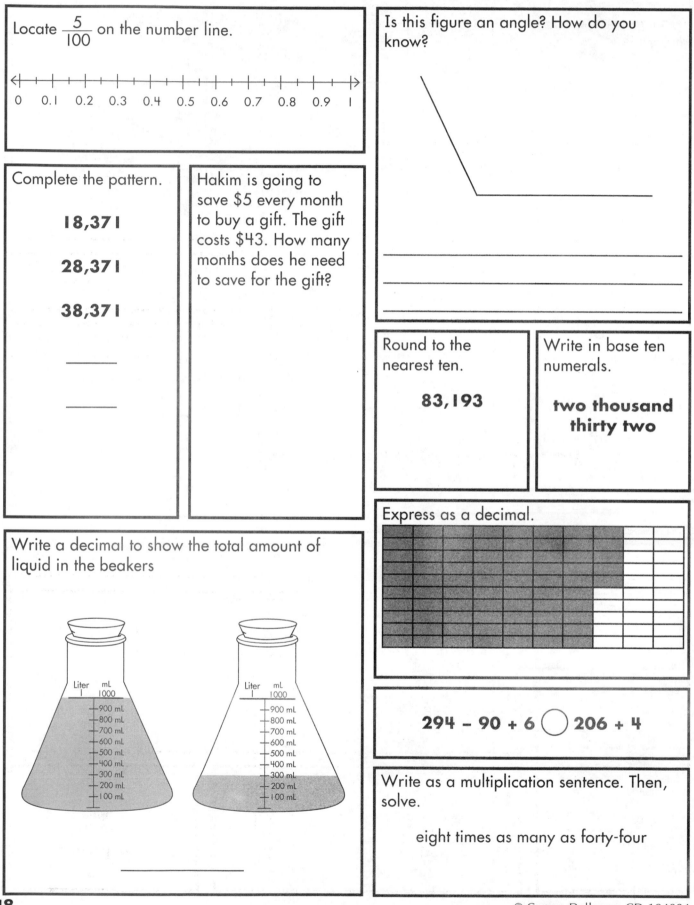

0   0.1   0.2   0.3   0.4   0.5   0.6   0.7   0.8   0.9   1

Complete the pattern.

18,371

28,371

38,371

_____

_____

Hakim is going to save $5 every month to buy a gift. The gift costs $43. How many months does he need to save for the gift?

Is this figure an angle? How do you know?

_____

_____

_____

Round to the nearest ten.

83,193

Write in base ten numerals.

two thousand thirty two

Express as a decimal.

Write a decimal to show the total amount of liquid in the beakers

_____

---

294 − 90 + 6 ◯ 206 + 4

Write as a multiplication sentence. Then, solve.

eight times as many as forty-four

What would you use to measure the height of an elephant?

meters

inches

grams

Measure the angle.

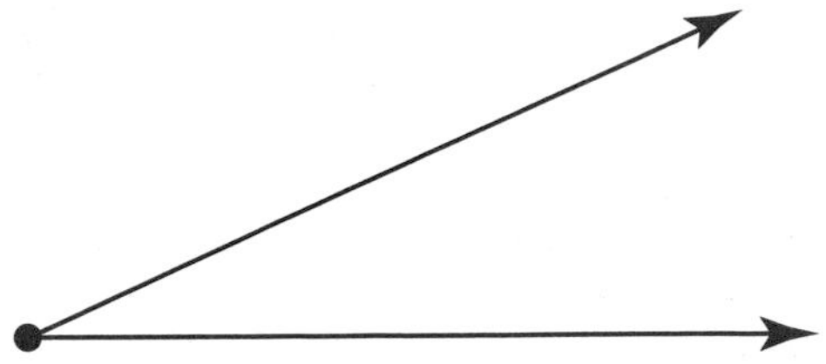

Tyra has $10. Sand for a sandbox costs $1.98 per pound. How many pounds of sand can she buy? Show your work.

Which has the highest value of **2**?
9,472   **3,204**

I am a number between 23 and 30. I am a multiple of 6 and 8. I am a factor of 48. What number am I?

What is the value of each **5**?

25,239 _____

53 _____

587 _____

Write in expanded form.

940,873

_____

Write the fraction as a sum of other fractions.

$\frac{4}{10}$ =

121

prime

composite

Find the least common multiple of 26 and 10.

Write the sums of adjacent numbers in the blocks above.

```
        ┌─────┐
        │     │
     ┌──┴──┬──┴──┐
     │  327 │
  ┌──┴──┬──┴──┬──┴──┐
  │     │ 109 │     │
┌─┴──┬──┴──┬──┴──┬──┴─┐
│ 13 │     │     │ 114 │
└────┴─────┴─────┴────┘
```

Rewrite as a decimal.

$\dfrac{176}{100} =$

Complete the Venn diagram with the factors of each number.

      21   **35**

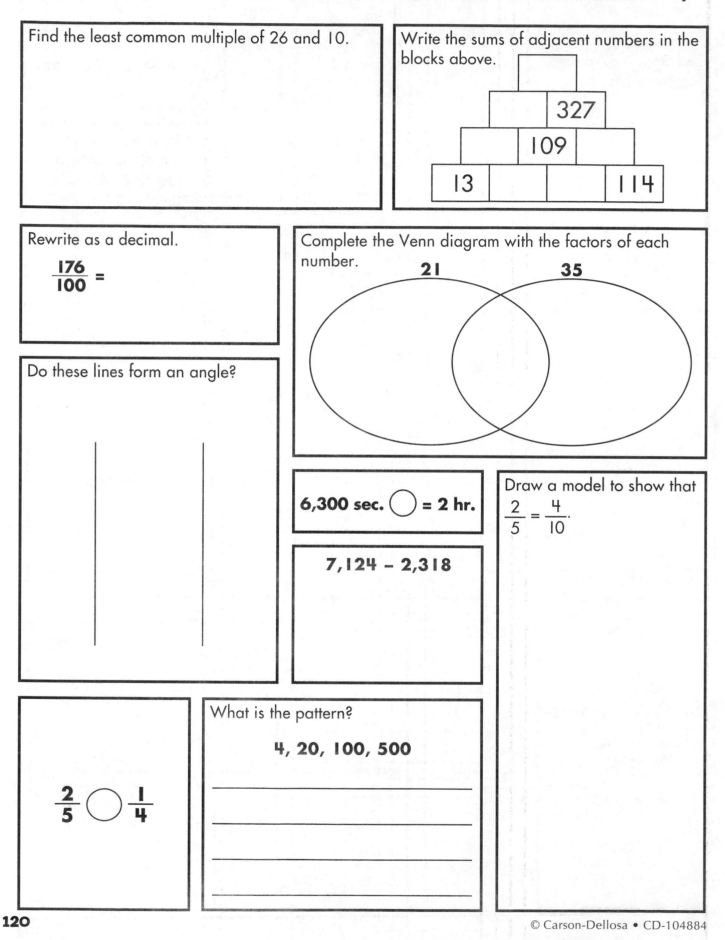

Do these lines form an angle?

6,300 sec. $\bigcirc$ = 2 hr.

7,124 – 2,318

Draw a model to show that $\dfrac{2}{5} = \dfrac{4}{10}$.

$\dfrac{2}{5} \bigcirc \dfrac{1}{4}$

What is the pattern?

4, 20, 100, 500

_____

_____

_____

_____

Start time: 2:18 pm
End time: 3:57 pm
Elapsed time:

Round to the nearest hundred thousand.

354,350

2.5 lb. ◯ 36 oz.

Write a word problem with a divisor of 4, a dividend of 68, and a quotient of 17.

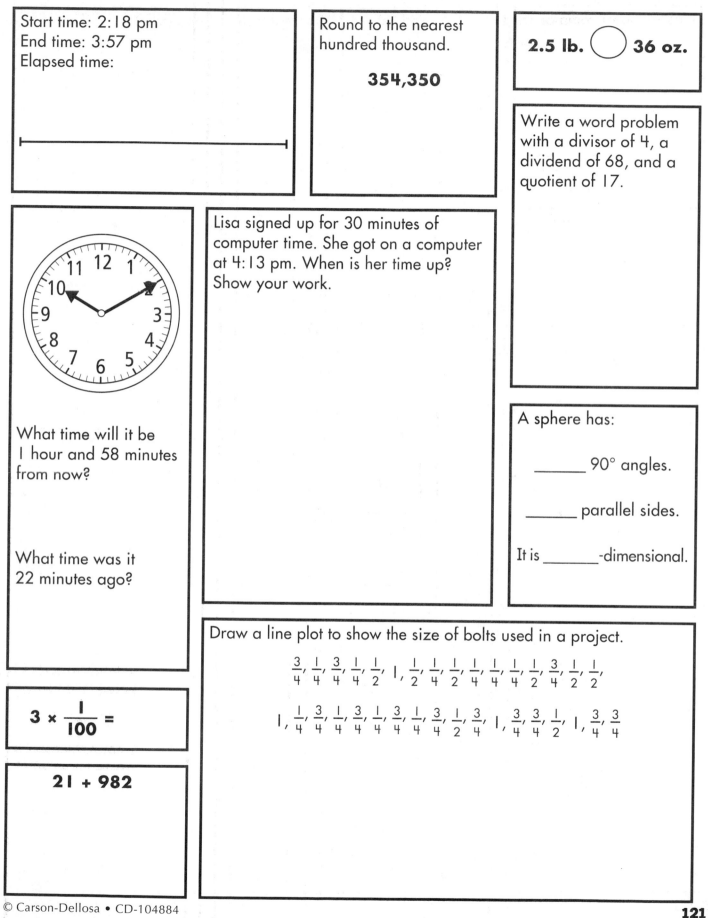

What time will it be 1 hour and 58 minutes from now?

What time was it 22 minutes ago?

Lisa signed up for 30 minutes of computer time. She got on a computer at 4:13 pm. When is her time up? Show your work.

A sphere has:

_____ 90° angles.

_____ parallel sides.

It is _____-dimensional.

$3 \times \dfrac{1}{100} =$

21 + 982

Draw a line plot to show the size of bolts used in a project.

$\dfrac{3}{4}, \dfrac{1}{4}, \dfrac{3}{4}, \dfrac{1}{4}, \dfrac{1}{2}, 1, \dfrac{1}{2}, \dfrac{1}{4}, \dfrac{1}{2}, \dfrac{1}{4}, \dfrac{1}{4}, \dfrac{1}{4}, \dfrac{1}{2}, \dfrac{3}{4}, \dfrac{1}{2}, \dfrac{1}{2},$

$1, \dfrac{1}{4}, \dfrac{3}{4}, \dfrac{1}{4}, \dfrac{3}{4}, \dfrac{1}{4}, \dfrac{3}{4}, \dfrac{1}{4}, \dfrac{3}{4}, \dfrac{1}{2}, \dfrac{3}{4}, 1, \dfrac{3}{4}, \dfrac{3}{4}, \dfrac{1}{2}, 1, \dfrac{3}{4}, \dfrac{3}{4}$

What number is 4 times as many as 1,922?

_____

What number is 767 times as many as 8?

_____

892 ÷ 4

365 ÷ 5

Draw a model to show that $\frac{1}{2} = \frac{2}{4}$.

Is this figure an angle?

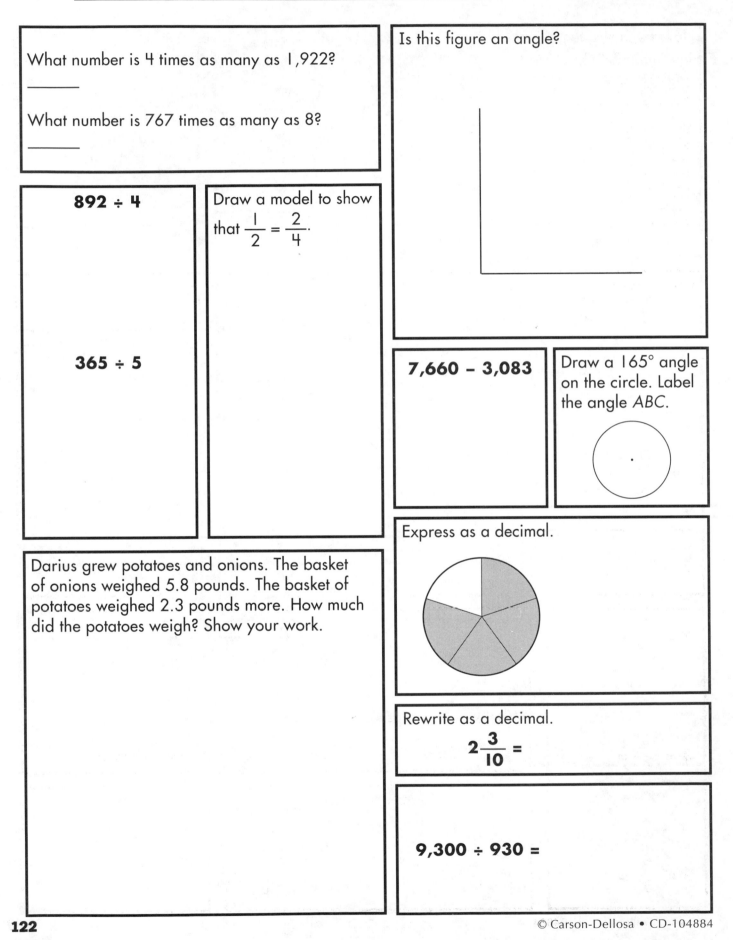

7,660 – 3,083

Draw a 165° angle on the circle. Label the angle *ABC*.

Express as a decimal.

Rewrite as a decimal.

$2\frac{3}{10} =$

9,300 ÷ 930 =

Darius grew potatoes and onions. The basket of onions weighed 5.8 pounds. The basket of potatoes weighed 2.3 pounds more. How much did the potatoes weigh? Show your work.

How much shorter is the book?

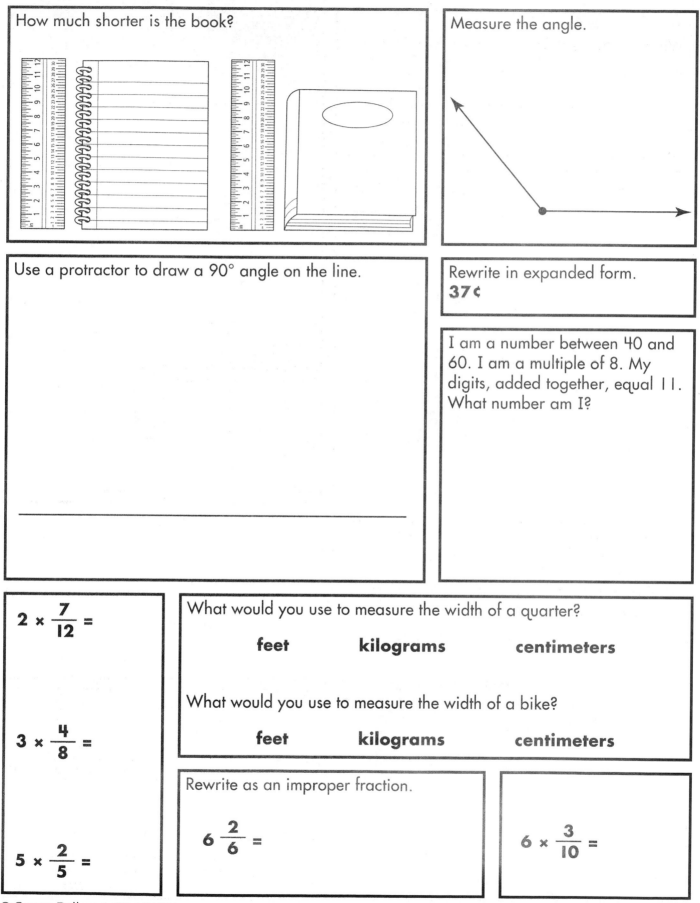

Measure the angle.

Use a protractor to draw a 90° angle on the line.

_____

Rewrite in expanded form.
37¢

I am a number between 40 and 60. I am a multiple of 8. My digits, added together, equal 11. What number am I?

$2 \times \dfrac{7}{12} =$

$3 \times \dfrac{4}{8} =$

$5 \times \dfrac{2}{5} =$

What would you use to measure the width of a quarter?

feet   **kilograms**   **centimeters**

What would you use to measure the width of a bike?

feet   **kilograms**   **centimeters**

Rewrite as an improper fraction.

$6 \dfrac{2}{6} =$

$6 \times \dfrac{3}{10} =$

Find the least common multiple of 2 and 6.

954 + 468

Draw a ray *AB*.

What would you use to measure the weight of a bowling ball?

pounds   **grams**   **feet**

What would you use to measure the weight of a cup of cereal?

pounds   **grams**   **feet**

Every morning that Karl milks his goat, he gets $1\frac{1}{4}$ gallons of milk. He milks the goat in the evening and gets another $\frac{1}{3}$ gallon. How much milk does Karl get each day? Show your work.

$\frac{1}{100}$ ◯ 0.1

Start time: 5:21 pm
End time: 6:28 am
Elapsed time:

|⎯⎯⎯⎯⎯⎯⎯⎯⎯⎯|

98
× 23

Draw a 41° angle.
Label the angle *JKL*.

635 ÷ 5

54
× 46

Start time: 10:23 pm
End time: 11:05 pm
Elapsed time:

|⊢──────────────────────────────⊣|

3,600 cm ◯ 30 m

4,000 cm ◯ 400 m

455 − 204

ABCD is a rectangle.
Angle BDA is 24°. Find
angle CDB.

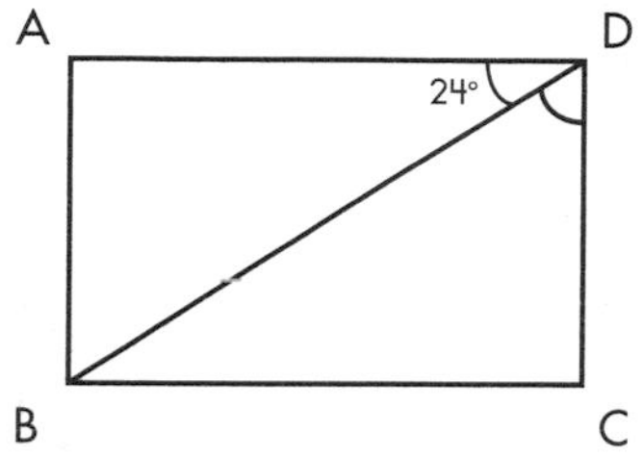

A _____ D
                24°
 /
B   C

What is the next shape
in the pattern?

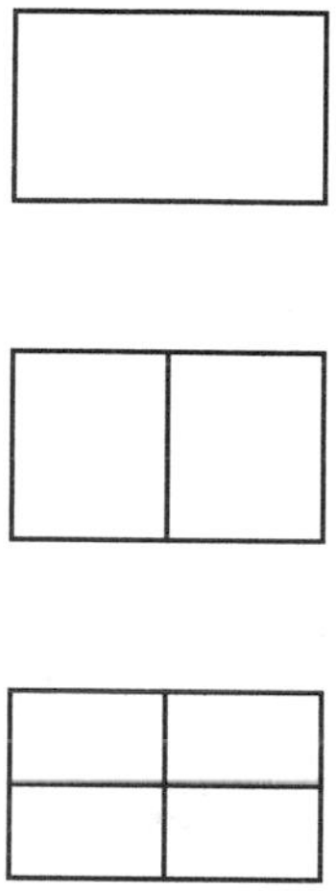

Draw a congruent shape.

Anderson purchased
one item. He gave the
clerk $7. He received
$0.95 in change. How
much did the item cost?

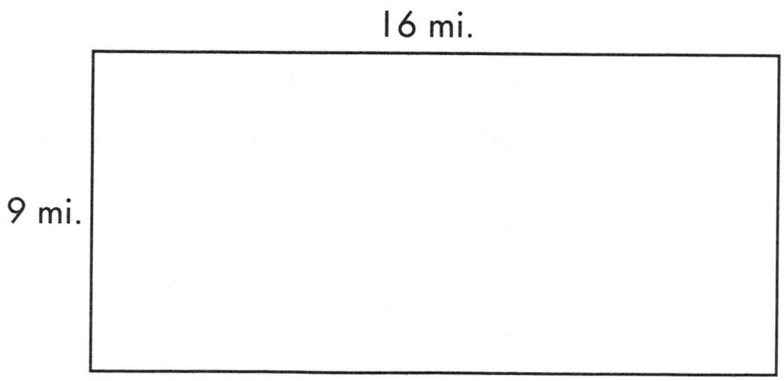

$3 \times \dfrac{1}{2} =$

Draw a model to show
that $\dfrac{1}{2} = \dfrac{3}{6}$.

What is the perimeter of the rectangle?

16 mi.

9 mi.

80,870

What is the value of each **8**? _____

_____

Is **51** composite or prime?

_____

Prove your answer.

207 ÷ 9 = ◯

161 ÷ ◯ = ◯

◯ × ◯ = 574

◯ ÷ 2 = ◯

◯ ÷ 5 = ◯

Hannah has $13.50 in savings. New hair bands cost $2.50 each. How many can she buy? Show your work.

Round to the nearest hundred.

31,903

Write **four thousand two hundred six** in base ten numbers.

29,844
+ 1,880
‾‾‾‾‾‾‾

Round **9,450** to the highest place value.

Write a decimal to show the total amount of liquid in the beakers.

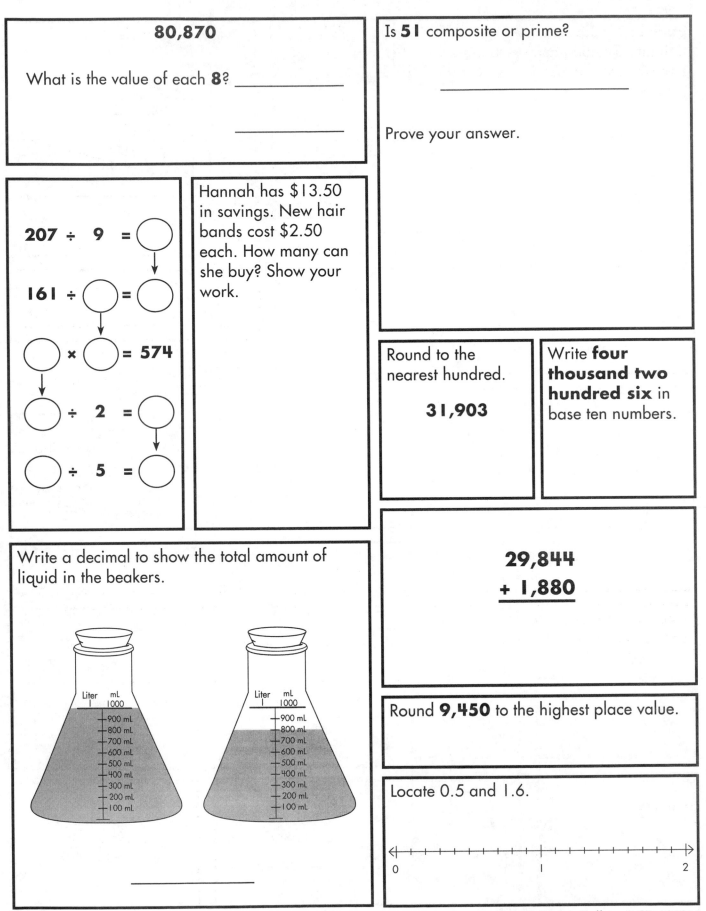

_____

Locate 0.5 and 1.6.

|←————|————|————|————|————|————|————|————|————|————|————|→|
0   1   2

Jada built a toy robot. The robot has 6 legs. Each leg has 3 joints. Building each joint used 4 screws. How many screws did Jada use to put the robot legs together? Show your work.

Measure the angle.

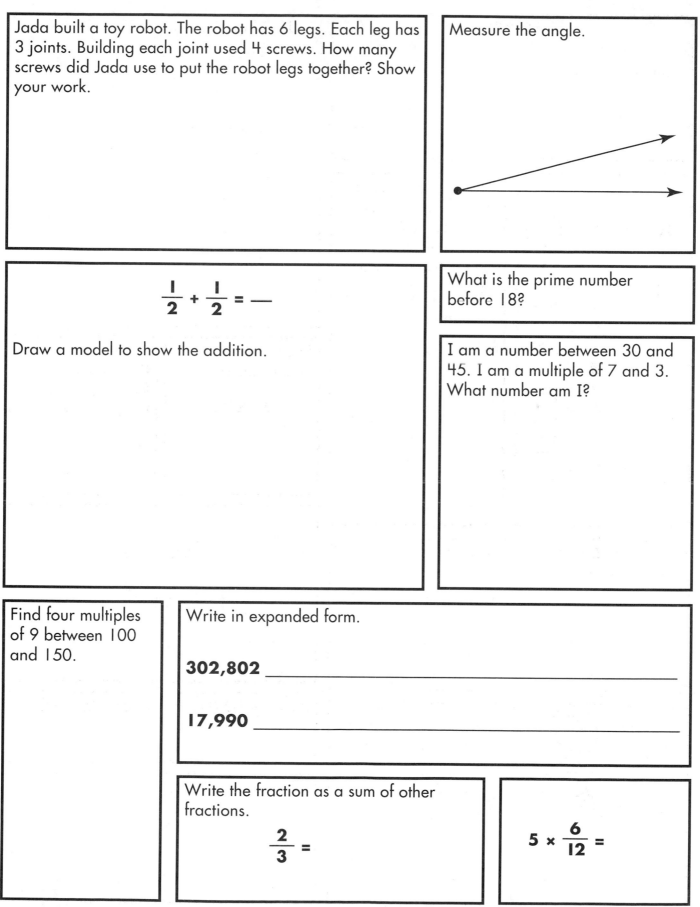

$\dfrac{1}{2} + \dfrac{1}{2} = $ ___

Draw a model to show the addition.

What is the prime number before 18?

I am a number between 30 and 45. I am a multiple of 7 and 3. What number am I?

Find four multiples of 9 between 100 and 150.

Write in expanded form.

302,802 _____

17,990 _____

Write the fraction as a sum of other fractions.

$\dfrac{2}{3} = $

$5 \times \dfrac{6}{12} = $

Locate $\frac{2}{10}$ on the number line.

0   0.1   0.2   0.3   0.4   0.5   0.6   0.7   0.8   0.9   1

103 + 160 =   133 + 158 =

Rewrite as a decimal.

$$\frac{50}{100} =$$

Divide into 6 equal parts.

What would you use to measure the length of a worm?

meters   centimeters   feet

What would you use to measure the length of a snake?

meters   centimeters   feet

0.31 ◯ 0.29

377 ÷ 9

Estimate: _____

Solve: _____

Draw a model to show that $\frac{4}{6} = \frac{12}{18}$.

$\frac{6}{8}$ ◯ $\frac{1}{2}$

$\frac{2}{3}$ ◯ $\frac{5}{6}$

Circle the image that has symmetry. Then, draw the line of symmetry.

Express as a decimal.

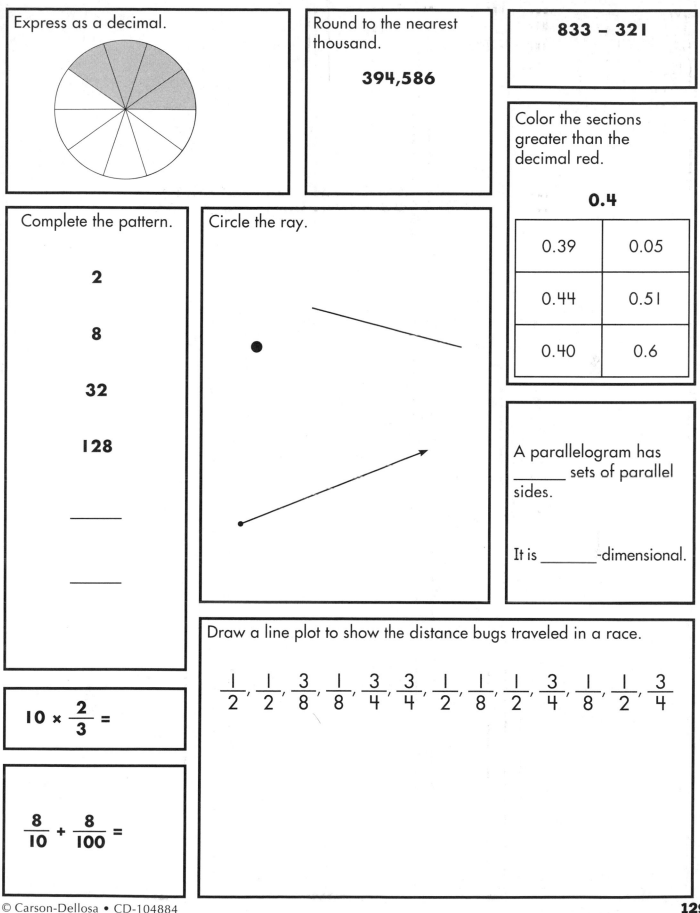

Round to the nearest thousand.

394,586

833 – 321

Color the sections greater than the decimal red.

0.4

0.39	0.05
0.44	0.51
0.40	0.6

Complete the pattern.

2

8

32

128

_____

_____

Circle the ray.

A parallelogram has _____ sets of parallel sides.

It is _____-dimensional.

$10 \times \dfrac{2}{3} =$

$\dfrac{8}{10} + \dfrac{8}{100} =$

Draw a line plot to show the distance bugs traveled in a race.

$$\frac{1}{2}, \frac{1}{2}, \frac{3}{8}, \frac{1}{8}, \frac{3}{4}, \frac{3}{4}, \frac{1}{2}, \frac{1}{8}, \frac{1}{2}, \frac{3}{4}, \frac{1}{8}, \frac{1}{2}, \frac{3}{4}$$

Name _____

Locate $\frac{50}{100}$ on the number line.

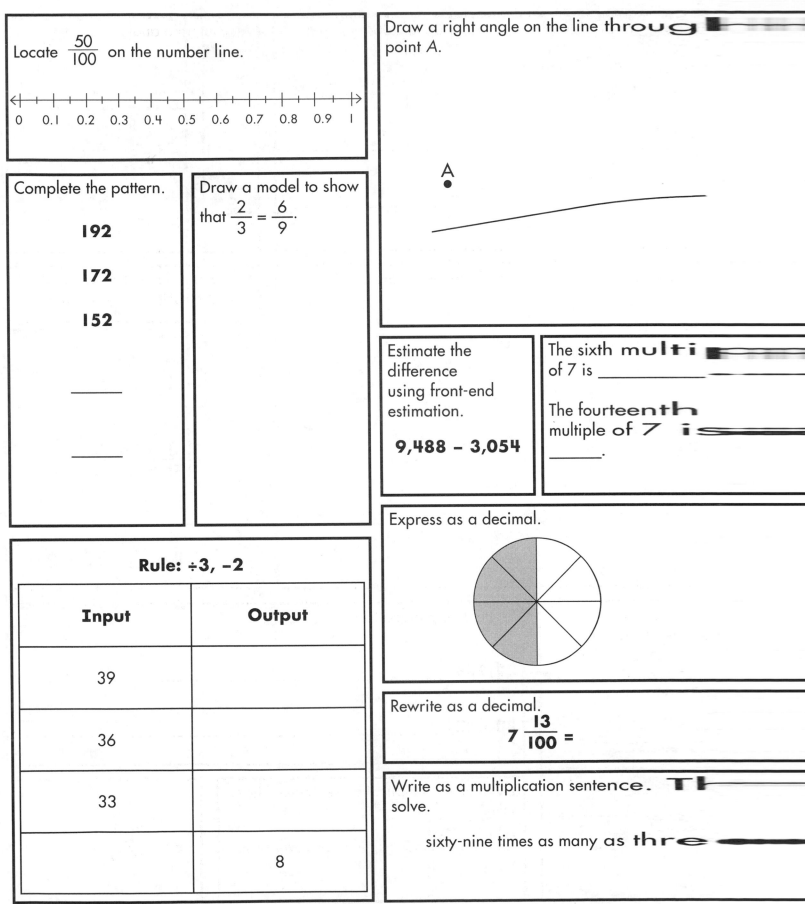

```
0   0.1  0.2  0.3  0.4  0.5  0.6  0.7  0.8  0.9   1
```

Complete the pattern.

192

172

152

_____

_____

Draw a model to show that $\frac{2}{3} = \frac{6}{9}$.

Draw a right angle on the line **throug**
point A.

A

Rule: ÷3, −2

Input	Output
39	
36	
33	
	8

Estimate the difference using front-end estimation.

9,488 − 3,054

The sixth **multi**
of 7 is _____

The fourteenth
multiple **of 7 i**
_____.

Express as a decimal.

Rewrite as a decimal.
$7\frac{13}{100} =$

Write as a multiplication sentence. **Th**
solve.

sixty-nine times as many **as thre**

Jada built a toy robot. The robot has 6 legs. Each leg has 3 joints. Building each joint used 4 screws. How many screws did Jada use to put the robot legs together? Show your work.

Measure the angle.

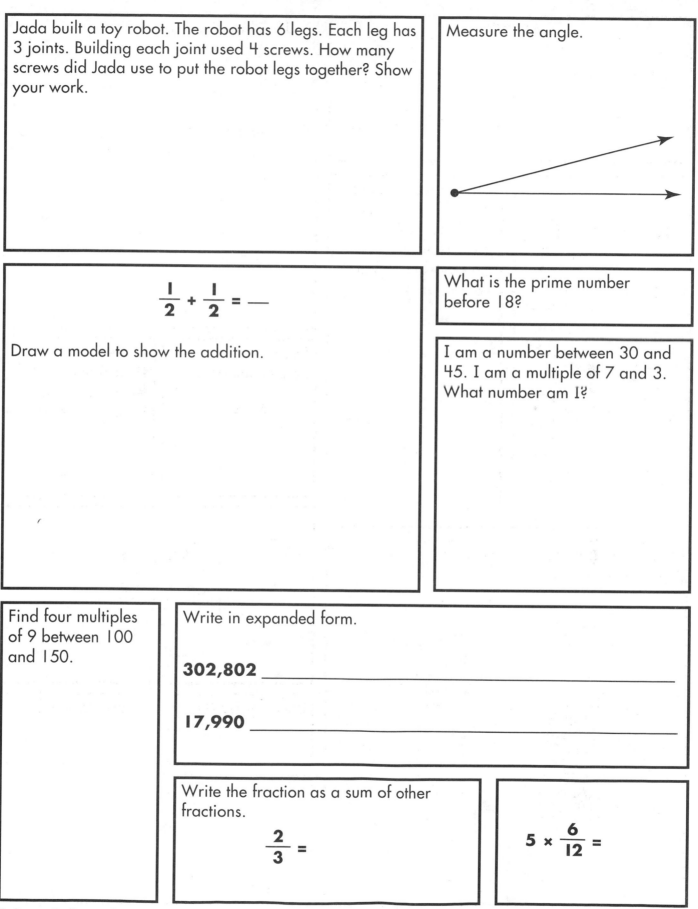

$$\frac{1}{2} + \frac{1}{2} = \text{—}$$

Draw a model to show the addition.

What is the prime number before 18?

I am a number between 30 and 45. I am a multiple of 7 and 3. What number am I?

Find four multiples of 9 between 100 and 150.

Write in expanded form.

302,802 _____

17,990 _____

Write the fraction as a sum of other fractions.

$$\frac{2}{3} =$$

$$5 \times \frac{6}{12} =$$

Locate $\frac{2}{10}$ on the number line.

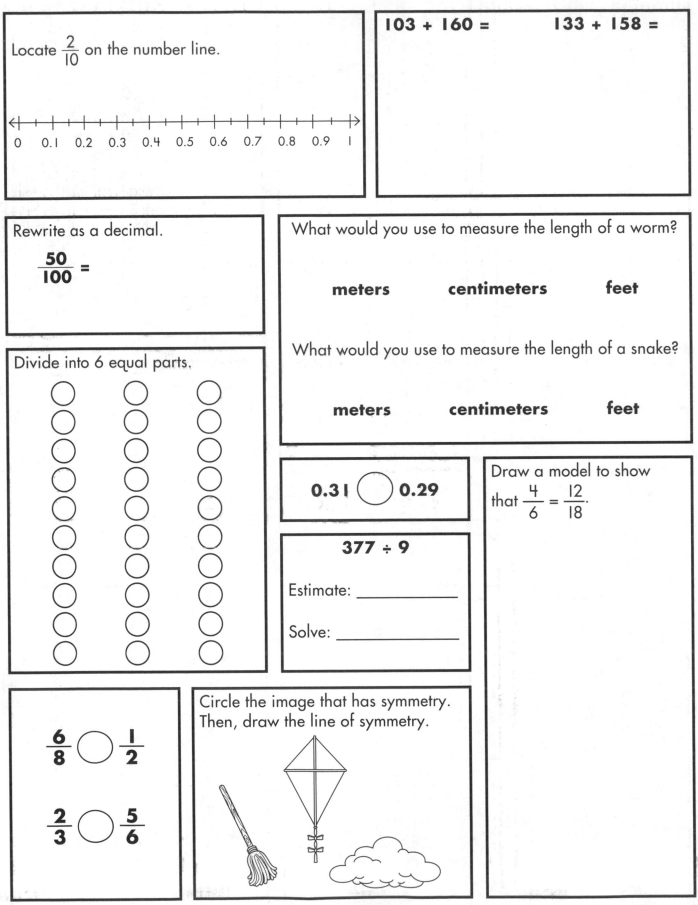

0   0.1   0.2   0.3   0.4   0.5   0.6   0.7   0.8   0.9   1

103 + 160 =   133 + 158 =

Rewrite as a decimal.

$$\frac{50}{100} =$$

Divide into 6 equal parts.

What would you use to measure the length of a worm?

meters   centimeters   feet

What would you use to measure the length of a snake?

meters   centimeters   feet

0.31 ◯ 0.29

377 ÷ 9

Estimate: _____

Solve: _____

Draw a model to show that $\frac{4}{6} = \frac{12}{18}$.

$\frac{6}{8}$ ◯ $\frac{1}{2}$

$\frac{2}{3}$ ◯ $\frac{5}{6}$

Circle the image that has symmetry.
Then, draw the line of symmetry.

Find the multiples of each number up to 200.

31 _____

37 _____

42 _____

Measure the angle.

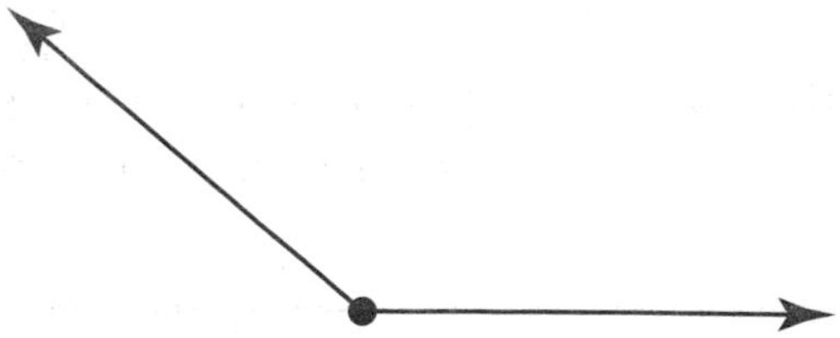

Use a protractor to draw a 50° angle on the line.

_____

Which has the highest value of **7**?
89,472   61,739

$\dfrac{6}{6}$ ◯ $\dfrac{6}{12}$

$\dfrac{3}{4}$ ◯ $\dfrac{4}{4}$

$\dfrac{5}{8}$ ◯ $\dfrac{8}{8}$

ABCD is a rectangle. Angle ACB is 60°. Find angle DCA.

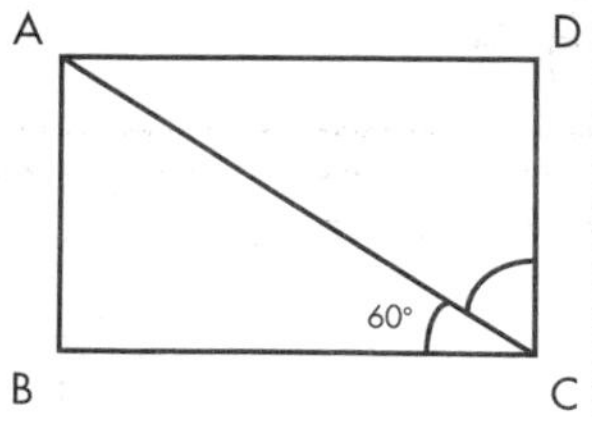

A   D

60°

B   C

Write in expanded form.

32,234 _____

700,821 _____

Write as a multiplication sentence. Then, solve.

thirty-four times as many as seventy-six

$6 \times \dfrac{32}{100} =$

Draw an obtuse angle on the line.

983 + 514

Draw a line segment labeled *OP*.

A goat is 3 feet tall. An elephant is 4 times as tall. How tall is the elephant? Show your work.

Laura made $2\frac{1}{4}$ cups of popcorn before the movie. Halfway through the movie, she made another $1\frac{1}{2}$ cups of popcorn. How much popcorn did Laura make in all?

$\frac{2}{3}$ ◯ **0.6**

Draw a model to show that $\frac{3}{8} = \frac{12}{32}$.

2,567 – 1,950

Draw a 155° angle on the circle. Label the angle *ABC*.

What is the pattern?

640, 160, 40, 10

_____

_____

_____

_____

Kelly walks every evening. She starts at 6:00 pm. She walks 2 miles. It takes her 20 minutes to walk 1 mile. What time will she finish? Show your work.

$1\frac{1}{2}$ L $\bigcirc$ 15,000 mL

3 L $\bigcirc$ 30,000 mL

5,475 + 2,057

Write a word problem with a divisor of 9 and a quotient of 15.

_____

_____

_____

_____

_____

What is the next shape in the pattern?

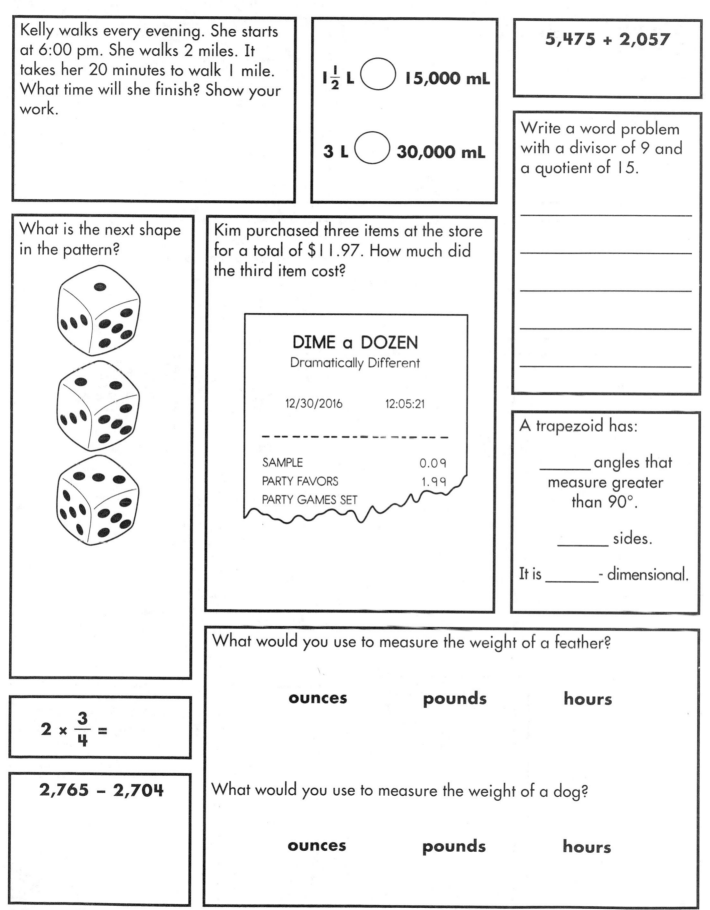

Kim purchased three items at the store for a total of $11.97. How much did the third item cost?

DIME a DOZEN
Dramatically Different

12/30/2016   12:05:21

— — — — — — — — — — — —

SAMPLE   0.09
PARTY FAVORS   1.99
PARTY GAMES SET

A trapezoid has:

_____ angles that measure greater than 90°.

_____ sides.

It is _____ - dimensional.

$2 \times \frac{3}{4} =$

2,765 – 2,704

What would you use to measure the weight of a feather?

ounces   **pounds**   **hours**

What would you use to measure the weight of a dog?

ounces   **pounds**   **hours**

1,072

What is the value of the **2**? _____

What is the value of the **7**? _____

Draw an acute angle through point *A*.

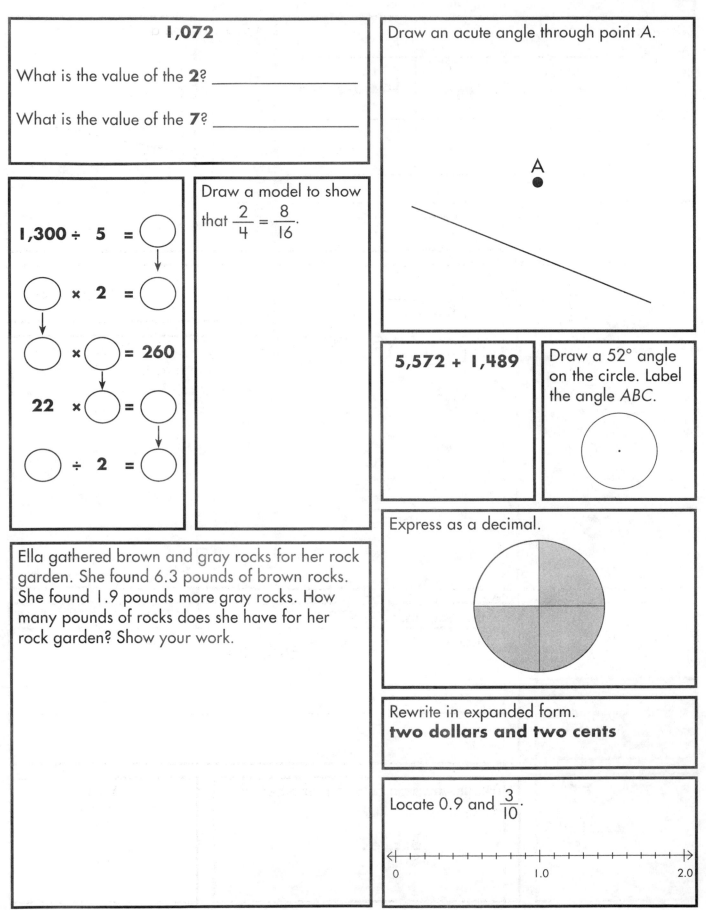

A

$1,300 \div 5 = \bigcirc$

$\bigcirc \times 2 = \bigcirc$

$\bigcirc \times \bigcirc = 260$

$22 \times \bigcirc = \bigcirc$

$\bigcirc \div 2 = \bigcirc$

Draw a model to show that $\dfrac{2}{4} = \dfrac{8}{16}$.

5,572 + 1,489

Draw a 52° angle on the circle. Label the angle *ABC*.

Express as a decimal.

Ella gathered brown and gray rocks for her rock garden. She found 6.3 pounds of brown rocks. She found 1.9 pounds more gray rocks. How many pounds of rocks does she have for her rock garden? Show your work.

Rewrite in expanded form.
two dollars and two cents

Locate 0.9 and $\dfrac{3}{10}$.

0   1.0   2.0

Rewrite as a decimal.

Ones	Tenths	Hundredths
		15

Measure the angle.

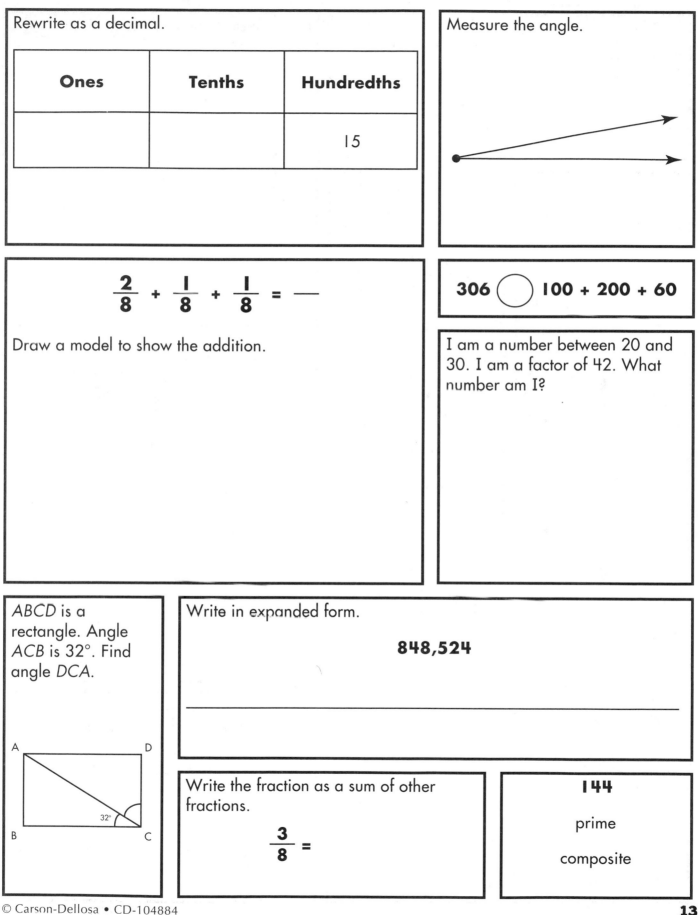

$$\frac{2}{8} + \frac{1}{8} + \frac{1}{8} = \text{---}$$

Draw a model to show the addition.

306 ◯ 100 + 200 + 60

I am a number between 20 and 30. I am a factor of 42. What number am I?

ABCD is a rectangle. Angle *ACB* is 32°. Find angle *DCA*.

A   D

32°

B   C

Write in expanded form.

848,524

_____

Write the fraction as a sum of other fractions.

$$\frac{3}{8} =$$

144

prime

composite

Find the least common multiple of 42 and 11.

Write the sums of adjacent numbers in the blocks above.

| 638 | |
| 104 |
| 78 | 39 |

40 hundreds = _____ tens

Complete the Venn diagram with the factors of each number.

40   **28**

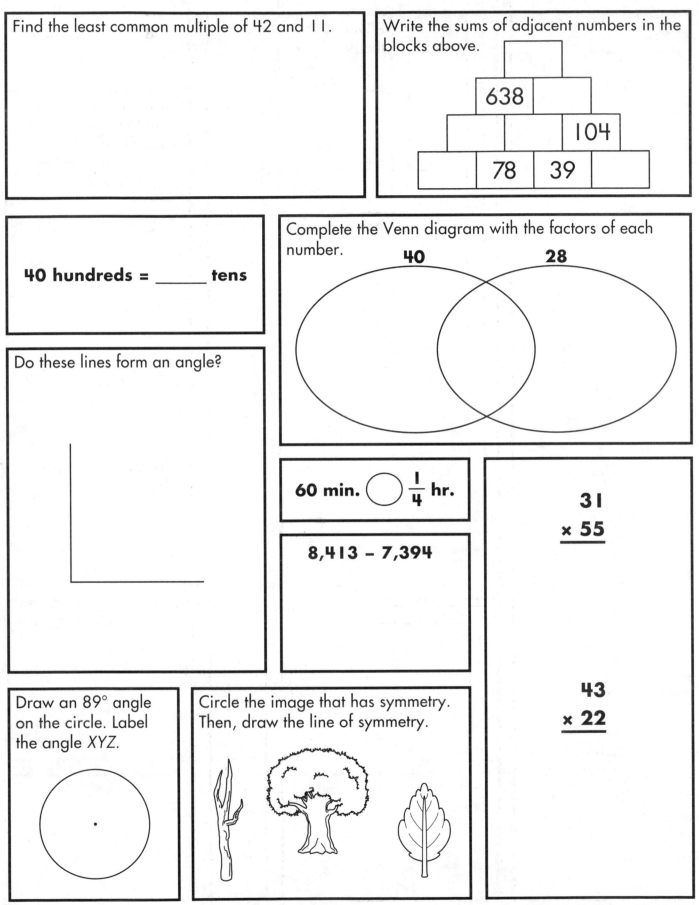

Do these lines form an angle?

60 min. ◯ $\frac{1}{4}$ hr.

8,413 – 7,394

31
× 55

43
× 22

Draw an 89° angle on the circle. Label the angle *XYZ*.

Circle the image that has symmetry. Then, draw the line of symmetry.

Find the first ten multiples of 4.

Find the first ten multiples of 5.

Circle the common multiples.

Round to the nearest ten thousand.

485,698

8,917 + 3,588

Color the sections equal to the decimal orange.

2.8

2.79	2.80
2.8	3.8
2.9	2.08

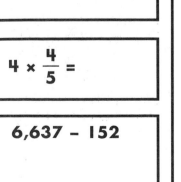

What time will it be 24 minutes from now?

What time was it 34 minutes ago?

Draw a congruent shape.

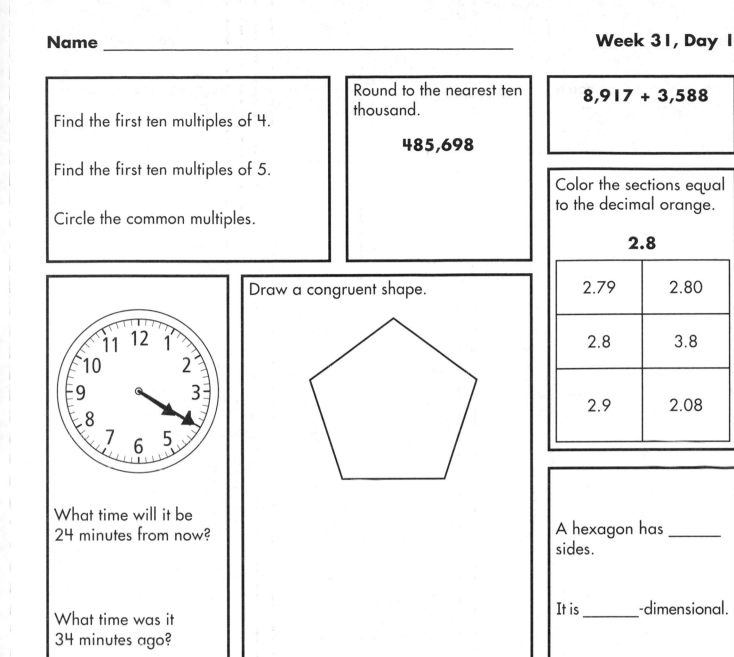

A hexagon has _____ sides.

It is _____-dimensional.

$4 \times \dfrac{4}{5} =$

6,637 − 152

What is the perimeter of the figure?

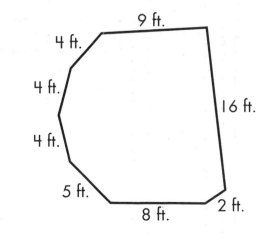

9 ft.

4 ft.

4 ft.

4 ft.

16 ft.

5 ft.

8 ft.

2 ft.

Locate 0.15 on the number line.

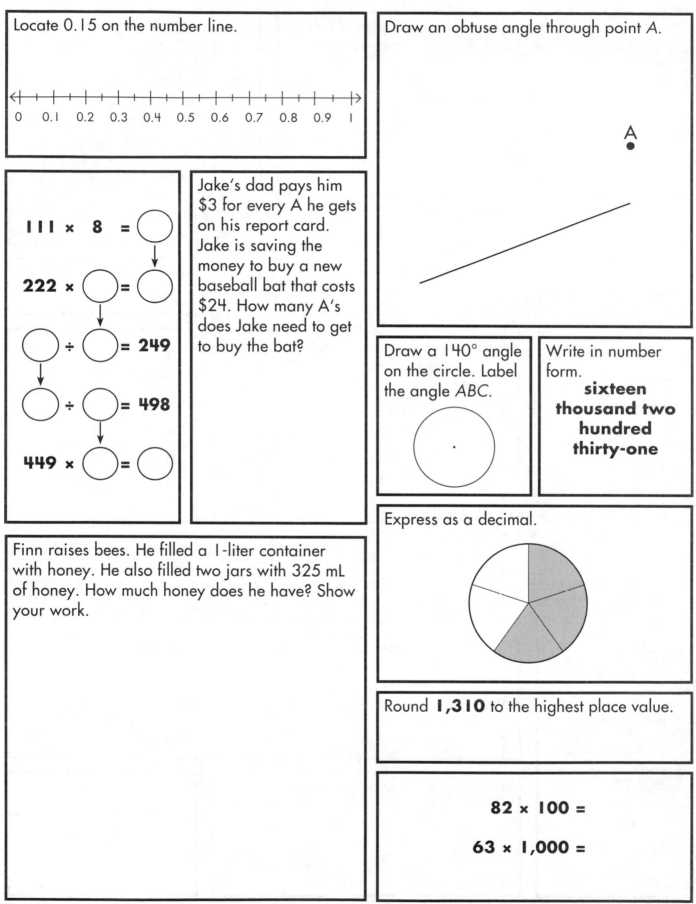

0   0.1   0.2   0.3   0.4   0.5   0.6   0.7   0.8   0.9   1

Draw an obtuse angle through point *A*.

A

111 × 8 = ◯

222 × ◯ = ◯

◯ ÷ ◯ = 249

◯ ÷ ◯ = 498

449 × ◯ = ◯

Jake's dad pays him $3 for every A he gets on his report card. Jake is saving the money to buy a new baseball bat that costs $24. How many A's does Jake need to get to buy the bat?

Draw a 140° angle on the circle. Label the angle *ABC*.

Write in number form.

sixteen thousand two hundred thirty-one

Express as a decimal.

Round **1,310** to the highest place value.

Finn raises bees. He filled a 1-liter container with honey. He also filled two jars with 325 mL of honey. How much honey does he have? Show your work.

82 × 100 =

63 × 1,000 =

Ted bought 2 pounds of apples. The apples cost $2.78 per pound. How much did he spend? Show your work.

Measure the angle.

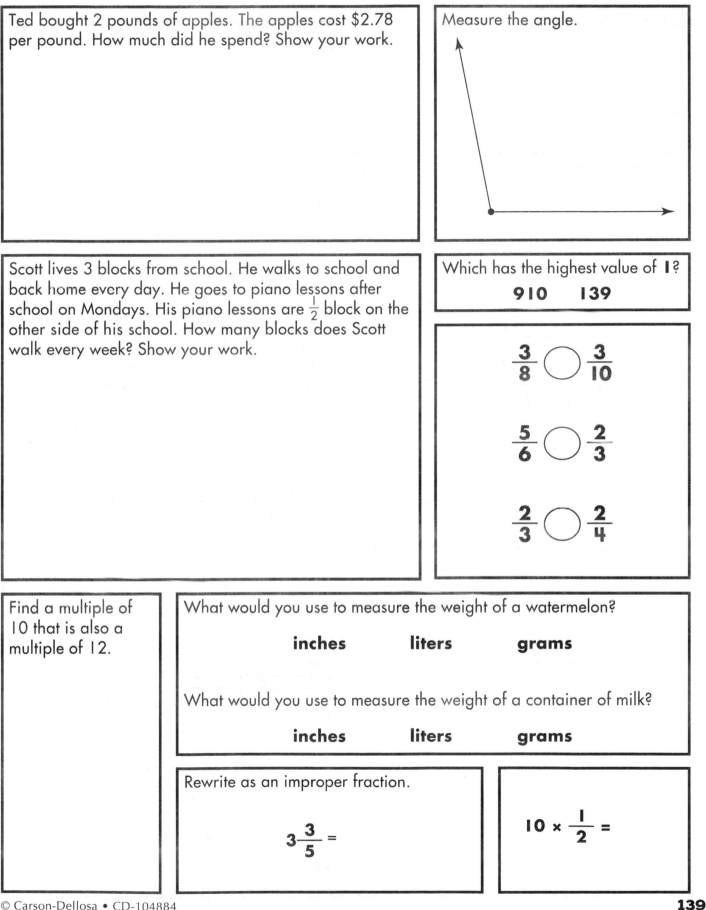

Scott lives 3 blocks from school. He walks to school and back home every day. He goes to piano lessons after school on Mondays. His piano lessons are $\frac{1}{2}$ block on the other side of his school. How many blocks does Scott walk every week? Show your work.

Which has the highest value of **1**?

910   139

$\frac{3}{8}$ ◯ $\frac{3}{10}$

$\frac{5}{6}$ ◯ $\frac{2}{3}$

$\frac{2}{3}$ ◯ $\frac{2}{4}$

Find a multiple of 10 that is also a multiple of 12.

What would you use to measure the weight of a watermelon?

inches   **liters**   **grams**

What would you use to measure the weight of a container of milk?

inches   **liters**   **grams**

Rewrite as an improper fraction.

$3\frac{3}{5} =$

$10 \times \frac{1}{2} =$

Find the least common multiple of 16 and 24.

Write **99,955** in word form.

_____

_____

Rewrite as a decimal.

$$\frac{199}{100} =$$

Yesterday, it snowed 2 inches. Today, it snowed half as much. How much did it snow in all? Show your work.

Max bought $5\frac{1}{2}$ pounds of screws. He used $3\frac{1}{4}$ pounds when he built a shed. How many pounds of screws does he have left? Show your work.

$\frac{3}{4}$ ◯ 0.12

Draw a model to show that $\frac{3}{10} = \frac{6}{20}$.

8,244 + 3,211

$\frac{6}{9}$ ◯ $\frac{2}{12}$

What is the pattern?

195, 190, 185, 180

_____

_____

_____

_____

Start time: 7:45 pm
End time: 9:55 pm
Elapsed time:

├─────────────────────────────┤

$\frac{3}{4}$ hr. ◯ 3,000 sec.

1.5 hr. ◯ 300,000 sec.

5,684 – 3,084

ABCD is a rectangle. Angle *DBC* is 36°. Find angle *ABD*.

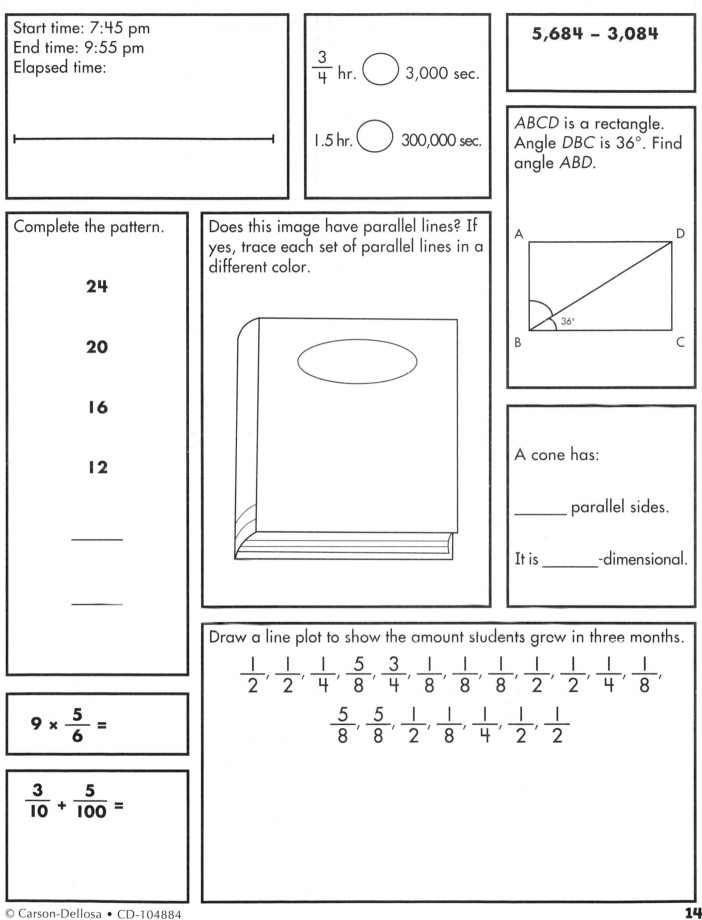

Complete the pattern.

24

20

16

12

_____

_____

Does this image have parallel lines? If yes, trace each set of parallel lines in a different color.

A cone has:

_____ parallel sides.

It is _____-dimensional.

$9 \times \frac{5}{6} =$

$\frac{3}{10} + \frac{5}{100} =$

Draw a line plot to show the amount students grew in three months.

$\frac{1}{2}$, $\frac{1}{2}$, $\frac{1}{4}$, $\frac{5}{8}$, $\frac{3}{4}$, $\frac{1}{8}$, $\frac{1}{8}$, $\frac{1}{8}$, $\frac{1}{2}$, $\frac{1}{2}$, $\frac{1}{4}$, $\frac{1}{8}$,

$\frac{5}{8}$, $\frac{5}{8}$, $\frac{1}{2}$, $\frac{1}{8}$, $\frac{1}{4}$, $\frac{1}{2}$, $\frac{1}{2}$

What number is 29 times as many as 67? _____

What number is 34 times as many as 38? _____

Is **27** composite or prime?

_____

Prove your answer.

Complete the pattern.

4,680

4,780

4,880

_____

_____

Draw a model to show that $\frac{3}{5} = \frac{6}{10}$.

Round to the nearest ten thousand.

43,923

The seventh multiple of 8 is _____.

Write a decimal to show the total amount of liquid in the beakers

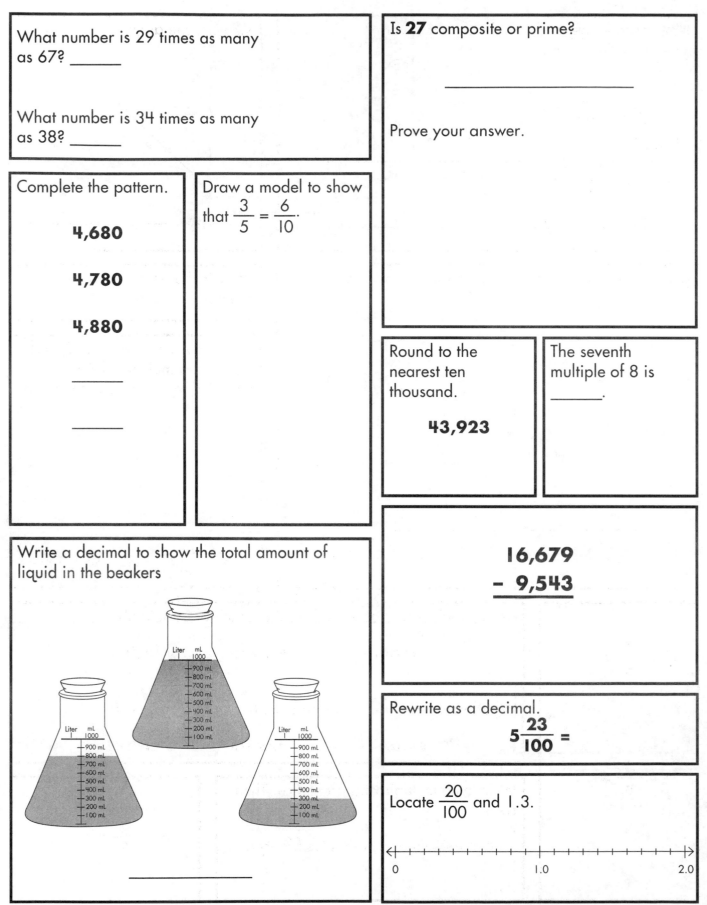

_____

16,679
- 9,543
_____

Rewrite as a decimal.

$5\frac{23}{100} =$

Locate $\frac{20}{100}$ and 1.3.

0   1.0   2.0

How much longer is the snake than the worm?

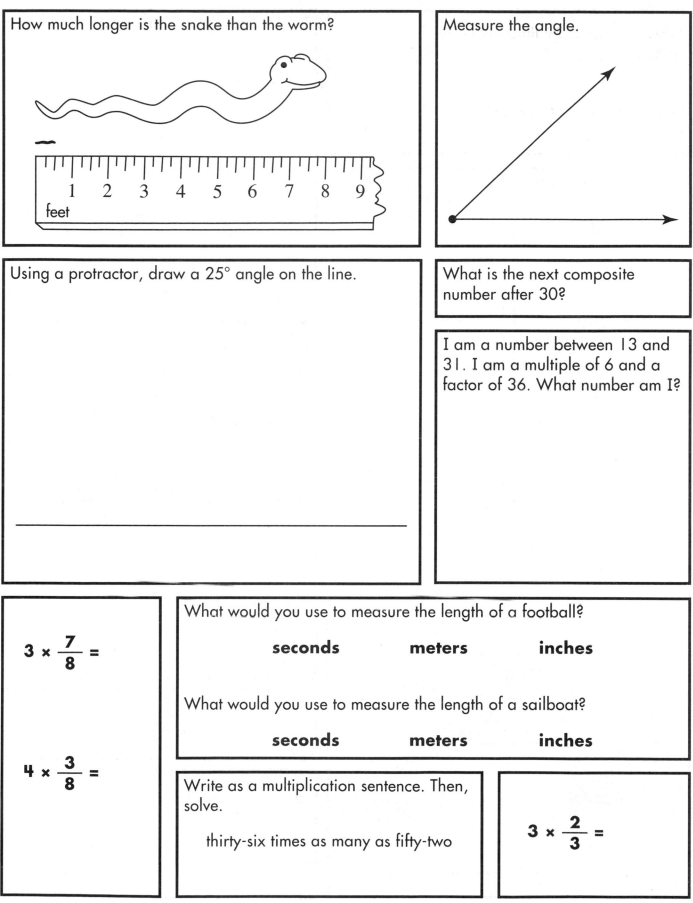

Measure the angle.

Using a protractor, draw a 25° angle on the line.

_____

What is the next composite number after 30?

I am a number between 13 and 31. I am a multiple of 6 and a factor of 36. What number am I?

$3 \times \dfrac{7}{8} =$

$4 \times \dfrac{3}{8} =$

What would you use to measure the length of a football?

seconds   **meters**   **inches**

What would you use to measure the length of a sailboat?

seconds   **meters**   **inches**

Write as a multiplication sentence. Then, solve.

thirty-six times as many as fifty-two

$3 \times \dfrac{2}{3} =$

Find the least common multiple of 27 and 9.

5,480 + 4,241

Rewrite as a decimal.

$$\frac{1}{10} =$$

What would you use to measure the height of a tower?

centimeters   meters   hours

What would you use to measure the height of an anthill?

centimeters   meters   hours

Divide into 3 equal parts.

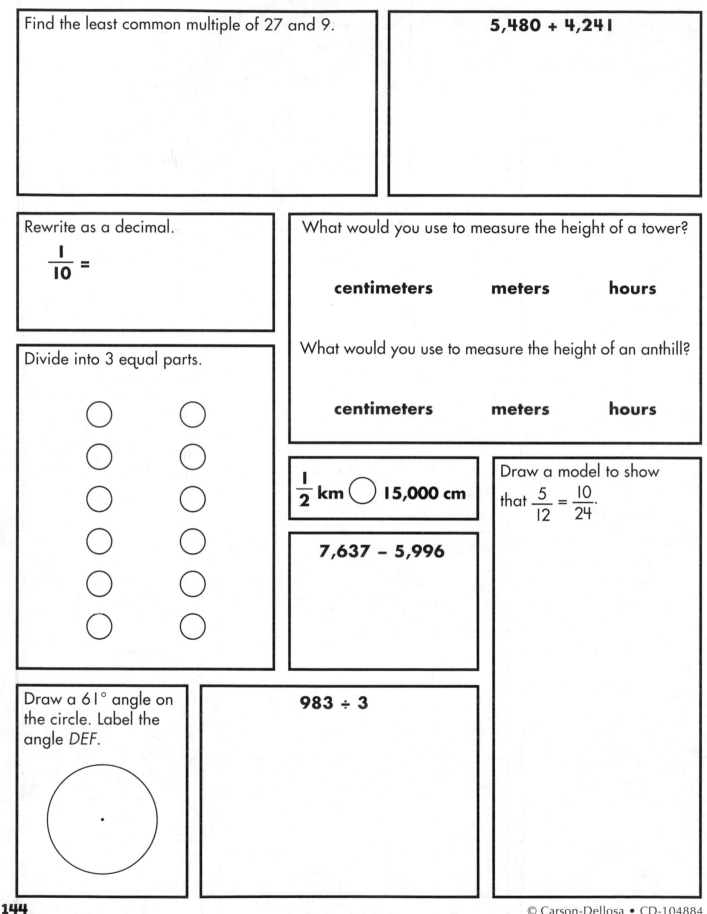

$\frac{1}{2}$ km ◯ 15,000 cm

7,637 – 5,996

Draw a model to show that $\frac{5}{12} = \frac{10}{24}$.

Draw a 61° angle on the circle. Label the angle *DEF*.

---

983 ÷ 3

Express as a decimal.

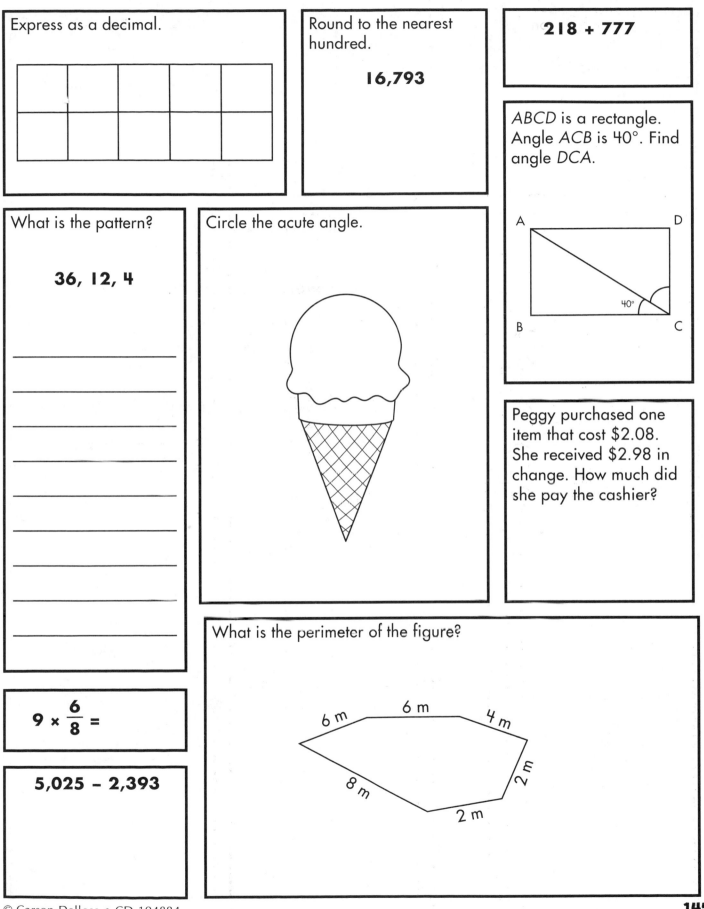

Round to the nearest hundred.

16,793

218 + 777

ABCD is a rectangle. Angle ACB is 40°. Find angle DCA.

A   D

40°

B   C

What is the pattern?

36, 12, 4

_____

_____

_____

_____

_____

_____

_____

_____

Circle the acute angle.

Peggy purchased one item that cost $2.08. She received $2.98 in change. How much did she pay the cashier?

$9 \times \dfrac{6}{8} =$

5,025 – 2,393

What is the perimeter of the figure?

6 m   6 m   4 m

8 m   2 m   2 m

502,584

What is the value of each **5**? _____

_____

Draw a parallel line through point C.

C
●

_____

What is the next shape in the pattern?

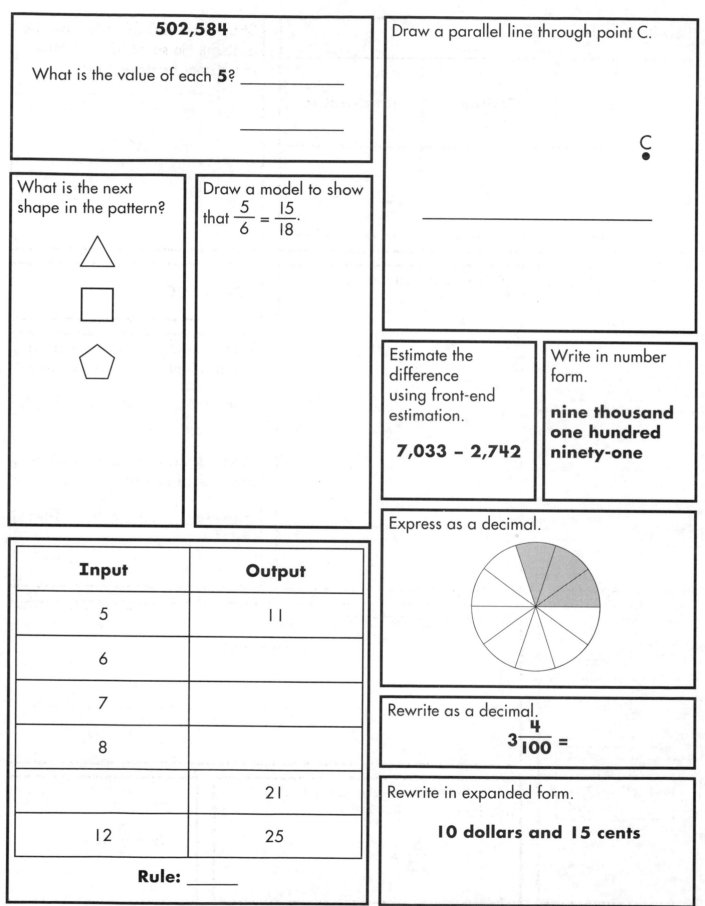

Draw a model to show that $\frac{5}{6} = \frac{15}{18}$.

Estimate the difference using front-end estimation.

7,033 – 2,742

Write in number form.

nine thousand one hundred ninety-one

Express as a decimal.

Rewrite as a decimal.

$3\frac{4}{100} =$

Rewrite in expanded form.

10 dollars and 15 cents

Input	Output
5	11
6	
7	
8	
	21
12	25

Rule: _____

Rewrite as a decimal.

Ones	Tenths	Hundredths
2	1	23

Shane had $75.38 in his savings account. He spent $31.14. How much does he have now?

Using a protractor, draw a 115° angle on the line.

_____

$70 \times 100 =$

What would you use to measure the length of a bus ride to school?

minutes   seconds   liters

What would you use to measure the blink of an eye?

minutes   seconds   liters

ABCD is a rectangle. Angle ACB is 65°. Find angle DCA.

Write in expanded form.

1,042,891

_____

Write the fraction as a sum of other fractions.

$$\frac{5}{12} =$$

$$3 \times \frac{3}{4} =$$

Locate $\frac{60}{100}$ on the number line.

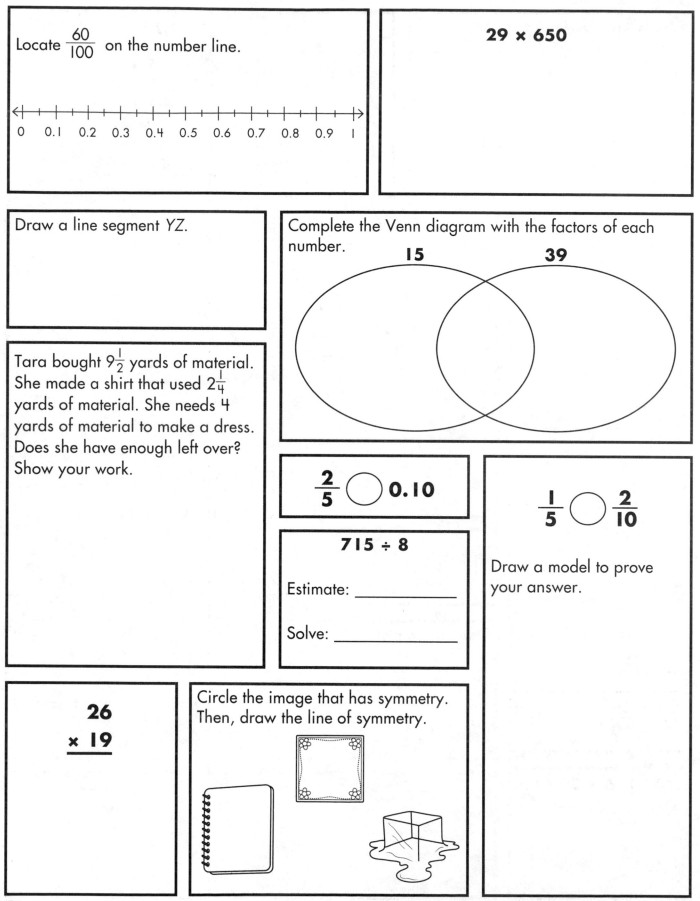

0   0.1   0.2   0.3   0.4   0.5   0.6   0.7   0.8   0.9   1

29 × 650

Draw a line segment *YZ*.

Tara bought $9\frac{1}{2}$ yards of material. She made a shirt that used $2\frac{1}{4}$ yards of material. She needs 4 yards of material to make a dress. Does she have enough left over? Show your work.

Complete the Venn diagram with the factors of each number.

15   **39**

$\frac{2}{5}$ ◯ **0.10**

715 ÷ 8

Estimate: _____

Solve: _____

$\frac{1}{5}$ ◯ $\frac{2}{10}$

Draw a model to prove your answer.

26
× 19

Circle the image that has symmetry. Then, draw the line of symmetry.

Express as a decimal.

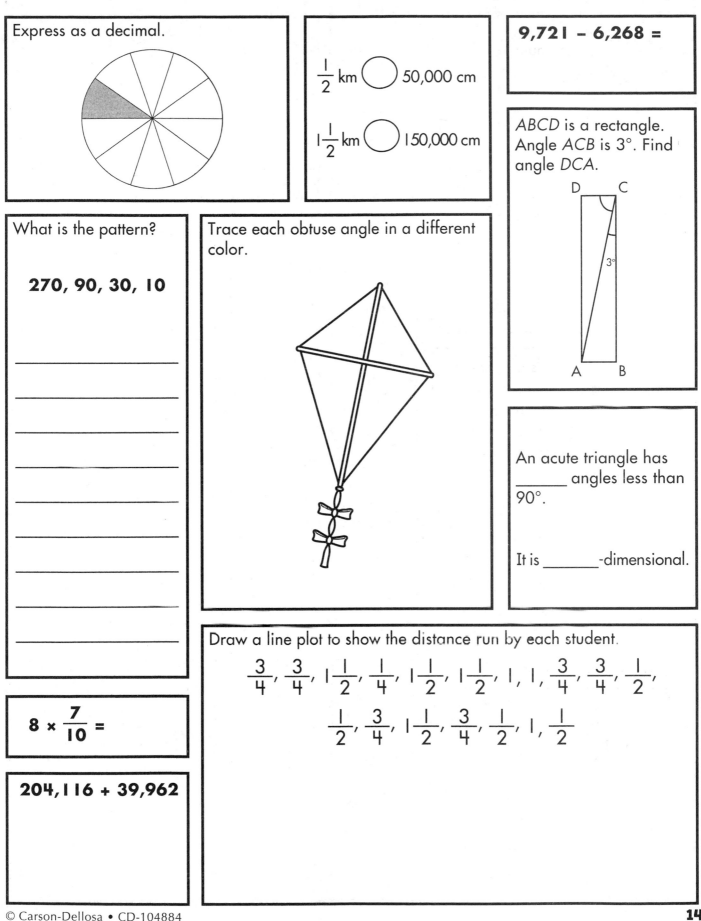

$\frac{1}{2}$ km ◯ 50,000 cm

$1\frac{1}{2}$ km ◯ 150,000 cm

9,721 – 6,268 =

ABCD is a rectangle. Angle ACB is 3°. Find angle DCA.

What is the pattern?

270, 90, 30, 10

_____
_____
_____
_____
_____
_____
_____
_____

Trace each obtuse angle in a different color.

An acute triangle has _____ angles less than 90°.

It is _____-dimensional.

$8 \times \frac{7}{10} =$

204,116 + 39,962

Draw a line plot to show the distance run by each student.

$\frac{3}{4}$, $\frac{3}{4}$, $1\frac{1}{2}$, $\frac{1}{4}$, $1\frac{1}{2}$, $1\frac{1}{2}$, 1, 1, $\frac{3}{4}$, $\frac{3}{4}$, $\frac{1}{2}$,

$\frac{1}{2}$, $\frac{3}{4}$, $1\frac{1}{2}$, $\frac{3}{4}$, $\frac{1}{2}$, 1, $\frac{1}{2}$

What is the pattern?

8, 16, 32, 64

_____

_____

Is **9** composite or prime?

_____

Prove your answer.

Complete the pattern.

5,968

5,978

5,988

_____

_____

Juanita mows lawns in her neighborhood. She charges $7.50 per lawn. She saves $2 from every lawn she mows. How many lawns must she mow to have more than $35 in savings?

Draw a 54° angle. Label the angle *TUV*.

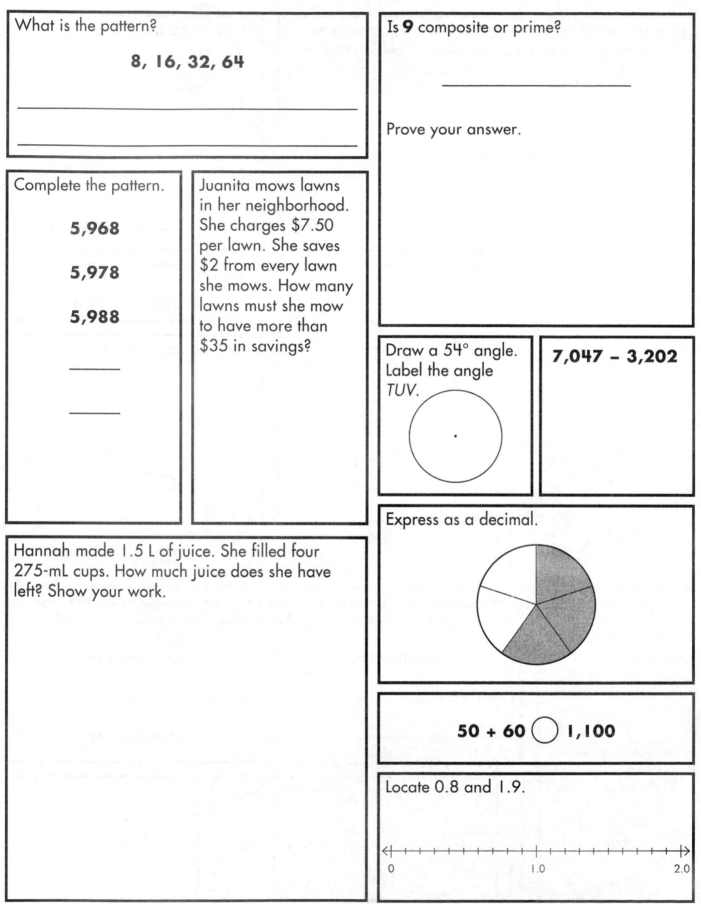

7,047 – 3,202

Express as a decimal.

Hannah made 1.5 L of juice. She filled four 275-mL cups. How much juice does she have left? Show your work.

50 + 60 ◯ **1,100**

Locate 0.8 and 1.9.

0   1.0   2.0

Mina is crocheting 12 pot holders for gifts. It takes her 35 minutes to crochet each pot holder. How long will it take her to finish all of the pot holders? Show your work.

Measure the angle.

Using a protractor, draw a 145° angle on the line.

_____

Which **5** has the greatest value?

4,599   4,905

Do these lines form an angle?

Find four multiples of 3 between 200 and 220.

What would you use to measure the height of a desk?

kilograms   feet   centimeters

What would you use to measure the length of a pencil?

kilograms   feet   centimeters

Write as a multiplication sentence. Then, solve.

thirteen times as many as fifty-seven

$5 \times \dfrac{4}{5} =$

Find the least common multiple of 48 and 24.

Write the sums of adjacent numbers in the blocks above.

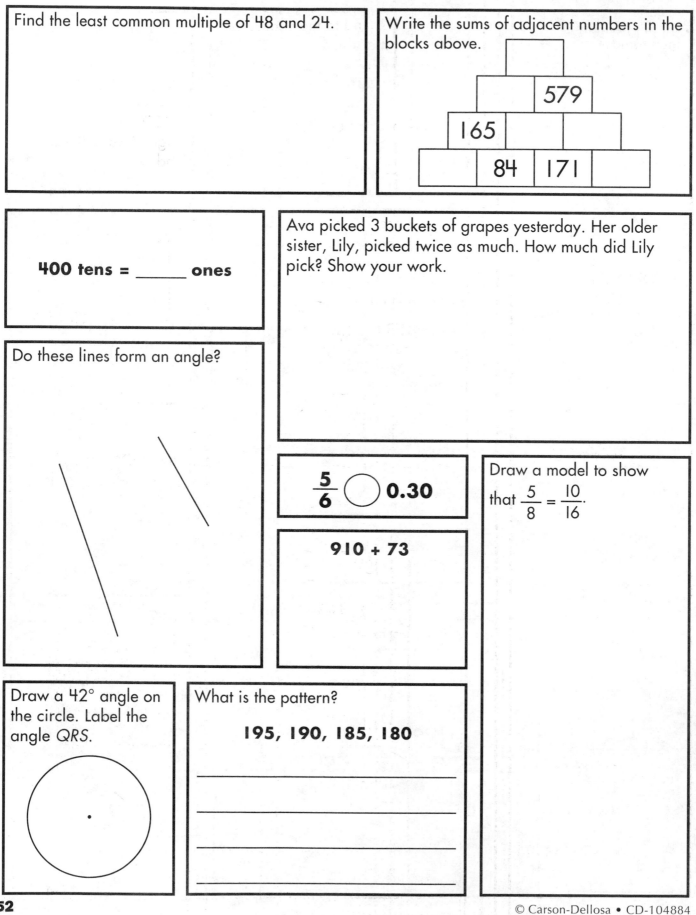

579

165

84 | 171

400 tens = _____ ones

Ava picked 3 buckets of grapes yesterday. Her older sister, Lily, picked twice as much. How much did Lily pick? Show your work.

Do these lines form an angle?

$\frac{5}{6}$ ◯ 0.30

Draw a model to show that $\frac{5}{8} = \frac{10}{16}$.

910 + 73

Draw a 42° angle on the circle. Label the angle QRS.

What is the pattern?

195, 190, 185, 180

_____

_____

_____

_____

What type of angle is formed by the clock hands?

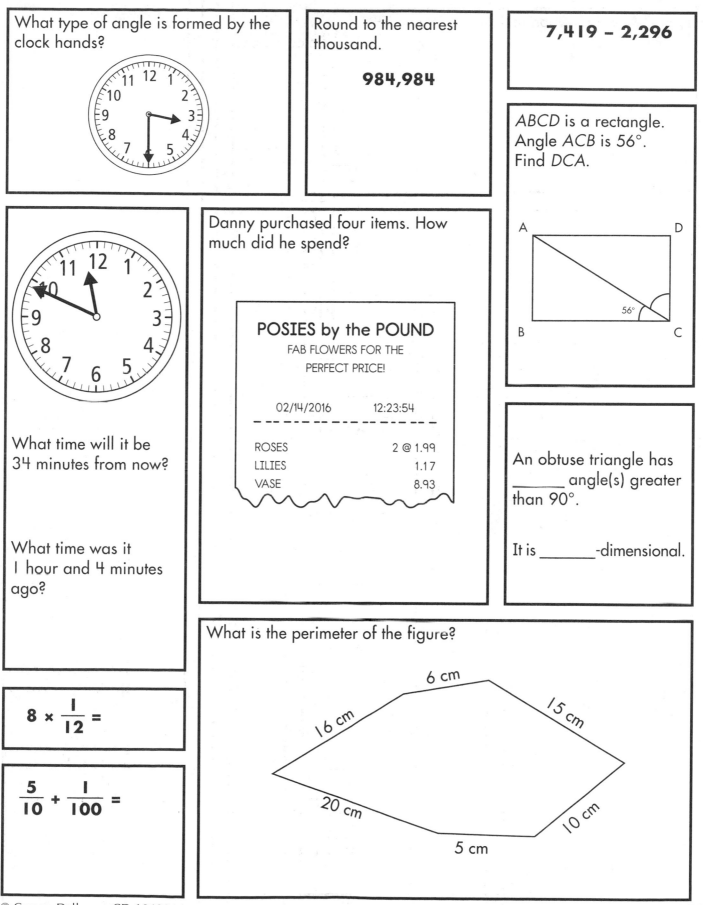

Round to the nearest thousand.

984,984

7,419 – 2,296

ABCD is a rectangle.
Angle *ACB* is 56°.
Find *DCA*.

A   D

B   C

56°

What time will it be 34 minutes from now?

What time was it 1 hour and 4 minutes ago?

Danny purchased four items. How much did he spend?

POSIES by the POUND
FAB FLOWERS FOR THE
PERFECT PRICE!

02/14/2016   12:23:54

ROSES   2 @ 1.99
LILIES   1.17
VASE   8.93

An obtuse triangle has _____ angle(s) greater than 90°.

It is _____-dimensional.

$8 \times \dfrac{1}{12} =$

$\dfrac{5}{10} + \dfrac{1}{100} =$

What is the perimeter of the figure?

6 cm
15 cm
16 cm
20 cm
5 cm
10 cm

Locate 0.8 on the number line.

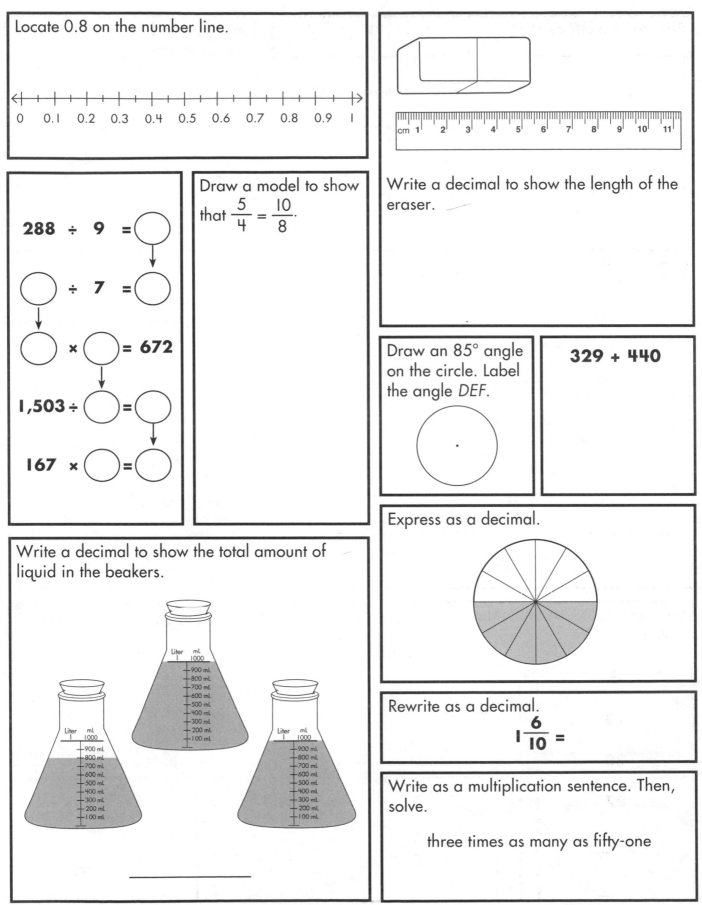

0   0.1   0.2   0.3   0.4   0.5   0.6   0.7   0.8   0.9   1

288 ÷ 9 = ◯

◯ ÷ 7 = ◯

◯ × ◯ = 672

1,503 ÷ ◯ = ◯

167 × ◯ = ◯

Draw a model to show that $\frac{5}{4} = \frac{10}{8}$.

Write a decimal to show the length of the eraser. _____

cm 1 2 3 4 5 6 7 8 9 10 11

Draw an 85° angle on the circle. Label the angle *DEF*.

329 + 440

Express as a decimal.

Rewrite as a decimal.
$1\frac{6}{10} =$

Write as a multiplication sentence. Then, solve.

three times as many as fifty-one

Write a decimal to show the total amount of liquid in the beakers.

Liter mL
1   1000
       900 mL
       800 mL
       700 mL
       600 mL
       500 mL
       400 mL
       300 mL
       200 mL
       100 mL

Liter mL
1   1000
       900 mL
       800 mL
       700 mL
       600 mL
       500 mL
       400 mL
       300 mL
       200 mL
       100 mL

Liter mL
1   1000
       900 mL
       800 mL
       700 mL
       600 mL
       500 mL
       400 mL
       300 mL
       200 mL
       100 mL

_____

Rewrite as a decimal.

Ones	Tenths	Hundredths
1	13	2

Sabrina had $23.95 in savings. She saved another $5.15. How much does she have in savings now? Show your work.

Using a protractor, draw a 170° angle on the line.

_____

$\frac{4}{10} \bigcirc \frac{5}{10}$

72×61

Complete the pattern.

6

13

20

27

_____

_____

What would you use to measure the width of a door?

feet   **hours**   **liters**

What would you use to measure the width of a bed?

feet   **hours**   **liters**

Write the fraction as a sum of other fractions.

$\frac{4}{8} =$

225

prime

composite

Find the least common multiple of 42 and 4.

$591 \div 3$

Rewrite as a decimal.

$\dfrac{123}{100} =$

What would you use to measure the width of a board?

inches　　　　**grams**　　　　**liters**

What would you use to measure the weight of a pea?

inches　　　　**grams**　　　　**liters**

Oscar bought 25 feet of rope. He used $2\frac{1}{4}$ feet to make a coaster. He needs $6\frac{1}{2}$ feet to make a place mat. Does he have enough rope left?

$\dfrac{3}{4}$ km ◯ **7,500 cm**

$510 \div 6 =$

Draw a model to show that $\dfrac{1}{2} = \dfrac{2}{4}$.

$\dfrac{3}{4}$ ◯ $\dfrac{2}{10}$

$\dfrac{4}{5}$ ◯ $\dfrac{2}{10}$

What is the pattern?

240, 120, 60, 30

_____

_____

_____

_____

Express as a decimal.

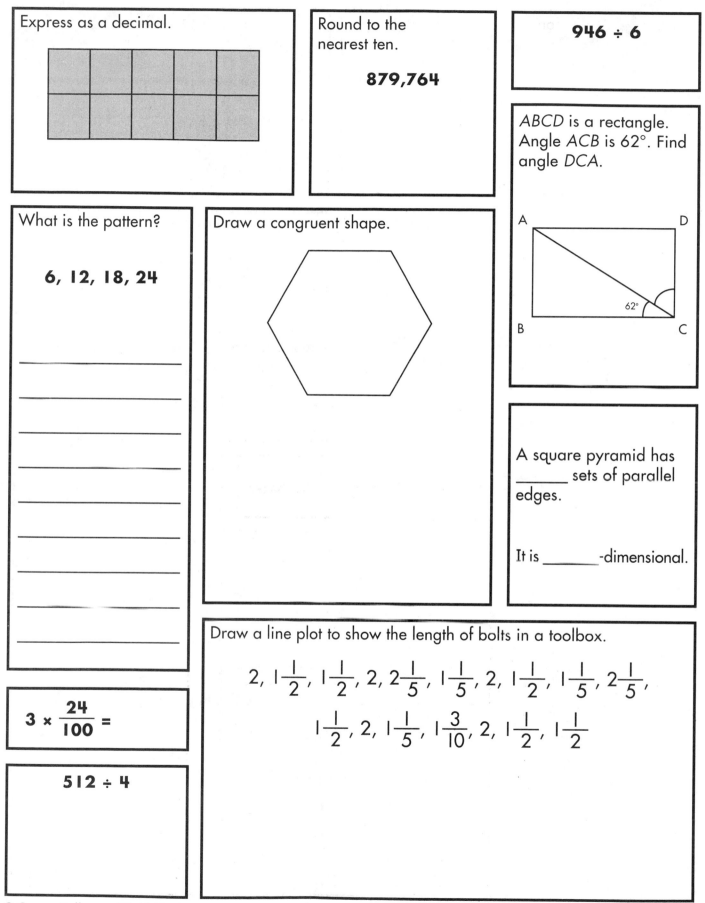

Round to the nearest ten.

879,764

946 ÷ 6

ABCD is a rectangle. Angle ACB is 62°. Find angle DCA.

A   D

B   62°   C

What is the pattern?

6, 12, 18, 24

_____

_____

_____

_____

_____

_____

_____

_____

_____

Draw a congruent shape.

A square pyramid has _____ sets of parallel edges.

It is _____ -dimensional.

$3 \times \dfrac{24}{100} =$

512 ÷ 4

Draw a line plot to show the length of bolts in a toolbox.

$2, 1\dfrac{1}{2}, 1\dfrac{1}{2}, 2, 2\dfrac{1}{5}, 1\dfrac{1}{5}, 2, 1\dfrac{1}{2}, 1\dfrac{1}{5}, 2\dfrac{1}{5},$

$1\dfrac{1}{2}, 2, 1\dfrac{1}{5}, 1\dfrac{3}{10}, 2, 1\dfrac{1}{2}, 1\dfrac{1}{2}$

What number is 75 times as many
as 41? _____

What number is 90 times as many
as 63? _____

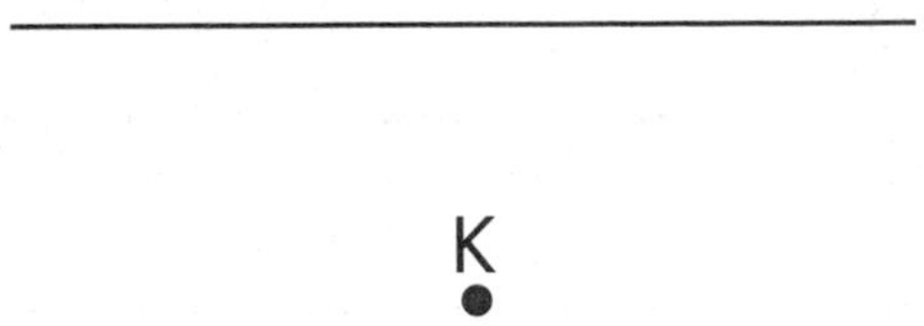

Complete the pattern.

3

9

27

81

_____

_____

Draw a model to show
that $\frac{7}{10} = \frac{14}{20}$.

Draw a perpendicular line through
point K.

_____

K
•

Round to the
nearest hundred
thousand.

349,989

Draw a 57° angle
on the circle. Label
your angle GHI.

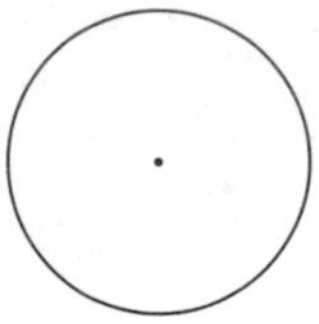

Rule: ×2, +2	
Input	**Output**
120	
130	
140	
	292

13,694
- 12,806

Round **935** to the highest place value.

731 × 10 =

731 × 100 =

731 × 1,000 =

Farmer Bill measured both animals in feet. How much longer is the horse?

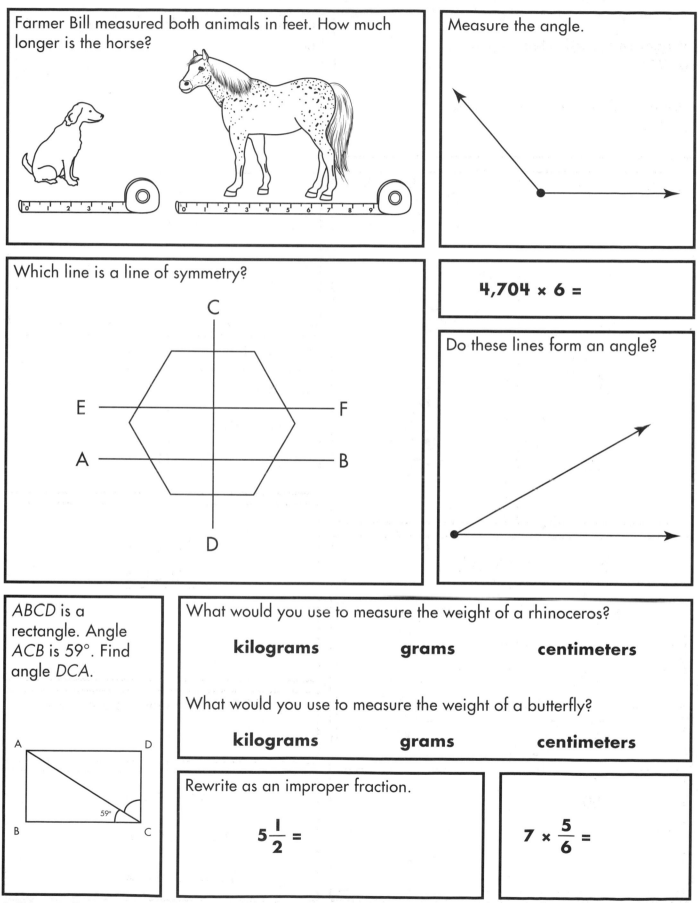

Measure the angle.

Which line is a line of symmetry?

4,704 × 6 =

Do these lines form an angle?

ABCD is a rectangle. Angle ACB is 59°. Find angle DCA.

What would you use to measure the weight of a rhinoceros?

kilograms   **grams**   **centimeters**

What would you use to measure the weight of a butterfly?

kilograms   **grams**   **centimeters**

Rewrite as an improper fraction.

$5\frac{1}{2} =$

$7 \times \frac{5}{6} =$

Locate $\frac{15}{100}$ on the number line.

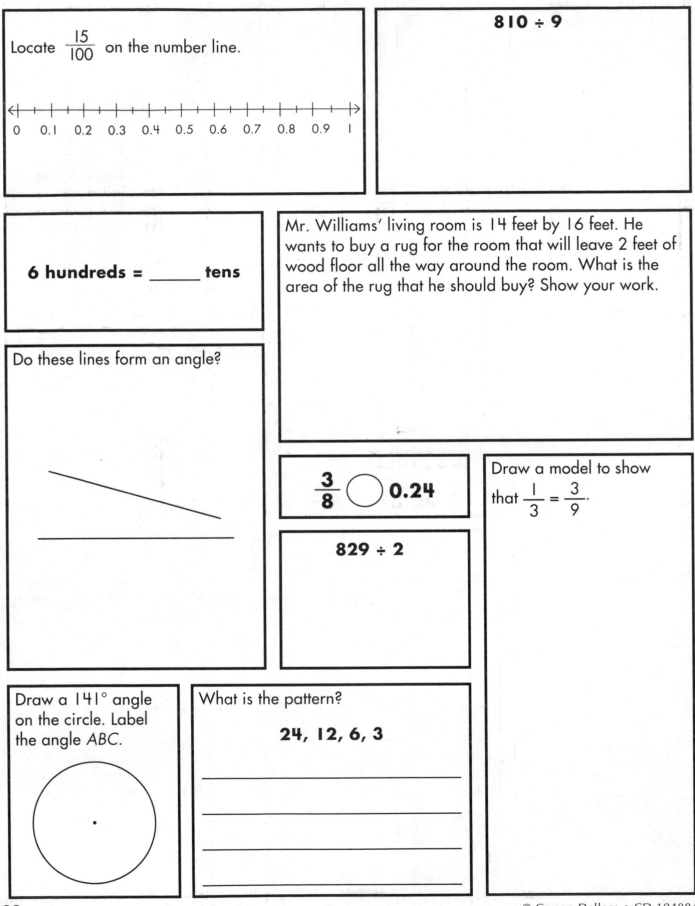

0   0.1   0.2   0.3   0.4   0.5   0.6   0.7   0.8   0.9   1

$810 \div 9$

6 hundreds = _____ tens

Mr. Williams' living room is 14 feet by 16 feet. He wants to buy a rug for the room that will leave 2 feet of wood floor all the way around the room. What is the area of the rug that he should buy? Show your work.

Do these lines form an angle?

$\frac{3}{8}$ ◯ **0.24**

$829 \div 2$

Draw a model to show that $\frac{1}{3} = \frac{3}{9}$.

Draw a 141° angle on the circle. Label the angle ABC.

What is the pattern?

24, 12, 6, 3

_____

_____

_____

Express as a decimal.

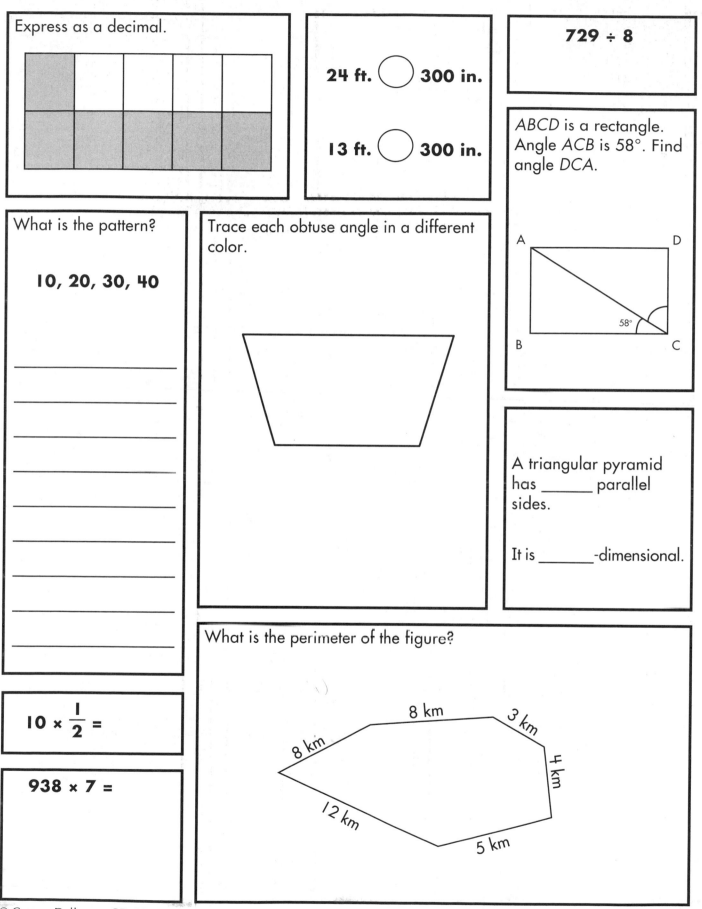

$729 \div 8$

24 ft. ◯ 300 in.

13 ft. ◯ 300 in.

ABCD is a rectangle. Angle *ACB* is 58°. Find angle *DCA*.

What is the pattern?

10, 20, 30, 40

_____

_____

_____

_____

_____

_____

_____

_____

_____

Trace each obtuse angle in a different color.

A triangular pyramid has _____ parallel sides.

It is _____-dimensional.

$10 \times \dfrac{1}{2} =$

$938 \times 7 =$

What is the perimeter of the figure?

8 km

3 km

8 km

4 km

12 km

5 km

30,850

What is the value of the **3**? _____

What is the value of the **5**? _____

Draw a ray through point B.

B
●

_____

What is the next shape in the pattern?

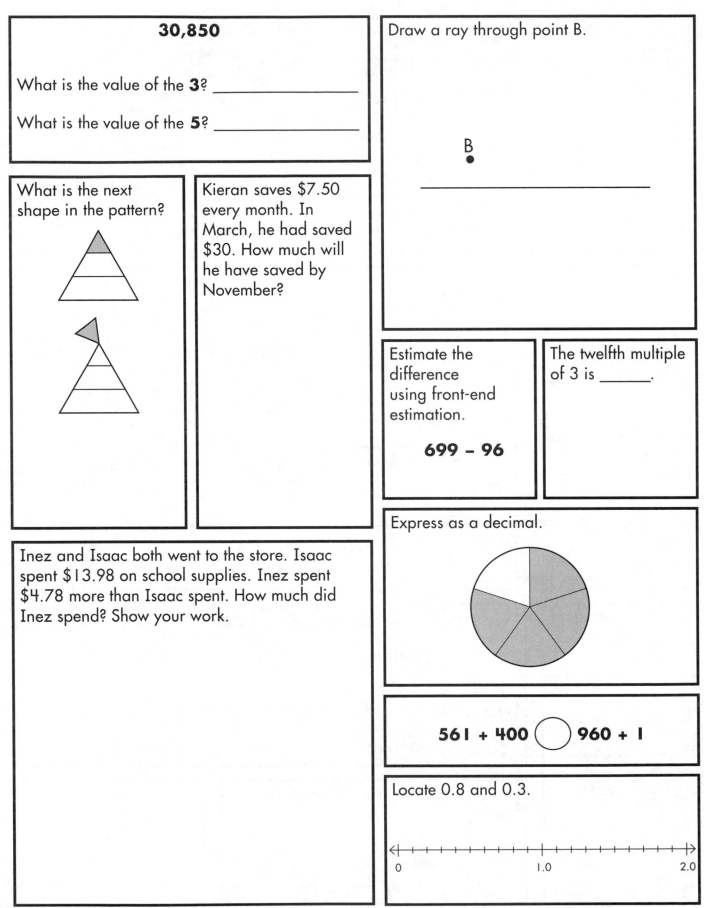

Kieran saves $7.50 every month. In March, he had saved $30. How much will he have saved by November?

Estimate the difference using front-end estimation.

699 – 96

The twelfth multiple of 3 is _____.

Express as a decimal.

Inez and Isaac both went to the store. Isaac spent $13.98 on school supplies. Inez spent $4.78 more than Isaac spent. How much did Inez spend? Show your work.

561 + 400 ◯ 960 + 1

Locate 0.8 and 0.3.

0   1.0   2.0

Rewrite as a decimal.

Ones	Tenths	Hundredths
1		357

Ryan spent $13.54 on various goods. He received $2.21 in change. How much did he give the cashier? Show your work.

$$\frac{2}{12} + \frac{3}{12} + \frac{5}{12} = \underline{\quad}$$

Draw a model to show the addition.

Rewrite in standard form.
$$30 + 3 + \left(8 \times \frac{1}{100}\right)$$

I am a number that is a multiple of 4. I am between 5 and 15. I am a factor of 16. What number am I?

Find four multiples of 12 between 150 and 200.

What would you use to measure the length of a racetrack?

meters   feet   grams

What would you use to measure the length of a jump rope?

meters   feet   grams

Write the fraction as a sum of other fractions.
$$\frac{5}{10} =$$

$$6 \times \frac{6}{8} =$$

Find the least common multiple of 42 and 20.

Write **77,256** in word form.

_____

_____

Rewrite as a decimal.

$$\frac{10}{100} =$$

Luke rode his horse 2 miles on Saturday. On Tuesday, he rode three times as far. How far did he ride on Tuesday? Show your work.

A recipe makes $3\frac{1}{2}$ dozen cookies. Pablo doubled the recipe. How many cookies did he make?

45 sec. ◯ $\frac{3}{4}$ min.

985 ÷ 5

92
× 48

45
× 33

Draw a 161° angle on the circle. Label the angle *FGH*.

Circle the image that has symmetry. Then, draw the line of symmetry.

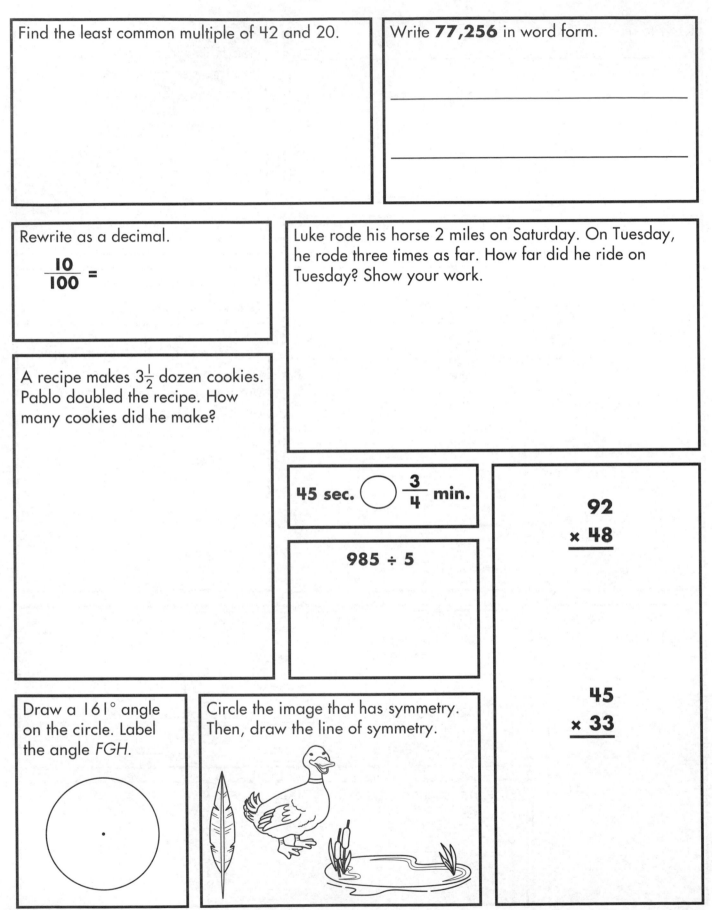

Express as a decimal.

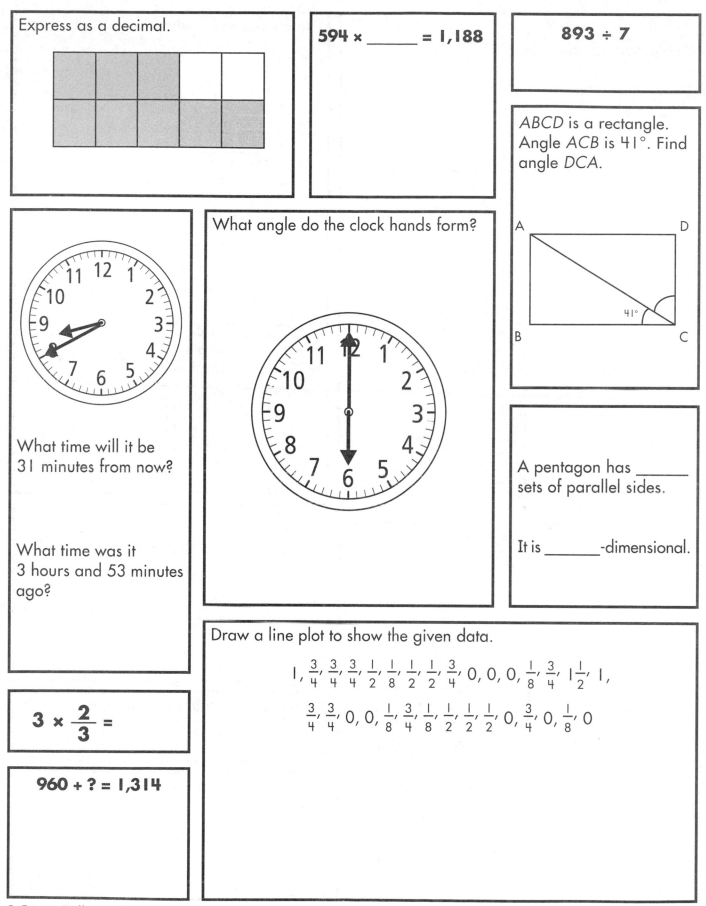

594 × _____ = 1,188

893 ÷ 7

ABCD is a rectangle. Angle ACB is 41°. Find angle DCA.

A   D

B   41°   C

What angle do the clock hands form?

What time will it be 31 minutes from now?

What time was it 3 hours and 53 minutes ago?

A pentagon has _____ sets of parallel sides.

It is _____-dimensional.

$3 \times \dfrac{2}{3} =$

960 + ? = 1,314

Draw a line plot to show the given data.

$1, \dfrac{3}{4}, \dfrac{3}{4}, \dfrac{3}{4}, \dfrac{1}{2}, \dfrac{1}{8}, \dfrac{1}{2}, \dfrac{1}{2}, \dfrac{3}{4}, 0, 0, 0, \dfrac{1}{8}, \dfrac{3}{4}, 1\dfrac{1}{2}, 1,$

$\dfrac{3}{4}, \dfrac{3}{4}, 0, 0, \dfrac{1}{8}, \dfrac{3}{4}, \dfrac{1}{8}, \dfrac{1}{2}, \dfrac{1}{2}, \dfrac{1}{2}, 0, \dfrac{3}{4}, 0, \dfrac{1}{8}, 0$

Locate $\frac{4}{10}$ on the number line.

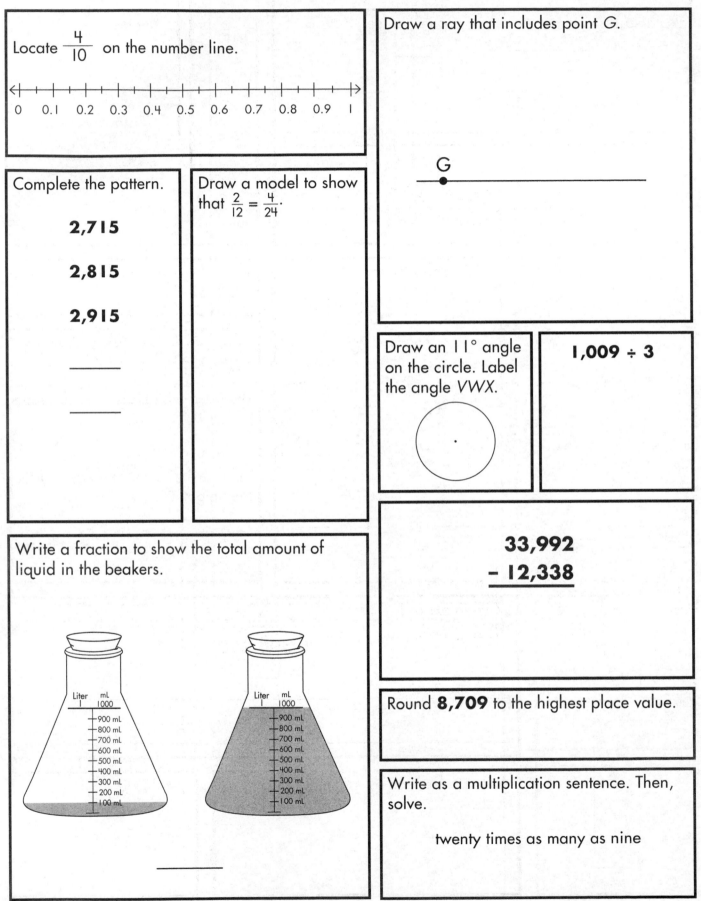

0   0.1   0.2   0.3   0.4   0.5   0.6   0.7   0.8   0.9   1

Complete the pattern.

2,715

2,815

2,915

_____

_____

Draw a model to show that $\frac{2}{12} = \frac{4}{24}$.

Draw a ray that includes point G.

G

Draw an 11° angle on the circle. Label the angle *VWX*.

1,009 ÷ 3

33,992
– 12,338

Round **8,709** to the highest place value.

Write a fraction to show the total amount of liquid in the beakers.

_____

Liter   mL
1   1000

─900 mL
─800 mL
─700 mL
─600 mL
─500 mL
─400 mL
─300 mL
─200 mL
─100 mL

Liter   mL
1   1000

─900 mL
─800 mL
─700 mL
─600 mL
─500 mL
─400 mL
─300 mL
─200 mL
─100 mL

Write as a multiplication sentence. Then, solve.

twenty times as many as nine

The zookeeper measured some reptiles in feet. How much shorter is the alligator?

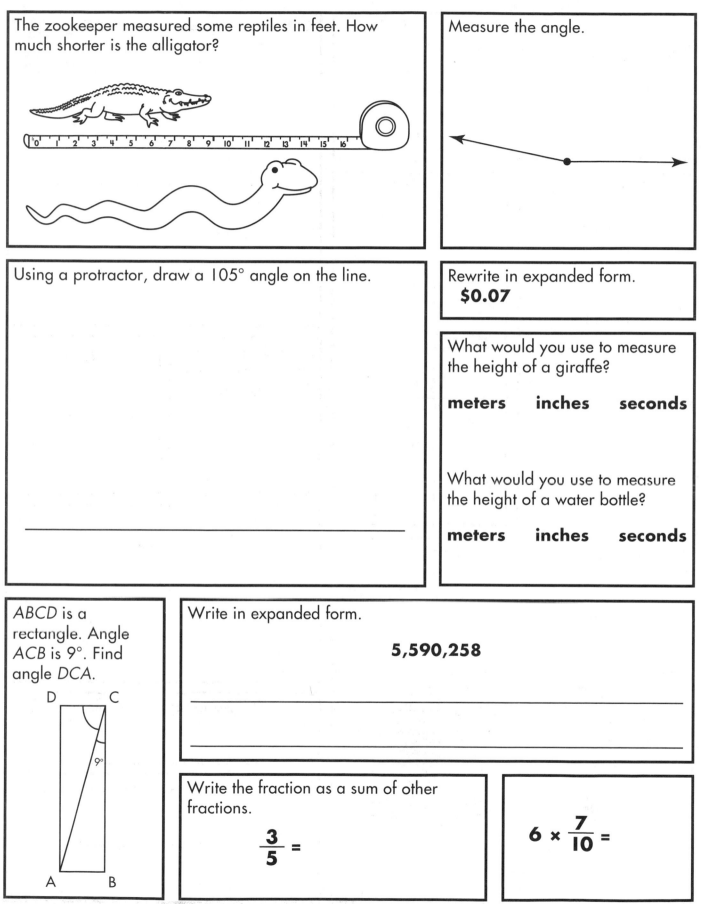

Measure the angle.

Using a protractor, draw a 105° angle on the line.

Rewrite in expanded form.
$0.07

What would you use to measure the height of a giraffe?

meters   inches   seconds

What would you use to measure the height of a water bottle?

meters   inches   seconds

ABCD is a rectangle. Angle ACB is 9°. Find angle DCA.

D   C

9°

A   B

Write in expanded form.

5,590,258

_____

_____

Write the fraction as a sum of other fractions.

$$\frac{3}{5} =$$

$$6 \times \frac{7}{10} =$$

Find the least common multiple of 10 and 7.

Write the sums of adjacent numbers in the blocks above.

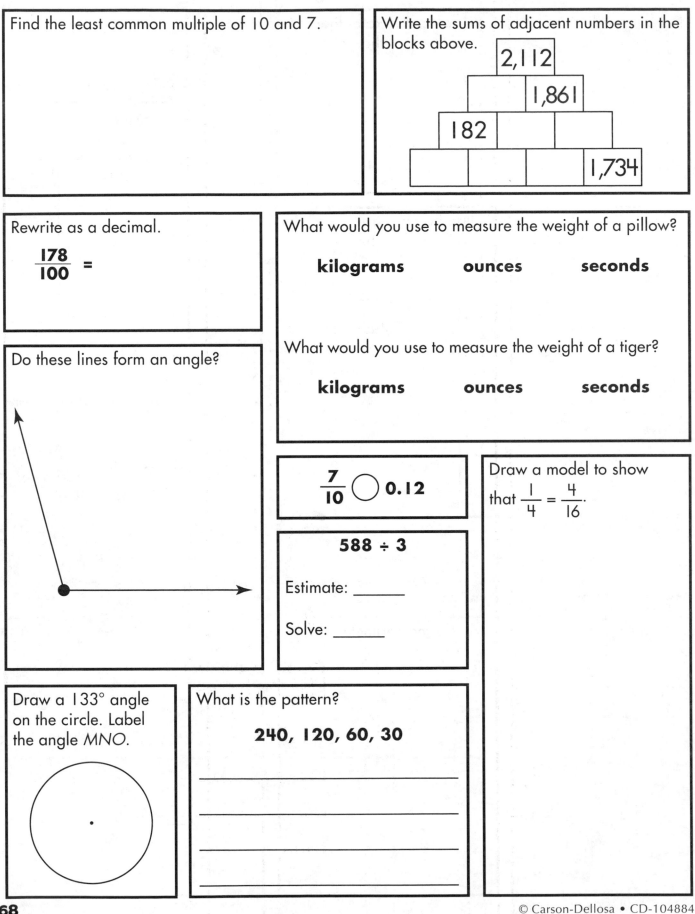

2,112

1,861

182

1,734

Rewrite as a decimal.

$\dfrac{178}{100} =$

What would you use to measure the weight of a pillow?

kilograms   **ounces**   **seconds**

What would you use to measure the weight of a tiger?

kilograms   **ounces**   **seconds**

Do these lines form an angle?

$\dfrac{7}{10} \bigcirc 0.12$

588 ÷ 3

Estimate: _____

Solve: _____

Draw a model to show that $\dfrac{1}{4} = \dfrac{4}{16}$.

Draw a 133° angle on the circle. Label the angle MNO.

What is the pattern?

240, 120, 60, 30

_____

_____

_____

How many degrees are in a circle?

Round to the nearest thousand.

874,957

755 ÷ 5

ABCD is a rectangle. Angle *ACB* is 6°. Find angle *DCA*.

_____ °

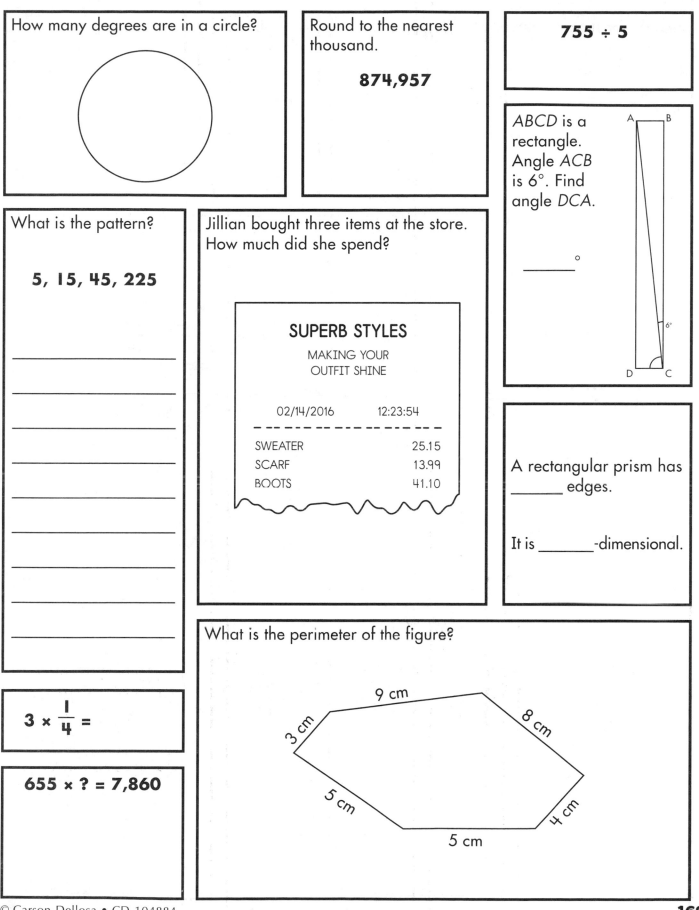

What is the pattern?

5, 15, 45, 225

_____

_____

_____

_____

_____

_____

_____

_____

Jillian bought three items at the store. How much did she spend?

SUPERB STYLES

MAKING YOUR
OUTFIT SHINE

02/14/2016   12:23:54
– – – – – – – – – – – – – – –
SWEATER   25.15
SCARF   13.99
BOOTS   41.10

A rectangular prism has _____ edges.

It is _____-dimensional.

$3 \times \dfrac{1}{4} =$

655 × ? = 7,860

What is the perimeter of the figure?

9 cm

8 cm

3 cm

5 cm

5 cm

4 cm

Locate 0.66 on the number line.

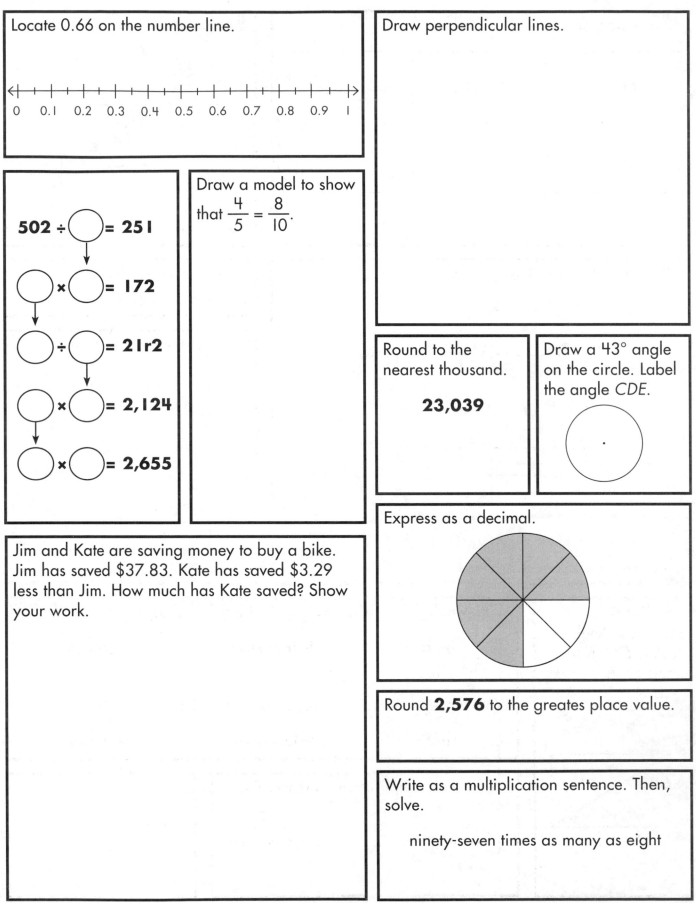

Draw perpendicular lines.

$502 \div \bigcirc = 251$

$\bigcirc \times \bigcirc = 172$

$\bigcirc \div \bigcirc = 21r2$

$\bigcirc \times \bigcirc = 2{,}124$

$\bigcirc \times \bigcirc = 2{,}655$

Draw a model to show that $\dfrac{4}{5} = \dfrac{8}{10}$.

Round to the nearest thousand.

23,039

Draw a 43° angle on the circle. Label the angle *CDE*.

Express as a decimal.

Round **2,576** to the greates place value.

Jim and Kate are saving money to buy a bike. Jim has saved $37.83. Kate has saved $3.29 less than Jim. How much has Kate saved? Show your work.

Write as a multiplication sentence. Then, solve.

ninety-seven times as many as eight

Rewrite as a decimal.

Ones	Tenths	Hundredths
	15	29

Measure the angle.

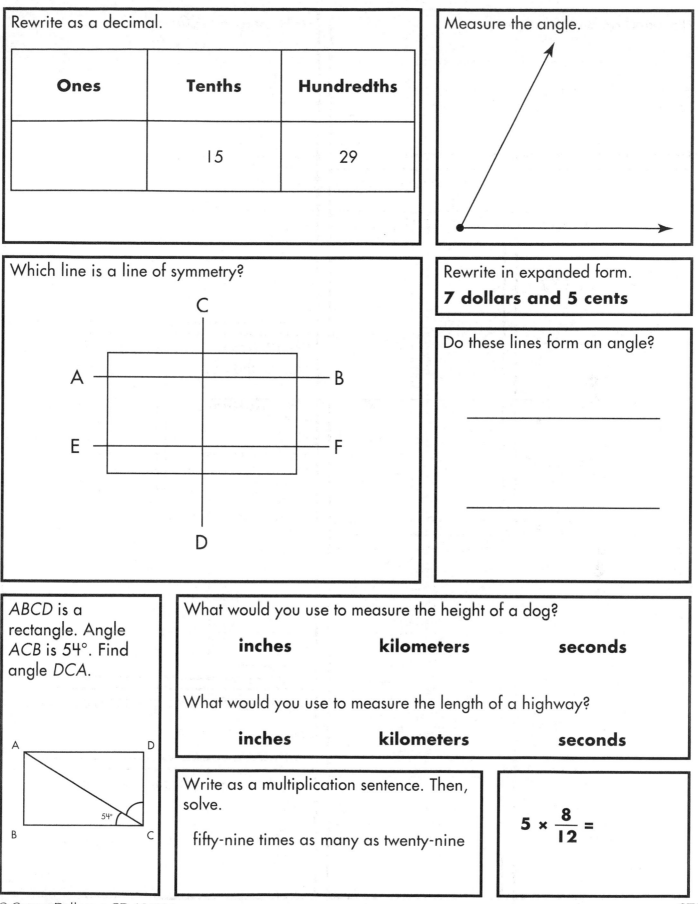

Which line is a line of symmetry?

Rewrite in expanded form.

7 dollars and 5 cents

Do these lines form an angle?

_____

_____

ABCD is a rectangle. Angle *ACB* is 54°. Find angle *DCA*.

What would you use to measure the height of a dog?

inches   **kilometers**   **seconds**

What would you use to measure the length of a highway?

inches   **kilometers**   **seconds**

Write as a multiplication sentence. Then, solve.

fifty-nine times as many as twenty-nine

$5 \times \dfrac{8}{12} =$

Write as a multiplication sentence. Then, solve.

seventy-five times as many as thirteen

---

900 ÷ 4

---

7 thousands =

_____ **hundreds**

What would you use to measure the length of a song?

milliseconds   inches   minutes

What would you use to measure the length of a comb?

milliseconds   inches   minutes

Rob wants to grill $\frac{2}{3}$-pound burgers for 12 people. How many pounds of meat does he need to buy? Show your work.

$\frac{3}{4}$ **lb.** ◯ **34 oz.**

1,025 × ? = 9,225

Draw a model to show that $\frac{1}{5} = \frac{2}{10}$.

$\frac{2}{6}$ ◯ $\frac{3}{12}$

What is the pattern?

625, 125, 25, 5

_____

_____

_____

Trace each set of parallel lines in a different color.

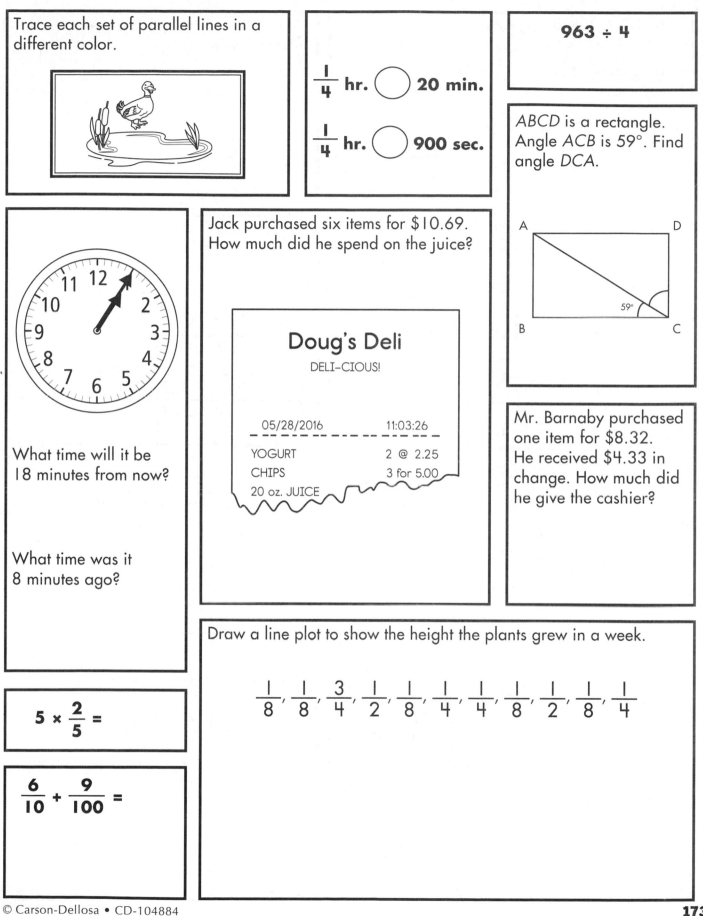

$\frac{1}{4}$ hr. ◯ 20 min.

$\frac{1}{4}$ hr. ◯ 900 sec.

963 ÷ 4

ABCD is a rectangle. Angle *ACB* is 59°. Find angle *DCA*.

What time will it be 18 minutes from now?

What time was it 8 minutes ago?

Jack purchased six items for $10.69. How much did he spend on the juice?

Doug's Deli

DELI–CIOUS!

05/28/2016   11:03:26

YOGURT   2 @ 2.25
CHIPS   3 for 5.00
20 oz. JUICE

Mr. Barnaby purchased one item for $8.32. He received $4.33 in change. How much did he give the cashier?

$5 \times \frac{2}{5} =$

$\frac{6}{10} + \frac{9}{100} =$

Draw a line plot to show the height the plants grew in a week.

$$\frac{1}{8}, \frac{1}{8}, \frac{3}{4}, \frac{1}{2}, \frac{1}{8}, \frac{1}{4}, \frac{1}{4}, \frac{1}{8}, \frac{1}{2}, \frac{1}{8}, \frac{1}{4}$$

5,715

What is the value of each **5**? _____

_____

Complete the pattern.

2

10

18

26

_____

_____

Harper gets $0.75 from the tooth fairy for every tooth she loses. She has lost 6 teeth so far. How much has the tooth fairy given her?

Draw parallel lines with a perpendicular intersecting line.

Use front-end estimation to estimate the difference.

2,037 – 379

The ninth multiple of 4 is _____.

The thirteenth multiple of 4 is _____.

15,324
– 9,803

---

315 ◯ 305 + 1

Locate 0.2 and 1.7.

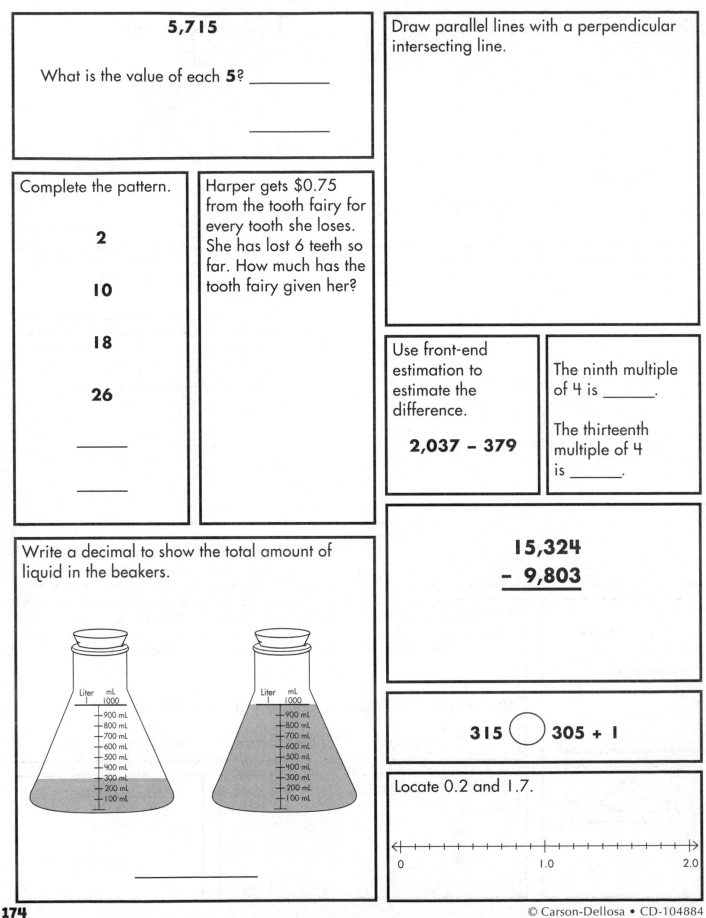

Write a decimal to show the total amount of liquid in the beakers.

_____

How much longer is the grasshopper?

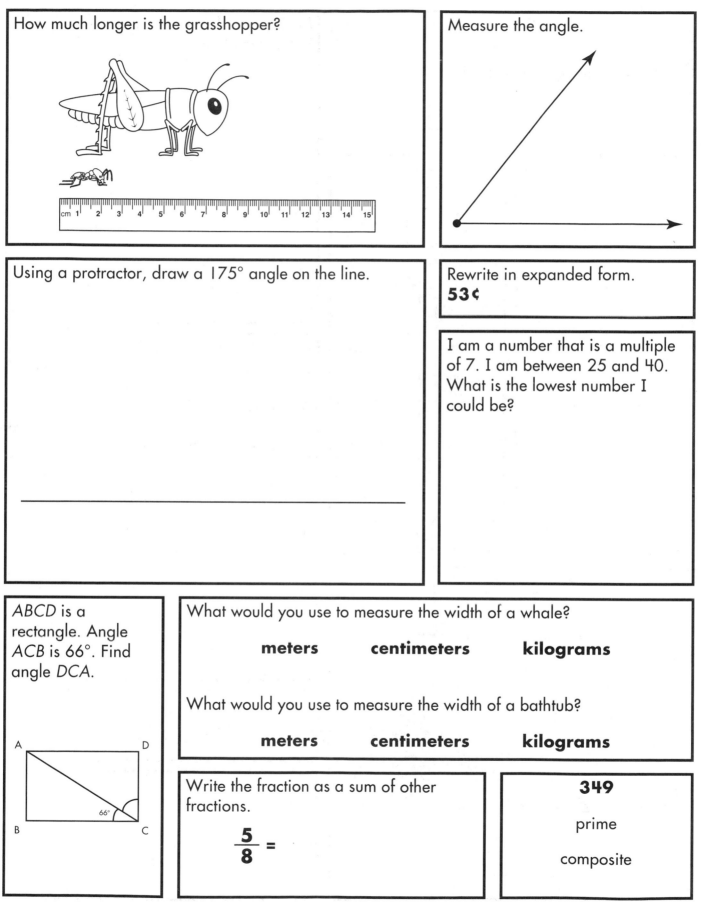

Measure the angle.

Using a protractor, draw a 175° angle on the line.

_____

Rewrite in expanded form.
53¢

I am a number that is a multiple of 7. I am between 25 and 40. What is the lowest number I could be?

ABCD is a rectangle. Angle *ACB* is 66°. Find angle *DCA*.

A   D

66°

B   C

What would you use to measure the width of a whale?

meters   centimeters   kilograms

What would you use to measure the width of a bathtub?

meters   centimeters   kilograms

Write the fraction as a sum of other fractions.

$$\frac{5}{8} =$$

349

prime

composite

Find the least common multiple of 48 and 3.

Write the sums of adjacent numbers in the blocks above.

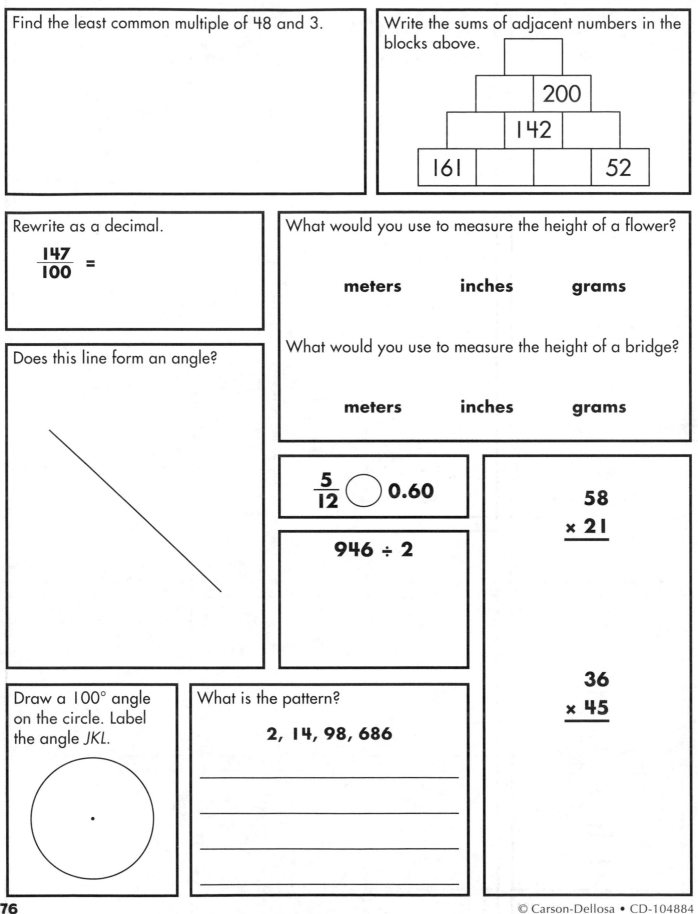

200
142
161		52

Rewrite as a decimal.

$$\frac{147}{100} =$$

What would you use to measure the height of a flower?

meters   inches   grams

What would you use to measure the height of a bridge?

meters   inches   grams

Does this line form an angle?

$$\frac{5}{12} \bigcirc 0.60$$

$$946 \div 2$$

$$58 \\ \times\, 21$$

$$36 \\ \times\, 45$$

Draw a 100° angle on the circle. Label the angle *JKL*.

What is the pattern?

2, 14, 98, 686

_____

_____

_____

_____

1 mi. = ____ ft.

1 km = ____ cm

1 lb. = ____ oz.

1 gal. = ____ qt.

1 yd. = ____ in.

1 km = ____ m

1 L = ____ mL

1 qt. = ____ pt.

1 yd. = ____ ft.

1 m = ____ cm

1 L = ____ cL

1 pt. = ____ c.

1 ft. = ____ in.

1 mi. = ____ yd.

1 kg = ____ g

1 t. = ____ lb.

5,280

36

3

12

100,000

1,000

100

1,760

16

1,000

10

1,000

4

2

2

2,000

1 qt. = ___ c.

1 min. = ___ sec.

1 decade = ___ years

1 millennium = ___ centuries

1 gal. = ___ c.

1 hr. = ___ sec.

1 year = ___ days

1 century = ___ decades

1 qt. = ___ pt.

1 c. = ___ oz.

1 day = ___ hr.

1 millennium = ___ years

1 gal. = ___ oz.

1 gal. = ___ pt.

1 hr. = ___ min.

1 century = ___ years

4	16		2	128
60	3,600	8	8
10	365	24	60
100	10	1,000	100

Answer Key

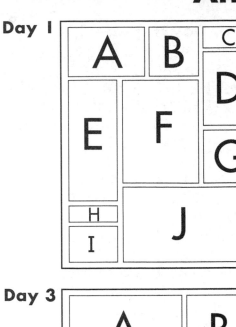

Day 1

A B C D E F G H I J

Day 2

A B C D E F G H I J

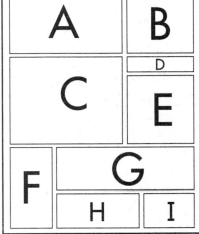

Day 3

A B C D E F G H I

Day 4

A B C D E F G H I J

Week 1, Day 1 (page 17)
A. The rectangle should show $\frac{1}{3}$ shaded.
B. $\frac{2}{8}$; C. >; D. 3 ft.; E. 60, 30, 2;
F. Students should draw a 12 by 15 array.
180; G. The butterfly should be divided into left and right, with a line going from top to bottom. H. 8; I. 680, 700; J. obtuse, acute, right

Week 1, Day 2 (page 18)
A. 1,000 + 400 + 30 + 8; B. less than;
C. 1 × 20, 2 × 10, 4 × 5; D. hundreds, ones, tens; E. 1,630; F. $\frac{5}{100}$; G. Students should draw a 24 by 6 array. H. $\frac{9}{12}$, $\frac{6}{126}$;
I. 32 quarts; J. 1,020

Week 1, Day 3 (page 19)
A. 6 inches; B. 15 × 15 = 225; C. top row: X, X, O; middle row: O, O, X; bottom row:

X, O, X; X won. D. 300; E. 137 × 4 = 548;
F. prime; G. 2,000 + 100 + 12; H. 8;
I. 4 × 3 = 12

Week 1, Day 4 (page 20)
A. 20,500, 35,000; B. multiplication;
C. >; D. 2; E. 7; F. 800; G. 315; H. The right triangle should be circled. I. 9,000;
J. square, rectangle

Week 2, Day 1 (page 21)
A. $\frac{1}{4}$, $\frac{1}{4}$, $\frac{1}{4}$; B. 2 and 5, 1 and 10;
C. 2; D. 24 inches; E. 3,168, 11,630;
F. Check drawings for perpendicular lines.
G. 3; H. 50; I. 6,981; J. 10 sq. ft.

Answer Key

Week 2, Day 2 (page 22)
A. $5 \times 2 = 10$; B. composite; C. from top to bottom, left to right: 9, 36, 9, 36, 12, 12, 4, 32, 4; D. 26 oranges; E. 870; F. 10,041; G. 4, 5, 5, 10, +2; H. Check students' work. I. >; J. 49,000

Week 2, Day 3 (page 23)
A. 45 baskets; B. $\frac{6}{8}$ or $\frac{3}{4}$, Check students' work. C. Students should draw four rows of 2 circles. D. 10; E. >, Check students' work. F. $1\frac{1}{3}$; G. $6,000 + 700 + 80 + 8$, $100,000 + 20,000 + 4,000 + 400 + 20 + 2$; H. $1\frac{2}{3}$, $2\frac{3}{4}$; I. 40

Week 2, Day 4 (page 24)
A. 6 times; B. five thousand eighty; C. 0.32; D. Check students' work. E. 2 feet; F. <; G. 1 hr. 30 min.; H. >, Check students' work. I. 1,035; J. 48×4, 32×6, 64×3, 24×8

Week 3, Day 1 (page 25)
A. 0.30; B. 740; C. 6r1, 5r1; D. Check students' work. 1,204, 1,202; E. $1.50; F. Check students' work. G. 4:45 pm; H. Check students' work. I. acute angle; J. multiples of 5: 5, 10, 15, 20, 25, 30, 35, 40, 45, 50, 55, 60, 65, 70, 75, 80, 85, 90, 95, multiples of 3: 3, 6, 9, 12, 15, 18, 21, 24, 27, common multiples: 15

Week 3, Day 2 (page 26)
A. 3,000, Answers will vary. B. less than; C. 8,000, 300, 20,000, 70, 2,000; D. $120; E. 13,000; F. 16; G. yes, $6.17; H. 3,124, 12,805; I. 3,446; J. 1.7

Week 3, Day 3 (page 27)
A. 3: 3, 6, 9, 12, 15, 18, 21, 24, 27, 30, 33, 36, 39, 42, 45, 48; 4: 4, 8, 12, 16, 20, 24, 28, 32, 36, 40, 44, 48; 8: 8, 16, 24, 32, 40, 48; B. $\frac{4}{7}$, $\frac{8}{14}$; C. $\frac{2}{4}$ is equal to $\frac{1}{2}$. D. 1,296; E. 14; F. 12, 24, 36, 48; G. $a = 3$, $b = 6$; H. 4; I. $\frac{1}{7}$, $\frac{1}{7}$, $\frac{1}{7}$

Week 3, Day 4 (page 28)
A. 240; B. 4,404, 6,340, 12,872; C. 20, 200; D. factors of 25: 1, 5, 25; factors of 10: 1, 2, 5, 10; common factors: 1, 5; E. Check students' work. F. 4:18; G. >; H. 90, 89; I. 1,606; J. from top to bottom, left to right: 1,416, 547, 443, 426, 81, 57

Week 4, Day 1 (page 29)
A. 6:15; B. 2, 36; C. 56; D. Check students' work. $36 \div 3 = 12$; E. 2:58; F. $10.01; G. 108; H. <; I. $\frac{64}{100}$; J. Check students' work.

Week 4, Day 2 (page 30)
A. 5,129, 5,921, 9,125; B. 1.7; C. 7, 8; D. Check students' work; E. 600; F. 1,110; G. 5, 6, 7, 5, +3; H. 0.4; I. =; J. $74 \times 1 = 74$

Week 4, Day 3 (page 31)
A. 10:23; B. $\frac{3}{5}$, $\frac{7}{10}$ (circled); C. CD; D. 4; E. 3×8, 24×5; F. 266; G. $2,000 + 500 + 20 + 1$, $500,000 + 8,000 + 600 + 30 + 3$; H. $\frac{1}{5}$, $\frac{1}{5}$, $\frac{1}{5}$, $\frac{1}{5}$; I. 3

Week 4, Day 4 (page 32)
A. Check students' work. B. Check students' work. C. 0.6; D. 5, Check students' reasoning. E. $\frac{3}{4}$ cup; F. <; G. 1 hr. 5 min.; H. =; I. 3,816; J. Check students' work. 5r1

Week 5, Day 1 (page 33)
A. 0.3; B. 120,000; C. <; D. 1 hour 35 minutes; E. 1,229, 5,662; F. Check students' work. $66 \div 11 = 6$; G. A line should be drawn in the middle of the clock from the top to the bottom. H. >; I. obtuse angle; J. rectangle

Week 5, Day 2 (page 34)
A. 4,000, Answers will vary. B. composite, Check students' work. C. blue: $\frac{4}{6}$, $\frac{2}{4}$, $\frac{5}{8}$, $\frac{2}{3}$; yellow: $\frac{1}{3}$, $\frac{3}{8}$, $\frac{3}{10}$, $\frac{1}{4}$; D. 1:08, 12:38; E. 56,000; F. 0.01; G. No, it would cost $5.18. H. 2,177; I. <; J. 117, 13

Answer Key

Week 5, Day 3 (page 35)
A. 2 songs; B. from bottom, left to right: 377, 21, 668, 1,523, 398, 1,087; C. Students should draw the third shape, with a triangle added to the left and right sides. D. 18,105; E. 25, 12; F. circled: 8, 12, 16, 28, 32, 36, 48; G. 30,000 + 2,000 + 200 + 3; H. $\frac{9}{4}, \frac{43}{8}$; I. prime

Week 5, Day 4 (page 36)
A. 82 × 81 = 6,642; B. 4; C. 30; D. 2 times; E. 2:07; F. <; G. 400, 443r4; H. 132, 504; I. Answers will vary but may iclude $\frac{1}{1}$, $\frac{2}{2}$, or $\frac{3}{3}$. J. Check students' work.

Week 6, Day 1 (page 37)
A. 1 hr. 3 min.; B. 1,000, 150,000, 200,000, 3, 300,000; C. >; D. Check students' work. E. 2:08, 12:48; F. 6, 2; G. $10.16; H. 10; I. 0.2 + 0.03 = 0.23; J. multiples of 4: 4, 8, 12, 16, 20, 24, 28, 32, 36, multiples of 3: 3, 6, 9, 12, 15, 18, 21, 24, 27, common multiples: 12, 24

Week 6, Day 2 (page 38)
A. 30,000, 800; B. more than; C. 5r2, 8r5; D. 33; E. 340,000; F. 9, 15; G. 8, 12, 16, 5, ×4; H. $\frac{6}{10}$, $\frac{2}{10}$; I. 36 ft.; J. 2,025

Week 6, Day 3 (page 39)
A. 25: 50, 75, 100, 125, 150, 175, 200; 50: 100, 150, 200; 75: 150; B. $\frac{6}{8}$ or $\frac{3}{4}$, Check students' drawings. C. are; D. 23,445; E. >, >; F. 4; G. $1\frac{1}{5}$, Check students' work. H. 6; I. 4; J. 50

Week 6, Day 4 (page 40)
A. Check students' work. B. five thousand two hundred twenty-three; C. 30, 300; D. factors of 42: 1, 2, 3, 6, 7, 14, 21, 42, factors of 4: 1, 2, 4, common factors: 1, 2, 4; E. 4 ft., 2 in.; F. 3,400; G. 18 m; H. 1,450; I. >, Check students' work. J. 3 hr. 45 min.

Week 7, Day 1 (page 41)
A. 0.20; B. 1.5, 1.6, 180; C. <; D. $\frac{4}{16}$, $\frac{2}{8}$, $\frac{3}{12}$; E. 46 ÷ 2 = 23, 2 × 23 = 46; F. 2 hr. 6 min.; G. 400,000; H. 1 hr. 6 min.; I. right angle; J. Check students' work.

Week 7, Day 2 (page 42)
A. 45, 56; B. 5.7; C. from top to bottom, left to right: 60, 3, 60, 3, 102, 6, 102, 6, 486; D. $260; E. 47,700; F. 12,627; G. $1.04; H. 0.40; I. <; J. 10, 100

Week 7, Day 3 (page 43)
A. 15; B. $\frac{2}{4}$ or $\frac{1}{2}$, Check students' work. C. *AB*; D. 374; E. 64; F. Answers will vary but may include 125, 130, 135, and 140. G. 7,000 + 60 + 3, 2,000 + 400 + 10 + 1; H. 71 × 38 = 2,698; I. >

Week 7, Day 4 (page 44)
A. 72; B. from bottom, left to right: 59, 108, 113, 519, 686, 966; C. 0.47; D. 4; E. Check students' work. F. >; G. prime; H. <, Check students' work. I. 2,117; J. 67

Week 8, Day 1 (page 45)
A. 252 in.; B. 1,650, 13,650; C. >; D. 864 sq. in.; E. 6:50, 6:03; F–G. Check students' work. H. 180; I. $\frac{51}{100}$; J. right triangle, rectangle

Week 8, Day 2 (page 46)
A. 7,000, 90,000; B. composite, Check students' work. C. 116, 101; D. 3,472; E. 29,600; F. $\frac{4}{8}$ or $\frac{1}{2}$; G. 20, 18, 9, 12; H. 32,051; I. 30,000; J. 45 × 65 = 2,925

Week 8, Day 3 (page 47)
A. multiples of 2: 2, 4, 6, 8, 10, 12, 14, 16, 18; multiples of 3: 3, 6, 9, 12, 15, 18, 21, 24, 27; common multiples: 12, 18; B. 0.0; C. are; D. 44; E. >, >; F. 7,752; G. $\frac{22}{6}$, $\frac{23}{5}$; H. $\frac{1}{8} + \frac{1}{8}$; I. 6

Answer Key

Week 8, Day 4 (page 48)
A. Check students' work. B. $322; C. 70;
D. 8; E. $5\frac{7}{8}$ feet; F. months; G. 3 hr. 45 min.;
H. Students should connect points X and Y.
Line XY; I. $2\frac{5}{8}$; J. Check students' work.

Week 9, Day 1 (page 49)
A. 17 min.; B. 34,600; C. <; D. $\frac{1}{3}$, $\frac{2}{7}$, $\frac{1}{5}$;
E. 384 ÷ 4 = 96, 4 × 96 = 384; F. 7:00 pm;
G. $14.17; H. $\frac{73}{100}$; I. 12,677; J. cone

Week 9, Day 2 (page 50)
A. 200,000, 1; B. more than; C. from top to
bottom, left to right: 9, 36, 9, 36, 12, 12, 4,
32, 4; D. 30; E. 79,900; F. 36, 45; G. no;
H. $\frac{1}{6}$ or $\frac{6}{12}$; I. <; J. 320, 3,200, 32,000

Week 9, Day 3 (page 51)
A. 8; B. $\frac{3}{12}$ or $\frac{1}{4}$; C. Students should draw
1 row of 7 squares; D. 3,240; E. 24;
F. Check students' work. G. Check students'
work. H. 12; I. composite

Week 9, Day 4 (page 52)
A. 83 × 76 = 6,308; B. from bottom, left to
right: 175, 276, 100, 340, 311, 751; C. 90;
D. $6; E. 224 sq. ft.; F. 1.5; G. 190, 188r4;
H. <, Check students' work. I. 429r2;
J. 7 bags, 4 baseballs left over

Week 10, Day 1 (page 53)
A. 0.9; B. 3,600; C. >; D. Check students'
work. E. 7:58, 7:08; F. obtuse; G. 870,000;
H. Students should draw lines. I. $\frac{99}{100}$;
J. Check students' work.

Week 10, Day 2 (page 54)
A. 25, 144; B. 0.80; C. 59r1, 112r3;
D. $150; E. 282,900; F. 0.68; G. 91 m;
H. 0.30; I. 8,384; J. 100, 1,000, 10,000

Week 10, Day 3 (page 55)
A. 5: 5, 10, 15, 20, 25, 30, 35, 40, 45, 50,
55, 60, 65, 70; 8: 8, 16, 24, 32, 40, 48,
56, 64; 12: 12, 24, 36, 48, 60; B. 1.0;
C. Check students' work. D. 4,984; E. Check
students' work. F. $\frac{7}{3}$ or $2\frac{1}{3}$, $\frac{9}{15}$ or $1\frac{2}{5}$;
G. 9,000 + 800, 5,000 + 40 + 2; H. $1\frac{3}{8}$;
I. 20

Week 10, Day 4 (page 56)
A. 20; B. two hundred thirty-nine thousand
nine hundred seventy-two; C. 0.4; D. factors
of 8: 1, 2, 4, 8; factors of 36: 1, 2, 3, 4, 6,
9, 12, 18, 36; common factors: 1, 2, 4;
E. 19 hr. 45 min.; F. <; G. 1 hr. 13 min.;
H. 4,455, 2,376; I. $6\frac{1}{4}$; J. 62°

Week 11, Day 1 (page 57)
A. 4 hr. 27 min.; B. 120, 7,200; C. $\frac{77}{100}$;
D. $\frac{1}{2}$, 1, $1\frac{1}{2}$, 120; E. 10:29, 8:35;
F. $40.15; G. 50,000; H. 360; I. prime;
J. multiples of 6: 6, 12, 18, 24, 30, 36, 42,
48, 54; multiples of 4: 4, 8, 12, 16, 20, 24,
28, 32, 36; common multiples: 12, 24

Week 11, Day 2 (page 58)
A. 50, 700; B. 6.5 cm; C. 4,865, 4,870;
D. 10,600, 7,332; E. 378,000; F. 21,550;
G. 22, 20, 12, 14, ×2, −6; H. 0.3;
I. 20,000; J. 42,023

Week 11, Day 3 (page 59)
A. *ADC* or *CDA*; B. $\frac{16}{12}$, $1\frac{4}{12}$, or $1\frac{1}{3}$, Check
students' work. C. *EF*; D. 17; E. >, >;
F. Answers will vary but may include 102,
108, 114, and 120. G. 6; H. $\frac{1}{10}$, $\frac{1}{10}$, $\frac{1}{10}$; I. 6

Week 11, Day 4 (page 60)
A. Check students' work. B. 12 sq. cm; C. 70;
D. 6; E. Check students' work. F. >; G. $4\frac{4}{5}$;
H. Students should circle the lines that form
an angle. I. >; J. Check students' work.

Week 12, Day 1 (page 61)
A. 2 hr. 15 min.; B. 300,000; C. >; D. 58;
E. a pyramid of 10 balls; F. Check students'
work. G. 2,469; H. 8; I. 5,464; J. hexagon,
pentagon

Answer Key

Week 12, Day 2 (page 62)
A. 2,000, 80; B. composite, Check students' work. C. 219, 66; D. Check students' work. E. $2\frac{2}{5}$; F. 30, 40; G. $60.25; H. <; I. 2,469; J. 74 × 35 = 2,590

Week 12, Day 3 (page 63)
A. 78; B. $\frac{4}{8}$ or $\frac{1}{2}$, Check students' work. C. are; D. 11; E. 8; F. $1\frac{1}{5}$, $1\frac{1}{2}$; G. Check students' work. H. 3; J. 9

Week 12, Day 4 (page 64)
A. 60; B. 81 sq. in.; C. 3,168; D. 2 hr.; E. yes, 45°; F. year; G. 1 hr. 58 min.; H. >, Check students' work. I. Check students' work. J. 545r2

Week 13, Day 1 (page 65)
A. Check students' work. B. >, <; C. 10" or 10 in.; D. 96, 24; E. 6:59, 4:29; F. $83.90; G. 2,600 g; H. $4\frac{2}{6}$ or $4\frac{1}{3}$; I. 27°; J. trapezoid

Week 13, Day 2 (page 66)
A. 24, 119; B. more than; C. 635, 636; D. 36; E. 19,500; F. $\frac{6}{7}$; G. Check students' work. H. 11,684, 34,867; I. 60,000 m; J. 9,100

Week 13, Day 3 (page 67)
A. 7: 7, 14, 21, 28, 35, 42, 49, 56, 63, 70, 77; 11: 11, 22, 33, 44, 55, 66, 77; 13: 13, 26, 39, 52, 65; B. 0.9; C. Students should draw one row of 2 triangles. D. 9,688; E. Check students' work. F. hundreds, ten thousands, thousands; G. 10,000 + 2,000 + 500 + 40 + 9, 10,000 + 900 + 20 + 7; H. $\frac{23}{6}$; I. 6,881

Week 13, Day 4 (page 68)
A. Check students' work. B. 7. C. 0.83; D. +6, ×10, −32, ÷7, ×4, ÷2; E. $2\frac{7}{12}$ yards; F. >; G. 60, 61r1; H. 975, 1,232; I. Check students' work. J. 2,798, Answers will vary.

Week 14, Day 1 (page 69)
A. 0.4; B. $\frac{1}{2}$, 1, 90; C. $12\frac{1}{12}$; D. Check students' work. E. 408 ÷ 8 = 51, 8 × 51 = 408; F. 12 min.; G. 10,000; H. Check students' work. I. 14,322; J. Students should circle the pentagon and the trapezoid.

Week 14, Day 2 (page 70)
A. 40,000, 400; B. 3.2 cm; C. 605r3, 1,266r2; D. $8.75; E. 7,000; F. $\frac{10}{10}$ or 1; G. 33 m; H. 0.2; I. =; J. 430, 4,300, 43,000

Week 14, Day 3 (page 71)
A. centimeters, meters; B. 26; C. Check students' work. D. 7; E. >, >, <; F. 2, 2; G. 60,000 + 8,000 + 80 + 2, 3,000 + 200 + 10 + 6; H. $\frac{1}{6}$, $\frac{1}{6}$; I. 7r2

Week 14, Day 4 (page 72)
A. 60; B. sixty-three thousand two hundred ten; C. 90; D. factors of 56: 1, 2, 4, 7, 8, 14, 28, 56; factors of 14: 1, 2, 7, 14; common factors: 1, 2, 7, 14; E. Check students' work. F. 12; G. $9\frac{1}{5}$; H. 112 sq. ft. I. >; J. Check students' work.

Week 15, Day 1 (page 73)
A. Check students' work. B. <, >; C. 4,919; D. $\frac{12}{15}$, $\frac{8}{10}$, $\frac{20}{25}$; E. 6:52, 5:56; F. $14.12; G. Check students' work. H. 90; I. $\frac{64}{100}$; J. multiples of 3: 3, 6, 9, 12, 15, 18, 21, 24, 27, 30, 33, 36, 39, 42, 45, 48, 51, 54, 57, 60, 63, 66, 69, 72, 75, 78, 81, 84, 87, 90, 93, 96, 99; multiples of 8: 8, 16, 24, 32, 40, 48, 56, 64, 72, 80, 88, 96; multiples of both: 24, 48, 72, 96

Week 15, Day 2 (page 74)
A. 100, 1; B. prime, Check students' work. C. from top to bottom, left to right: 108, 3, 108, 14, 3, 14, 7, 7, 112; D. Check students' work. E. 239,100; F. 20,000 + 2,000 + 300 + 40; G. 19, 21, 13, 27; ×2, −1; H. 0.50; I. 3,000; J. 68 × 16 = 1,088

Answer Key

Week 15, Day 3 (page 75)
A. 5, 10, 15, 20, 25, 30, 35, 40, 45; 7, 14, 21, 28, 35, 42, 49, 56, 63; 35; B. 0.80; C. $\frac{10}{12}$ or $\frac{5}{6}$, Check students' work. D. 2; E. Check students' work. F. Answers will vary but may include 105, 112, 119, and 126. G. 6; H. 4; I. 90

Week 15, Day 4 (page 76)
A. 18; B. 2 cm; C. 50; D. 36; E. 7; F. >; G. 270, 268r6; H. >, Check students' work. I. 42 cousins; J. A, Check students' work.

Week 16, Day 1 (page 77)
A. 1 hr. 57 min.; B. $\frac{1}{2}$, $\frac{3}{4}$, 1, 200; C. <; D. 49 cm; E. 15, 18, 21; F. 0; G. $1.17; H. =; I. 38; J. 38, Check students' work.

Week 16, Day 2 (page 78)
A. 24, 72; B. $5\frac{1}{10}$; C. 3,242, 2,242; D. Check students' work. E. 1,564; F. 27; G. 48 cm; H. true; I. 7; J. 810

Week 16, Day 3 (page 79)
A. $\frac{3}{4}$; B. 154°; C. $\frac{2}{5}$, Check students' work. D. 5,803; E. Check students' work. F. 75°; G. 12,328, 524, 5,215; H. $\frac{11}{4}$; I. composite, Check students' work.

Week 16, Day 4 (page 80)
A. 44; B. 28; C. 0.9; D. 3.3; E. 2 wallets; F. >; G. 3 hr. 37 min.; H. 3,404, 1,104; I. $1\frac{5}{7}$; J. 311r1

Week 17, Day 1 (page 81)
A. 6 hr. 57 min.; B. 120,000; C. 12,760; D. $\frac{4}{6}$, $\frac{5}{12}$, $\frac{2}{4}$, $\frac{3}{10}$; E. Students should draw two dice rolled to a 6; F. 5:30 pm; G. yellow; H. 2.5; I. 8,678; J. square

Week 17, Day 2 (page 82)
A. 0, 9,000; B. 20,118, 28,035; C. 63r5, 202r1; D. $195; E. 60,000; F. $\frac{4}{5}$; G. 1.9 L; H. 0.50; I. <; J. 136

Week 17, Day 3 (page 83)
A. 16: 16, 32, 48, 64, 80, 96, 112, 128, 144; 31: 31, 62, 93, 124; 35: 35, 70, 105, 140; B. 0.7; C. Students should draw 2 rows of 3 circles. D. 80,080; E. <, <; F. 5; G. 3; H. 42 × 93 = 3,906; I. 489

Week 17, Day 4 (page 84)
A. Check students' work. B. 78 sq. ft.; C. 70; D. factors of 64: 1, 2, 4, 8, 16, 32, 64; factors of 8: 1, 2, 4, 8; common factors: 1, 2, 4, 8; E. Check students' work. F. <; G. 9,678; H. 274 coins; I. 3,072; J. V

Week 18, Day 1 (page 85)
A. 0.5; B. <, >; C. >; D. Check students' work. E. 11:09, 9:41; F. Check students' work. G. $8.43; H. 3,475; I. 47; J. prism, pyramid

Week 18, Day 2 (page 86)
A. 40, 10,000; B. 5.40; C. from top to bottom, left to right: 12, 15, 12, 15, 3, 13, 3, 6, 13; D. 1,057r3, 797; E. 130,000; F. $\frac{8}{7}$ or $1\frac{1}{7}$; G. 12 sq. ft.; H. 1.2, 1.02 I. 64 oz. ; J. 72

Week 18, Day 3 (page 87)
A. 12; B. 37°; C. Check students' work. D. 2; E. 4, Answers will vary. F. hundred thousands, ones, ten thousands; G. 2,000 + 400 + 2, 10,000 + 8,000 + 100 + 1; H. Answers will vary but may include $\frac{4}{8} + \frac{3}{8}$. I. 60

Week 18, Day 4 (page 88)
A. Check students' work. B. from bottom, left to right: 153, 218, 390, 715, 826, 1,541; C. 1.10; D. 15; E. 3 hr. 5 min.; F. >; G. yes; H. Check students' work. I. >; J. 785

Week 19, Day 1 (page 89)
A. Check students' work. B. 0.5, 1, 1.75, 2,800; C. >; D. 8 sq. m; E. Students should shade four of the six sections of the next hexagon. F. $8.59; G. Check students' work. H. 9; I. $\frac{83}{100}$; J. prism, hexagon, pyramid

Answer Key

Week 19, Day 2 (page 90)
A. 42, 117; B. prime, Check students' work.
C. triangle; D. Check students' work.
E. 38,000; F. 24; G. $\frac{2}{4}$ and $\frac{2}{6}$; H. 0.25;
I. 200,001; J. 900 + 70 + 3

Week 19, Day 3 (page 91)
A. $\frac{5}{6} > \frac{3}{4}$; B. 0.2; C. $\frac{1}{6}$, Check students'
work. D. <; E. Check students' work. F. 128,
136, 144, and 152; G. 100,000 + 7,000 +
500 + 40 + 9, 6,000 + 400 + 10 + 2; H. 3;
I. 1,448

Week 19, Day 4 (page 92)
A. 96; B. seventy-three thousand nine
hundred ninety-six; C. 20; D. Check students'
work. E. Check students' work. F. >;
G. 1 hr. 41 min. H. Check students' work.
I. 1,581; J. D

Week 20, Day 1 (page 93)
A. 0.5; B. 500, 750, 1.75; C. 733; D. Check
students' work. E. 28, 32, 36; F. 7:55 am;
G. 34,560; H. $\frac{2}{3}$; I. Check students' work.
J. multiples of 5: 5, 10, 15, 20, 25, 30, 35,
40, 45, 50, 55, 60, 65, 70, 75, 80, 85, 90,
95, 100; multiples of 2: 2, 4, 6, 8, 10, 12,
14, 16, 18, 20, 22, 24, 26, 28, 30, 32, 34,
36, 38, 40, 42, 44, 46, 48, 50, 52, 54, 56,
58, 60, 62, 64, 66, 68, 70, 72, 74, 76, 78,
80, 82, 84, 86, 88, 90, 92, 94, 96, 98,
100; multiples of both: 10, 20, 30, 40, 50,
60, 70, 80, 90, 100

Week 20, Day 2 (page 94)
A. 2,000, 2; B. 3.2 cm; C. 14 in.; D. Check
students' work. E. 123,000; F. 1,020;
G. 45, 48, 51, 54; H. 0.6; I. 4.6; J. Check
students' work.

Week 20, Day 3 (page 95)
A. 14: 14, 28, 42, 56, 70, 84, 98; 18: 18,
36, 54, 72, 90; 22: 22, 44, 66, 88; B. $\frac{4}{5}$
, Check students' work. C. Check students'
work. D. 4,071; E. <, >, =; F. $\frac{4}{3}$ or $1\frac{1}{3}$, $\frac{15}{8}$
or $1\frac{7}{8}$; G. 300,000 + 10,000 + 5,000 + 700
+ 80 + 4; H. $\frac{28}{5}$; I. 7

Week 20, Day 4 (page 96)
A. 90; 90 m; C. 10; D. 14; E. 1.75 years;
F. <; 60, 55r16; H. >, Check students' work.
I. 1,323; J. line *EF*

Week 21, Day 1 (page 97)
A. Check students' work. B. 200,000;
C. 173; D. 16 cm; E. 4:08, 2:46; F. $14.07;
G. $4.76; H. $2\frac{1}{2}$; I. Check students' work.
J. 18, 34

Week 21, Day 2 (page 98)
A. 500, 20,000; B. 7.60 cm; C. 3,759,
3,809; D. Ms. Jackson; E. 300,000; F. $\frac{4}{4}$ or
1; G. 64; H. 800; I. <; J. 10 + 1 +
$\frac{1}{10} + \frac{2}{100}$

Week 21, Day 3 (page 99)
A. 11 times; B. 177°; C. $\frac{5}{12}$, Check students'
work. D. 5,200; E. Check students' work.
F. 87°; G. 100,000 + 10,000 + 9,000 + 30
+ 40 + 5, 300,000 + 20,000 + 8,000 + 40
+ 50 + 2; H. 25 × 4 = 100; I. 7,947

Week 21, Day 4 (page 100)
A–B. Check students' work. C. 0.28;
D. 8 lawns; E. Check students' work. F. ;
G. 8; H. Check students' work. I. no; J

Week 22, Day 1 (page 101)
A. 0.3; B. 500, 1, 1.2, 2.3; C. 1,927 D. 8;
E. domino with three pips over six pips;
F. bottom left angle; G. 35,000; H. $\frac{1}{5}$;
I. $\frac{69}{100}$; J. Check students' work.

Week 22, Day 2 (page 102)
A. 72, 90; B. yes, Answers will vary.
C. 295r2, 606r1; D. 107,613, 112,296;
E. 70,000; F. 40; G. 8.5 ft.; H. .1 L; I. 1.9;
J. 89 × 64 = 5,696

Week 22, Day 3 (page 103)
A. 4; B. 71; C. Check students' work.
D. 49; E. Check students' work. F. ten
thousands, hundreds, thousands; G. circle,
square, pentagon; H. $\frac{1}{12}$, $\frac{1}{12}$, $\frac{1}{12}$, $\frac{1}{12}$; I.
composite

Answer Key

Week 22, Day 4 (page 104)
A. Check students' work. B. from bottom, left to right: 33, 77, 320, 576, 494, 1,070; C. Check students' work. D. factors of 54: 1, 2, 3, 6, 9, 18, 27, 54; factors of 18: 1, 2, 3, 6, 9, 18; common factors: 1, 2, 3, 6, 9, 18; E. 6 hr. 5 min.; F. =; G. 15,112; H. >, Check students' work. I. 24,164; J. 862

Week 23, Day 1 (page 105)
A. 1 hr. 29 min.; B. 10,000; C. >; D. Check students' work. E. 27, 33; F. 5:35 pm; G. 90, 4, 2; H. $\frac{1}{8}$; I–J. Check students' work.

Week 23, Day 2 (page 106)
A. 30, 900; B. 8.4 cm; C. from top to bottom, left to right: 256, 16, 256, 16, 6, 6, 12, 20, 12; D. $90; E. 10,900; F. 4,224; G. 5.32 km; H. 0.2; I. 7,000; J. 38

Week 23, Day 3 (page 107)
A. multiples of 3: 3, 6, 9, 12, 15, 18, 21, 24, 27; multiples of 4: 4, 8, 12, 16, 20, 24, 28, 32, 36; common multiples: 12, 24; B. 42°; C. $4.21; D. 429; E. >, <; F. $\frac{15}{12}$ or $\frac{5}{4}$ or $1\frac{1}{4}$, $\frac{12}{5}$ or $2\frac{2}{5}$; G. 200,000 + 2,000 + 900 + 60 + 8; H. $\frac{1}{6} + \frac{1}{6} + \frac{1}{6}$; I. 13,532

Week 23, Day 4 (page 108)
A. 1,435; B. 6; C. 1.04; D–E. Check students' work. F. hour; G. 8 min.; H. 16,496, 14,536; I. Check students' work. J. –3

Week 24, Day 1 (page 109)
A. 2 hr. 34 min.; B. 1, 12, 38,000; C. 1,959; D. no; E. 3:11, 10:11; F. Check students' work. G. $196.67; H. $\frac{3}{4}$; I. Check students' work. J. Students should circle the triangle.

Week 24, Day 2 (page 110)
A. 78, 369; B. prime, Check students' work. C. 3, $1\frac{1}{2}$; D. Check students' work. E. 980,000; F. 11,044; G. $1\frac{6}{10}$ L; H. 1.0; I. 26,352; J. 46 × 9 = 414

Week 24, Day 3 (page 111)
A. 1.5 hr.; B. 172°; C. $\frac{12}{12}$ or 1, Check students' work. D. $0.20; E. 15; F. Students should circle both acute triangles. G. 300,000 + 30,000 + 2,000 + 700 + 9; H. $\frac{23}{10}$; I. $4\frac{2}{3}$

Week 24, Day 4 (page 112)
A–C. Check students' work. D. centimeters, inches; E. 2 hr. 15 min.; F. <; G. 90, 86r2; H. =, Check students' work. I. 1,734; J. U

Week 25, Day 1 (page 113)
A. 0.6; B. >, >; C. 4; D. Check students' work. E. P should be rotated 90° clockwise. F. Check students' work. G. 14,330; H. $\frac{1}{10}$; I. 8,313; J. 80 cm

Week 25, Day 2 (page 114)
A. 1,000, 800; B. 5.1 cm; C. 263r2, 97r5; D. domino with one pip beside four pips; E. 16,000; F. 24, 64; G. 50, 45, 44, 40, 70; H. 1,990; I. 3.9; J. 100

Week 25, Day 3 (page 115)
A. 19: 19, 38, 57, 76, 95, 114, 133; 23: 23, 46, 69, 92, 115, 138; 29: 29, 58, 87, 116, 145; B. 161°; C. Students should shade two sections of the circle. D. 47; E. >, <; F. $\frac{168}{100}$ or $1\frac{17}{25}$, $\frac{111}{100}$ or $1\frac{11}{100}$; G. 70,000 + 3,000 + 300 + 30; H. Answers will vary but may include $\frac{1}{12} + \frac{1}{12} + \frac{1}{12}$. I. $5\frac{1}{4}$

Week 25, Day 4 (page 116)
A. Check students' work. B. eighty-five thousand five hundred five; C. 0.03; D. 9 books; E. Check students' work. F. <; G. 96; H–I. Check students' work. J. butterfly

Week 26, Day 1 (page 117)
A. Check students' work. B. 0.50, 1, 2, 48; C. 40,850; D. $\frac{3}{10}$, $\frac{4}{12}$, $\frac{1}{4}$; E. 162, 486, 1,458; F. $26.99; G. 90, 3, 2; H. $\frac{1}{3}$; I. $\frac{71}{100}$; J. Check students' work.

Answer Key

Week 26, Day 2 (page 118)
A. Check students' work. B. yes, Answers will vary. C. 48,371, 58,371; D. 9 months; E. 83,190; F. 2,032; G. 1.3 L; H. 0.75; I. =; J. 8 × 44 = 352

Week 26, Day 3 (page 119)
A. meters; B. 25°; C. 5 lb.; D. 3,204; E. 24; F. thousands, tens, hundreds; G. 900,000 + 40,000 + 800 + 70 + 3; H. Answers will vary but may include $\frac{2}{10} + \frac{1}{10} + \frac{1}{10}$. I. composite

Week 26, Day 4 (page 120)
A. 130; B. from bottom, left to right: 5, 104, 18, 218, 127, 454; C. 1.76; D. factors of 35: 1, 5, 7, 35; factors of 21: 1, 3, 7, 21; common factors: 1, 7; E. no; F. >; G. 4,806; H. Check students' work. I. >; J. ×5

Week 27, Day 1 (page 121)
A. 1 hr. 39 min. B. 400,000; c. >; D. Check students' work. E. 12:08, 9:48; F. 4:43 pm; G. 0, 0, 3; H. $\frac{3}{100}$; I. 1,003; J. Check students' work.

Week 27, Day 2 (page 122)
A. 7,688, 6,136; B. yes; C. 223; D. Check students' work. E. 4,577; F. Check students' work. G. 8.1 lb.; H. 0.8; I. 2.3; J. 10

Week 27, Day 3 (page 123)
A. $1\frac{1}{4}$ in.; B. 129°; C. Check students' work. D. $0.37; E. 56; F. $\frac{7}{6}$ or $1\frac{1}{6}$, $\frac{12}{8}$ or $1\frac{1}{2}$, $\frac{10}{5}$ or 2; G. centimeters, feet; H. $\frac{38}{6}$ or $\frac{19}{3}$; I. $1\frac{4}{5}$

Week 27, Day 4 (page 124)
A. 6; B. 1,422; C. Check students' work. D. pounds, grams; E. $1\frac{7}{12}$ gal.; F. <; G. 13 hr. 7 min.; H. 2,254, 2,484; I. Check students' work. J. 127

Week 28, Day 1 (page 125)
A. 42 min.; B. >, <; C. 251; D. 66; E. rectangle divided into eighths; F. Check students' work. G. $6.05; H. $1\frac{1}{2}$; I. Check students' work. J. 50 mi.

Week 28, Day 2 (page 126)
A. 80,000, 800; B. composite, Check students' work. C. from top to bottom, left to right: 23, 7, 23, 82, 7, 82, 41, 205, 41; D. 5 hair bands; E. 31,900; F. 4,206; G. 1.8 L; H. 31,724; I. 9,000; J. Check students' work.

Week 28, Day 3 (page 127)
A. 72 screws; B. 15°; C. $\frac{2}{2}$ or 1, Check students' work. D. 17; E. 42; F. Answers will vary but may include 108, 117, 126, and 135. G. 300,000 + 2,000 + 800 + 2, 10,000 + 7,000 + 900 + 90; H. Answers will vary must may include $\frac{1}{3} + \frac{1}{3} + \frac{1}{3}$. I. $2\frac{1}{2}$

Week 28, Day 4 (page 128)
A. Check students' work. B. 554; C. 0.50; D. centimeters, feet; E. Check students' work. F. >; G. 40, 41r8; H. Check students' work. I. >, <; J. kite

Week 29, Day 1 (page 129)
A. 0.4; B. 395,000; C. 512; D. 0.44, 0.51, 0.6; E. 512, 2,048, 8,192, 32,768; F. Check students' work. G. 2, 2; H. $6\frac{1}{10}$; I. $\frac{88}{100}$; J. Check students' work.

Week 29, Day 2 (page 130)
A–B. Check students' work. C. 132, 112; D. Check students' work. E. 6,000; F. 42, 98; G. 13, 12, 11, 30; H. 0.5; I. 7.13; J. 69 × 3 = 207

Week 29, Day 3 (page 131)
A. 31: 31, 62, 93, 124, 155, 186; 37: 37, 74, 111, 148, 185; 42: 42, 84, 126, 168; B. 139°; C. Check students' work. D. 61,739; E. >, <, <; F. 30°; G. 30,000 + 2,000 + 200 + 30 + 4, 700,000 + 800 + 20 + 1; H. 34 × 76 = 2,584; I. $1\frac{23}{25}$

Week 29, Day 4 (page 132)
A. Check students' work. B. 1,497; C. Check students' work. D. 12 ft.; E. $3\frac{3}{4}$ cups; F. >; G. 617; H–I. Check students' work. J. ÷4

Answer Key

Week 30, Day 1 (page 133)
A. 6:40 pm; B. >, <; C. 7,532; D. Check students' work. E. die rolled to a 4; F. $9.89; G. 2, 4, 2; H. $1\frac{1}{2}$; I. 61; J. ounces, pounds

Week 30, Day 2 (page 134)
A. 2, 70; B. Check students' work. C. from top to bottom, left to right: 260, 130, 260, 130, 2, 2, 44, 88, 44; D. Check students' work. E. 7,061; F. Check students' work. G. 8.2 lb.; H. 0.75; I. 200 + 2; J. Check students' work.

Week 30, Day 3 (page 135)
A. 0.15; B. 11°; C. $\frac{4}{8}$ or $\frac{1}{2}$, Check students' work. D. <; E. 21; F. 58°; G. 800,000 + 40,000 + 8,000 + 500 + 20 + 4; H. Answers will vary but may include $\frac{1}{8} + \frac{1}{8} + \frac{1}{8}$. I. composite

Week 30, Day 4 (page 136)
A. 462; B. from bottom, left to right: 443, 65, 521, 117, 221, 859; C. 400; D. factors of 28: 1, 2, 4, 7, 14, 28, factors of 40: 1, 2, 4, 5, 8, 10, 20, 40, common factors: 1, 2, 4; E. yes; F. >; G. 1,019; H. 1,705, 946; I. Check students' work. J. leaf

Week 31, Day 1 (page 137)
A. multiples of 4: 4, 8, 12, 16, 20, 24, 28, 32, 36, 40; multiples of 5: 5, 10, 15, 20, 25, 30, 35, 40, 45, 50; common multiples: 20; B. 490,000; C. 12,505; D. 2.80, 2.8; E. 4:44, 3:46; F. Check students' work. G. 6, 2; H. $3\frac{1}{5}$; I. 6,485; J. 52 ft.

Week 31, Day 2 (page 138)
A–B. Check students' work. C. from top to bottom, left to right: 888, 4, 888, 996, 4, 996, 2, 2, 898; D. 8 A's; E. Check students' work. F. 16,231; G. 1 L 650 mL or 1.65 L; H. 0.6; I. 1,000; J. 8,200, 63,000

Week 31, Day 3 (page 139)
A. $5.56; B. 101°; C. 31 blocks; D. 139; E. >, >, <; F. Answers will vary but may include 60 or 120. G. grams, liters; H. $\frac{18}{5}$; I. 5

Week 31, Day 4 (page 140)
A. 48; B. ninety-nine thousand nine hundred fifty-five; C. 1.99; D. 3 in.; E. $2\frac{1}{4}$ lb.; F. >; G. 11,455; H. Check students' work. I. >; J. –5

Week 32, Day 1 (page 141)
A. 2 hr. 10 min.; B. <, <; C. 2,600; D. 54°; E. 8, 4; F. yes, Check students' work. G. 0, 3; H. $7\frac{1}{2}$; I. $\frac{35}{100}$; J. yes, Check students' work.

Week 32, Day 2 (page 142)
A. 1,943, 1,292; B. composite, Check students' work. C. 4,980, 5,080; D. Check students' work. E. 40,000; F. 56; G. 2.10 L; H. 7,136; I. 5.23; J. Check students' work.

Week 32, Day 3 (page 143)
A. $7\frac{1}{2}$ feet; B. 44°; C. Check students' work. D. 32; E. 18; F. $2\frac{5}{8}$, $1\frac{4}{8}$ or $1\frac{1}{2}$; G. inches, meters; H. 36 × 52 = 1,872; I. 2

Week 32, Day 4 (page 144)
A. 27; B. 9,721; C. 0.1; D. meters, centimeters; E. Check students' work. F. >; G. 1,641; H. Check students' work. I. Check students' work. J. 327r2

Week 33, Day 1 (page 145)
A. 0.0; B. 16,800; C. 995; D. 50°; E. ÷3; F. Check students' work. G. $5.06; H. $6\frac{3}{4}$; I. 2,632; J. 28 m

Week 33, Day 2 (page 146)
A. 500,000, 500; B. Check students' work. C. hexagon; D. Check students' work. E. 4,000; F. 9,191; G. 13, 15, 17, 10; ×2, +1; H. 0.3; I. 3.04; J. 10 + $\frac{1}{10}$ + $\frac{5}{100}$

Week 33, Day 3 (page 147)
A. 2.33; B. $44.24; C. Check students' work. D. 7,000; E. minutes, seconds; F. 25°; G. 1,000,000 + 40,000 + 2,000 + 800 + 90 + 1; H. Answers will vary but may include $\frac{3}{12}$ + $\frac{1}{12}$ + $\frac{1}{12}$. I. $2\frac{1}{4}$

Answer Key

Week 33, Day 4 (page 148)
A. Check students' work. B. 18,850;
C. Check students' work. D. factors of 39:
1, 3, 13, 39; factors of 15: 1, 3, 5, 15;
common factors: 1, 3; E. yes; F. >; G. 90,
89r3; H. =, Check students' work. I. 494;
J. handkerchief

Week 34, Day 1 (page 149)
A. 0.1; B. =, =; C. 3,453; D. 87°; E. ÷3;
F. Check students' work. G. 3, 2; H. $5\frac{3}{5}$;
I. 244,078; J. Check students' work.

Week 34, Day 2 (page 150)
A. ×2; B. composite, Check students' work.
C. 5,998, 6,008; D. 18 lawns; E. Check
students' work. F. 3,845; G. 400 mL;
H. 0.6; I. =; J. Check students' work.

Week 34, Day 3 (page 151)
A. 7 hours; B. 95°; C. Check students' work.
D. 4,599; E. no; F. Answers will vary but may
include 201, 204, 207, and 210. G. feet,
centimeters; H. 13 × 57 = 741; I. 4

Week 34, Day 4 (page 152)
A. 48; B. from bottom, left to right: 81, 153,
255, 324, 420, 999; C. 4,000; D. 6 baskets;
E. no; F. >; G. 983; H. Check students' work.
I. Check students' work. J. −5

Week 35, Day 1 (page 153)
A. acute angle; B. 985,000; C. 5,123;
D. 34°; E. 12:23, 10:45; F. $14.08; G. 1, 2;
H. $5\frac{1}{3}$; I. $\frac{51}{100}$; J. 72 cm

Week 35, Day 2 (page 154)
A. Check students' work. B. 5.4 cm; C. from
top to bottom, left to right: 32, 224, 32, 224,
3, 3, 501, 3, 501; D. Check students' work.
E. Check students' work. F. 769; G. 2.8 L;
H. 0.5; I. 1.6; J. 3 × 51 = 153

Week 35, Day 3 (page 155)
A. 2.32; B. $29.10; C. Check students' work.
D. <; E. 4,392; F. 34, 41; G. feet, feet;
H. $\frac{1}{8}$, $\frac{1}{8}$, $\frac{2}{8}$; I. composite

Week 35, Day 4 (page 156)
A. 84; B. 197; C. 1.23; D. inches, grams;
E. yes; F. >; G. 85; H. Check students' work.
I. >, =; J. ÷2

Week 36, Day 1 (page 157)
A. 1.0; B. 879,760; C. 157r4; D. 28°;
E. +6; F. Check students' work. G. 2, 2;
H. $\frac{18}{25}$; I. 128; J. Check students' work.

Week 36, Day 2 (page 158)
A. 3,075, 5,670; B. Check students' work.
C. 243, 729; D. Check students' work.
E. 300,000. F. Check students' work. G. 242,
262, 282, 145; H. 888; I. 900; J. 7,310,
73,100, 731,000

Week 36, Day 3 (page 159)
A. 4.5 ft.; B. 130°; C. *CD*; D. 28,224;
E. yes; F. 31°; G. kilograms, grams; H. $1\frac{1}{2}$;
I. $5\frac{5}{6}$

Week 36, Day 4 (page 160)
A. Check students' work. B. 90; C. 60;
D. 168 sq. ft.; E. no; F. >; G. 414r1;
H–I. Check students' work. J. ×$\frac{1}{2}$ or ÷2

Week 37, Day 1 (page 161)
A. 0.6; B. <, <; C. 91r1; D. 32°; E. +10;
F. Check students' work. G. 0, 3; H. 5;
I. 6,566; J. 40 km

Week 37, Day 2 (page 162)
A. 30,000, 50; B. Check students' work.
C. Students should draw a triangle with
the shaded triangle rotated $\frac{2}{3}$ of the way
clockwise. D. $90; E. 600; F. 36; G. $18.76;
H. 0.8; I. =; J. Check students' work.

Week 37, Day 3 (page 163)
A. 4.57; B. $15.75; C. $\frac{10}{12}$ or $\frac{5}{6}$, Check
students' drawings. D. 33.08; E. 8;
F. Answers will vary but may include 156,
168, 180, and 192. G. meters, feet;
H. Answers will vary but may include
$\frac{2}{10} + \frac{2}{10} + \frac{1}{10}$. I. $4\frac{1}{2}$

Answer Key

Week 37, Day 4 (page 164)
A. 420; B. seventy-seven thousand two hundred fifty-six; C. 0.10; D. 6 miles; E. 7 dozen or 84 cookies; F. =; G. 197; H. 4,416, 1,485; I. Check students' work. J. feather

Week 38, Day 1 (page 165)
A. 0.8; B. 2; C. 127r4; D. 49°; E. 9:11, 4:47; F. straight; G. 0 or 1, 2; H. 2; I. 354; J. Check students' work.

Week 38, Day 2 (page 166)
A–B. Check students' work. C. 3,015, 3,115; D. Check students' work. E. Check students' work. F. 336r1; G. $1\frac{100}{1000}$ L or $1\frac{1}{10}$ L; H. 21,654; I. 9,000; J. 20 × 9 = 180

Week 38, Day 3 (page 167)
A. 5.5 ft.; B. 168°; C. Check students' work. D. $(7 \times \frac{1}{100})$; E. meters, inches; F. 81°; G. 5,000,000 + 500,000 + 90,000 + 200 + 50 + 8; H. $\frac{1}{5} + \frac{1}{5} + \frac{1}{5}$; I. $4\frac{1}{5}$

Week 38, Day 4 (page 168)
A. 70; B. from bottom to top, left to right: 171, 11, 58, 69, 1,792, 251; C. 1.78; D. ounces, kilograms; E. yes; F. >; G. 200, 196; H. Check students' work. I. Check students' work. J. ÷2

Week 39, Day 1 (page 169)
A. 360°; B. 875,000; C. 151; D. 84°; E. ×3; F. $80.24; G. 12, 3; H. $\frac{3}{4}$; I. 12; J. 34 cm

Week 39, Day 2 (page 170)
A–B. Check students' work. C. from top to bottom, left to right: 2, 86, 2, 86, 4, 531, 4, 531, 5; D. Check students' work. E. 23,000; F. Check students' work. G. $34.54; H. 0.75; I. 3,000; J. 97 × 8 = 776

Week 39, Day 3 (page 171)
A. 1.79; B. 64°; C. CD; D. $7.05; E. no; F. 36°; G. inches, kilometers; H. 59 × 29 = 1,711; I. $3\frac{1}{3}$

Week 39, Day 4 (page 172)
A. 75 × 13 = 975; B. 225; C. 70; D. minutes, inches; E. 8 lb.; F. <; G. 9; H. Check students' work. I. >; J. ÷5

Week 40, Day 1 (page 173)
A. Check students' work. B. <, =; C. 240r3; D. 31°; E. 1:23, 12:57; F. $1.19; G. $12.65; H. 2; I. $\frac{69}{100}$; J. Check students' work.

Week 40, Day 2 (page 174)
A. 5,000, 5; B. Check students' work. C. 34, 42; D. $4.50; E. 1,600; F. 36, 52; G. 1.3 L; H. 5,521; I. >; J. Check students' work.

Week 40, Day 3 (page 175)
A. 6.5 cm; B. 52°; C. Check students' work. D. $0.53; E. 28; F. 24°; G. meters, centimeters; H. Answers will vary but may include $\frac{3}{8} + \frac{2}{8}$. I. prime

Week 40, Day 4 (page 176)
A. 48; B. from bottom, left to right: 136, 6, 297, 58, 439, 639; C. 1.47; D. inches, meters; E. no; F. <; G. 473; H. 1,218, 1,620; I. Check students' work. J. ×7